SpringerBriefs in Philosophy

SpringerBriefs present concise summaries of cutting-edge research and practical applications across a wide spectrum of fields. Featuring compact volumes of 50 to 125 pages, the series covers a range of content from professional to academic. Typical topics might include:

- A timely report of state-of-the art analytical techniques
- A bridge between new research results, as published in journal articles, and a contextual literature review
- A snapshot of a hot or emerging topic
- An in-depth case study or clinical example
- A presentation of core concepts that students must understand in order to make independent contributions

SpringerBriefs in Philosophy cover a broad range of philosophical fields including: Philosophy of Science, Logic, Non-Western Thinking and Western Philosophy. We also consider biographies, full or partial, of key thinkers and pioneers.

SpringerBriefs are characterized by fast, global electronic dissemination, standard publishing contracts, standardized manuscript preparation and formatting guidelines, and expedited production schedules. Both solicited and unsolicited manuscripts are considered for publication in the SpringerBriefs in Philosophy series. Potential authors are warmly invited to complete and submit the Briefs Author Proposal form. All projects will be submitted to editorial review by external advisors.

SpringerBriefs are characterized by expedited production schedules with the aim for publication 8 to 12 weeks after acceptance and fast, global electronic dissemination through our online platform SpringerLink. The standard concise author contracts guarantee that

- an individual ISBN is assigned to each manuscript
- each manuscript is copyrighted in the name of the author
- the author retains the right to post the pre-publication version on his/her website or that of his/her institution.

Rosa Fioravante · Antonino Vaccaro
Editors

Humanism and Artificial Intelligence

Springer

Editors
Rosa Fioravante
Catholic Lisbon School of Business and Economics
Catholic University of Portugal
Lisboa, Portugal

Antonino Vaccaro
IESE Business School
Barcelona, Spain

ISSN 2211-4548 ISSN 2211-4556 (electronic)
SpringerBriefs in Philosophy
ISBN 978-3-031-85477-4 ISBN 978-3-031-85478-1 (eBook)
https://doi.org/10.1007/978-3-031-85478-1

This Springer imprint is published by the registered company Springer Nature Switzerland AG
The registered company address is: Gewerbestrasse 11, 6330 Cham, Switzerland

Introduction

Foundations: Why Humanism in and Upon Artificial Intelligence

The Rationale of This Book

Actual and potential disruptions tied to Artificial Intelligence (AI) are spreading in virtually all facets of human life. For each and all human dimensions, whether personal, professional, private, or public, leaders, scholars, professionals, and public opinion are debating whether such technology will bring about dehumanizing threats or will better humans' capabilities to thrive.

The World Economic Forum Global Risks Report 2024 lists the flood of misinformation and disinformation that AI can bring about in our social systems worldwide as Number 1, and adverse outcomes of AI technologies are ranked 6th in a 10-year span, second as a category, after five environmental-based risks. McKinsey reports, among many others, are circulating numbers on the majority of the workforce to be displaced, reskilled, or upskilled, and enlisting radical changes in how business and work are organized, at various degrees, in all industries.

The primary, phenomenologically driven rationale for this book is to be found in the observed distance between claims of "Human-centered AI" fostered by CEOs, managers, political leaders, governmental representatives, and experts in general and the actual and potential ethical impact of AI on humanity, both understood as singular persons and humankind at large. Likewise, a similar discrepancy can be observed between optimistic claims of Artificial Intelligence's ability to augment human and organizational capabilities and everyday life's ethical shortcomings and dilemmas arising from its usage. Although claims of human-centered AI present a clear and sharp sensibility towards human-led aims of technological development, they often do not answer crucial foundational questions posed by humanistic ethics, such as, among others, why is this technology needed? To which human needs, purposes, and ends does it answer? What scopes can it seek? What human intrinsic features, such as dignity, rights, and capabilities, support or hinder? These concerns have vast applied implications. Questions underpinning humanistic ethics are across each and all aspects of ethics of AI listed in the current Stanford Encyclopedia of Philosophy ("Ethics of Artificial Intelligence and Robotics" (Muller, V.C., 2020, 2018): "Privacy and Surveillance, Manipulation of Behaviour, Opacity of AI systems, Bias in Decision Systems, Human-Robot Interaction, Automation and Employment, Autonomous Systems, Machine Ethics, Artificial Moral Agents, Singularity." Two are the main dimensions involved in debates on the ethics of AI. The first dimension involved is AI's ethical design, which can optimize profit maximization and competitive advantage of big techs, race towards new frontiers of innovation, or serve shared prosperity and the common good. The second dimension is AI's ethical use, which can lead to planning increased productivity and efficiency regardless of its impact or changing productivity by freeing humans from undesirable existing drivers of psychological, physical, and moral distress and fatigue (Widder and Whittaker n.d.). These choices, confronted by institutions, organizations, and individuals in their professional and personal lives, are informed by ethical stances in which decision-making processes and AI purposes are enrooted. This book seeks to provide an ethical underpinning to decision-making developed in both dimensions concerned with ethical AI design and ethical AI use, arguing for humanistic control over both as a central feature of responsible, fair, and sustainable AI. Indeed, the book challenges current views on technological and moral neutrality (Cheruvalath 2018; Turilli et al. 2012) to reassess human development and flourishing as the ultimate end of technological advancement, avoiding all tendencies of reducing humans to means of technological optimization as the sole rationale of our civilization's progress (Reeves and Sinnicks 2023).

A more theory-driven, nuanced rationale for this volume rests on the inevitable sense of overwhelming confusion that all scholars are confronted with when entering the field of AI ethics. The quantity of production on the topic is justified, as already mentioned, more than just it being a "hot topic": as challenges connected with AI are complex, stratified, everchanging, and difficult even to analyze, let alone propose ready solutions, it is no wonder that scholars and practitioners are tirelessly trying to schematize its domains and provide suitable guidelines (Attard-Frost et al. 2023; Ryan and Stahl 2021) and to identify guidelines and principles able to be operationalized into policies, practices, and processes to meet such challenges (Goglin 2023). However, even when common ethical principles are identified, criticism arises as they often remain vague in their self-regulation effort (van Maanen 2022) and their inefficacy in providing organizations with practical tools to tame and prevent unethical consequences of AI (Munn 2023). Regardless of such numerosity, we could not help but notice how humanistic ethics, often recalled in contemporary production, had not yet acquired its distinctive production body within AI debates. This book adds to a widening discussion comprising countless debated ethical approaches to AI. It provides a so far lacking distinctive perspective on humanistic ethics: its foundational concepts, main normative propositions, and some of its most exemplary applications. All of this contributes to assessing the role and value of humanism in underpinning applied ethics when confronted with AI and, particularly, AI in business and working contexts. This book presents humanistic ethics as a stream of applied ethics informing various organizational contexts and policy-making suggestions relevant to facing ethical shortcomings of everyday AI design and deployment and confronting ambitious projects of General Artificial Intelligence, Artificial Super Intelligence, and others. Such projects elicit a wide range of reflections on ethical theories looking "beyond human" dimensions, such as posthumanism and transhumanism (Nath and Manna 2023; Sayers et al. 2022), raising the need for humanistic ethics to reaffirm its valuable contribution.

Why Is Humanistic Ethics the Primary Approach of Applied Ethics to AI?

Humanism as a theoretical framework, as well as an epistemological choice (Dierksmeier 2016; Spitzeck et al. 2010), poses challenges to the neoclassical *homo oeconomicus*, thus providing useful conceptual tools to understand non-strictly efficiency-related and utility-maximizing multiple combined drivers for human behavior (and misbehavior) (Colander 2000; Fontrodona and Sison 2006; Jensen 2002). Anthropological assumptions on the social nature of human beings, as well as their natural tendency to *eudaimonia* (human flourishing), are among those theoretical stances informing the humanistic perspective on people-centered organizations, *i.e.,* organizations in which leadership, governance, culture, and values are integrally ethical and oriented towards internal and external stakeholders' wellbeing (Melé 2003; Melé and Cantón 2014; Sandelands 2009). In this way, humanism provides analysis able to conceive profit and utility maximization goals into a broader set of moral, psychological, and spiritual concerns, thus providing more realistic models of the interplay between personal, social, and economic variables (Keleher 2018; Pirson and Lawrence 2010). One relevant example is proving a thorough evaluation of working context and organizational life as the setting of a broader quest for meaningful life and transcendental purposes. Such an approach extensively affects how AI is deployed within a working context (Kim and Scheller-Wolf 2022). Furthermore, it focuses on human development critical goals: it underlines the relevance and purpose of ethical behavior to foster personal and organizational wellbeing beyond its instrumental deployment to reach satisfying economic performances (Rosanas 2008). By focusing on both means and ends of economic and business development, humanism provides an understanding of means and ends to both business engagements and technological advancements (Kim et al. 2021; Melé 2012; Schlag and Melé 2020).

It is worth mentioning that the humanistic tradition holds both secular and religious roots. The former recalls the classic Western perspective rooted in the well-known motto of Protagoras of Abdera (485–415 B.C.): "Of all things the measure is Man, of the things that are, that they are, and of the things that are not, that they are not" (DK 80B1) (Dierksmeier 2016; Wagner-Tsukamoto 2013). On the other, humanistic tradition has been developed in light of the Catholic Social Teaching body of documents and the Integral Humanism principles—often recalled in literature in their organizational applications (Melé 2021; Zigarelli 1993; Costa and Ramus 2012). Both the secular and religious streams, by leveraging universalistic principles and scopes, have proven valuable in developing solutions within crisis contexts, in extreme contexts focusing on marginalized groups (Mongelli et al. 2018), to navigate uncertainty and complexity tied to ethical and legal compliance (das Neves and Melé 2013; das Neves and Vaccaro 2013).

Lastly, Human-centered AI is central to many debates among policymakers and legislators. It is not by chance that, in 2020, the European Parliament adopted the "Framework of ethical aspects of artificial intelligence, robotics, and related technologies" (2020/2012INL), explicitly focusing on human-centered concerns. The exemplary document provides preliminary indications on how companies might create market and job opportunities through AI without losing sight of how to guarantee human rights and address ethical values intrinsic to the EU constitution. Fairness and inequality at the macro and micro levels are a widespread concern. At the macro level, all the above-mentioned major issues in AI and ethics present an additional challenge strictly tied to organizational and governance responsibility: those who are the most affected by undesirable consequences of AI design and implementation are those with the least power to tackle and tame them (Derry 2012; Kim and Scheller-Wolf 2022). In this regard, humanism has long addressed the importance of subsidiarity as a value and a moral duty for organizations (Melé 2005). When deployed in organizations, subsidiarity, often in connection with solidarity, entails a body of normative prescriptions to address topics related to power asymmetries and multilevel integral responsibility. This paradigm is relevant to organizations engaging in private-public partnerships on AI development and implementation and organizations aiming to participate in legal framework regulation processes. Even more so to those seeking to anticipate additional legal compliance duties possibly arising from future legislation by tackling critical consequences of AI use through an ethically integral compliance approach (Vaccaro 2023). Power imbalances, social exclusion, and sharpening inequalities are at stake in ethical AI, at least on two levels. At the macro level, the perils of AI's increasing social divide and polarization have been addressed by scholars looking at the economics of its infrastructures and pipelines (Crawford 2021; Johnson and Acemoglu 2023). At the micro-level, the risk of dehumanizing stakeholders and fueling further social exclusion has been addressed through proposals for democratizing AI processes (Buhmann and Fieseler 2023).

Furthermore, widening discrimination fostered by AI has been at the center of concerns and claims on the fairness of AI (Bietti 2021; Tilmes 2022). The topic is highly relevant for organizations already failing to address inequality or committed to a process of reform aimed at reducing social imbalances (AMIS et al. 2021; Amis et al. 2020; Thomason et al. 2023). AI can hinder such processes if bias and sources of discrimination are overlooked from an ethical perspective; broad examples of such issues are observed within human resource management through recruiting and selecting (Fritts and Cabrera 2021). Indeed, relevant literature has been underlying how algorithms increase social inequality (whether based on gender, race, nationality, or class discrimination). This can be done by reinforcing discrimination, including prejudices affecting decision-making, ultimately displaying moral biases that reinforce previously existing social exclusion and disadvantage for marginalized groups. Rising inequality, at large and as the specific output of AI bias, presents distinctive features of opposition to humanistic values and perspectives. All of this points to an ethical failure to respect the intrinsic dignity of each person, which should be recognized and protected by organizations regardless of gender, nationality, and wealth (Burgos and Melé 2018; Melé 2015). This book addresses such topics by looking into moral norms able to underpin ethical conduct, which can, in turn, influence law-making and regulatory frameworks (de Colle et al. 2023): humanistic ethics is therefore identified as an ethical stance able to draw from moral principles while informing practical wisdom and inspiring juridical debates over transparency, accountability, and responsibility.

This volume foresees four significant contributions (to see the detailed list of contributions, refer to the last Chapter, "Concluding Remarks"). First, it proposes humanistic ethics as a holistic framework able to confront AI challenges. Fioravante and Vaccaro propose a debate on Humanistic Ethics as applied to the design and use of AI by avoiding dehumanization, calling for an "ex-ante" prevention of unethical organizational behavior in AI. Dehumanization in the form of human alienation is at the center of Simona Chiodo's reflection on "automating humans through predicting humans". John Tasioulas further details the prerequisites of humanistic ethics to underpin human-centered AI, thus highlighting inconsistencies of human-centered AI and falling short of coping with all the presented domains. This body of contributions is detailed in Chaps. 1–3.

Second, following the humanistic doctrine, Chaps. 4–6 highlight the role of Spirituality and Virtues in AI in the workplace and business organizations, posing the need to include moral norms and transcendental dimensions to evaluate AI's personal, organizational, and social impact. This issue is explored in the Chapters by Schlag on Christian Ethics and contemplation and Ferrero et al.'s Chapter on virtues and AI in the workplace. Furthermore, Ferrante's Chapter links algorithmics and Canonical Law, relying on CST as the only juridical document explicitly enrooted in humanistic ethics.

Third, the book contributes to assessing AI ethics debates focusing on boundaries between humans and non-humans, highlighting human integral responsibility in AI design and use. Indeed, in Chap. 7, das Neves details pretentious claims for machines' intelligence, and Gunkel discusses machines' morality in Chap. 8, highlighting how debates on responsible AI cannot but start with human moral responsibility in shaping rights and duties connected to AI development. Additionally, Chap. 9 presents Romele's analysis of AI communication and contributes to assessing human social responsibility towards discourse revolving around technological advancements, which can be used to enhance rather than diminishing current social inequalities and imbalances.

Fourth, the book contributes to assessing humanistic ethics as a source of guidelines for data governance and management and AI deployment in sensitive contexts, such as healthcare facilities. Hence, the book contributes to research on organizational automation (Lindebaum et al. 2023; Raisch and Krakowski 2021) by raising concerns about the cross-awareness of ethical risks throughout all organizational dimensions. In Chap. 10, Peggy Tsai develops a holistic model of ethical data governance, which allows professionals to pair normative ethical guidelines with deontological approaches and organizations to foresee strict processes of guardrail for ample data use. In Chap. 11, Boddington thoroughly discusses AI's grey areas, where AI used to increase efficiency falls short of meeting fragile groups' needs, thus highlighting organizational duties to evaluate AI with humanistic-based criteria rather than solely economic guiding rationale.

Overall, this volume represents an interdisciplinary attempt to analyze AI ethical issues from a humanistic perspective. Bridging the literature on the Ethics of AI, Business Ethics, and Catholic Social Teaching aims to provide scholars and practitioners with a unifying, although heterogeneous, humanistic perspective able to inform organizational studies in light of ethically challenging technological innovations.

The following paragraphs present some highlights of each Chapter's content, summarized by the editors:

Part I Humanistic Ethics and Dehumanization in AI

Chapter 1: Humanism, Dehumanization, Integral Human Development: An Overview of Boundaries and Capabilities of Human-Centered Artificial Intelligence in Business and Organizations (Fioravante Rosa, CLSBE-IESE & Vaccaro Antonino, IESE)

Rosa Fioravante and Antonino Vaccaro discuss the perils of dehumanization entailed by AI design and deployment within business and working organizations. Authors discuss current approaches of "human-centered AI," "AI that benefits humanity," "responsible AI," and other ethical AI streams by arguing how their ethical shortcomings are tied to an absence of humanistic ethics underpinning them. Fioravante and Vaccaro propose a humanistic model of AI deployment in organizations that deals "ex-ante" (i.e., foreseeing ethical risks) with the negative impact of AI in terms of human flourishing, organizational wellbeing, and humanizing stakeholders. This Chapter contributes to the literature on humanism in business by detailing how humanistic ethics represents a unifying approach to ethical AI: able at the same time to overcome the burgeoning number of different stances adopted by corporate ethical codes and principles lists and to tackle different ethical shortcomings in a variety of organizational applications altogether.

Chapter 2: 21st-Century Alienation: From Engineered Humans to Predicted Humans (Chiodo Simona, Politecnico of Milan)

Simona Chiodo proposes a contribution focused on human alienation as a consequence of engineered humans: looking into how language changes to progressively support a vision of human performance to be optimized to be closer to values of efficiency; the Chapter highlights a process of paradoxically automating humans through the use of automated technologies. Furthermore, the Chapter discusses ancient to modern humankind's quests for prediction in Western culture. It proposes a critical assessment of the use of technology to determine rather than predicting humans' future.

Chapter 3: Artificial Intelligence, Humanistic Ethics (Tasioulas Jhon, Oxford University)

Jhon Tasioulas provides an overview of three critical dimensions of humanistic ethics to be deployed in theoretical debates on the ethics of AI and the practical unfolding of AI design and use. He argues how the three dimensions qualify humanistic ethics since they all are required to foresee human-centered technological development, thus being a distinguished ethical perspective from many others deployed in the ethics of AI. By looking into the plurality of values, relevance of procedures rather than sole focus on outcomes, and centrality of individual and collective participation as three main humanistic principles of AI ethics, the Chapter contributes to detailed contents and values of humanistic holistic approaches.

Part II Humanism, Law, and Spirituality in AI

Chapter 4: Algorethics: On the Relationship Among Artificial Intelligence, Law and Religion (Ferrante Mario, University of Palermo)

Mario Ferrante presents "algorithmics" as a realm of reflection upon artificial intelligence within which religion and faith can inform policy regulations on upcoming ethical challenges in AI. Considering religious-based perspectives on AI regulations, such as the "Rome Call for AI Ethics" at the Vatican joined by representatives of the three Abrahamic religions, the Chapter discusses the contribution of spirituality in determining rules and practices to guardrail AI's development and use as well as documents enrooted in religious traditions able to inform also secular law-making upon its ethical challenges.

Chapter 5: Christian Humanism and Technology: New Frontiers for Contemplation (Schlag Martin, University of St. Thomas)

Martin Schlag draws on Catholic Social Teaching (CST) and its body of literature focused on the technology and ethics of AI to assess the value of contemplation, its meaning, and its role in informing ethical stances towards AI. The Chapter argues how Christian spirituality, particularly contemplation, can shape a human-centered approach that aligns technology with human dignity, freedom, subsidiarity, solidarity, and the preferential option for the poor. By arguing for new virtues to confront socio-ethical challenges derived from artificial intelligence, the Chapter contributes to the debate on the role of spirituality and contemplation in business and working contexts.

Chapter 6: AI and the Future of Virtues in the Workplace (Ferrero Muñoz Ignacio, University of Navarra; Rocchi Marta, Dublin City University, Giarmoleo Francesco Vincenzo, University of Navarra)

Ignacio Ferrero Muñoz, Marta Rocchi, and Francesco Vincenzo Giarmoleo present the implications of applying a Virtue Ethics approach to deploying AI in the workplace. As Virtue Ethics promotes ethical behavior in the design, deployment, and use of AI technology, it challenges developers to create AI that enhances excellent character traits in individuals and contributes to societal good. Such a perspective helps organizations foresee AI, enhancing the workplace's virtuous personal and professional characters. To contribute to this perspective, the Chapter discusses the impact of AI utilization in workplaces on developing cardinal virtues, namely practical wisdom, justice, courage, and temperance. The Chapter contributes to debates on practical wisdom and virtues in AI design and use.

Part III Humanism, Anti-humanism, and Human Responsibility in AI

Chapter 7: What's in a Name? Anti-Humanism and the AI Claim (das Neves João César, Catholic University Lisbon)

João César das Neves describes Artificial Intelligence's origin, nature, and effects as a troublesome manifestation. By addressing the history of the career of the concept of Artificial Intelligence, the Chapter highlights its misuse to address its questionable scientific background and semantic perimeter. The Chapter links ideological and ethical stances concerning AI to its practical deployment and its foreseen role in the future of humanity by addressing social, political, and economic choices revolving around AI as an instrument to be used for the welfare of humanity or as a dangerous and deceiving concept used by humanity's quest to acquire God-like features.

Chapter 8: Nonhuman Persons and Other Things (Gunkel David, Northern Illinois University)

David Gunkel proposes a thorough discussion of current debates to assess the ontological status of AI by drawing on the classical distinction between "person" and "thing". Such debates inform virtually all considerations upon legal regulation of AI, human-machine relations, and ethical stances toward how to use such technologies. By presenting the pros and cons of different options—ignoring AI-specific features that distinguish such systems from other technologies and framing a sharp dichotomy between considering an entity as a person or non-person—the author argues for overcoming current dichotomic debates. Ultimately, by bestowing responsibility toward moral considerations of AI on humans, it is possible to assess the social function and the social role of AI, robots, and other anthropomorphized artifacts.

Chapter 9: |Ethics of AI| as a Floating Signifier; or Towards a Politics of AI Ethics (Romele Alberto, ICM, Sorbonne Nouvelle)

Alberto Romele presents a text analysis of major newspapers involved in the communication of |the ethics of AI as a source of reflection upon its being a "floating signifier". The term, borrowed from Laclau and Mouffe's work, drawing on a "neo-Gramscian" theory of discourse, analyzes contemporary public debates in light of their construction towards hegemonic scopes. The concept of hegemony results as a key concept to understanding how discourses upon ethics of AI are built and how its communication is channeled and popularized. In this way, actors involved in ethics of AI debates, whether scholars, companies, and media outlets, address AI in a manner that leaves most ethical implications untacked by relying on companies' abilities to perform what is called "techno-solutionism," i.e., autonomously foreseeing and self-regulating AI best development.

Part IV Humanism, Technical, and Values-laden AI

Chapter 10: How to Build an AI Governance Framework with Data Governance (Tsai Peggy, Carnegie Mellon University)

Peggy Tsai focuses on Generative Artificial Intelligence and the widespread popularization of Large Language Models in their ubiquitous use for profit and non-profit purposes. By looking into the benefits of business deployment of technologies based on large datasets, the author stresses the opacity of accountability rules for extensive data management and use. More in detail, the Chapter reflects upon the quality of data used to feed Generative AI as a focal point to assess to ensure the ethical functioning of technologies, averting the risk of so-called "black box" AI. By applying the principles of accountability, transparency, trustworthiness, bias management, and ethics to data management, the author conveys a framework for the "three Lines of Defense Roles and Governing Council for AI Governance" to guardrail ethical shortcomings of unfettered business data use.

Chapter 11: Dementia Care: A Test Case for the Humanity of AI in Health and Nursing Care (Boddington Paula, University of West London)

Paula Boddington presents an empirical study on dementia care facilities to illustrate dehumanizing processes enacted by AI use in the context of healthcare. The Chapter draws on reflections upon literature on dehumanizing practices in healthcare before the advent of AI and their changes, as well as debating ethical approaches concerned with AI and its relation to human nature. Boddington inquiries into relevant variables affecting the use of AI in dementia care facilities, such as speed and urgency, the use of data, an agency of AI, and others, to support her claim that AI has far-reaching impacts on dehumanization practices. The case serves as an explanation for a variety of ethical issues tied to AI usage for control and optimization purposes.

Acknowledgements This edited book is part of the research efforts undertaken by "IESE Artificial Intelligence and the Future of Management Initiative" that the Authors acknowledge for the support and encouragement.

Fioravante Rosa
CLSBE-IESE

Vaccaro Antonino
IESE

References

Amis J, Brickson S, Haack P, Hernadez M (2021) Taking inequality seriously. Acad Manag Rev 46(3):431–439. https://doi.org/10.5465/AMR.2021.0222

Amis JM, Mair J, Munir KA (2020) The organizational reproduction of inequality. Acad Manag Ann 14(1):195–230. https://doi.org/10.5465/ANNALS.2017.0033

Attard-Frost B, De los Ríos, A. (2023) The ethics of AI business practices: a review of 47 AI ethics guidelines. AI and Ethics 3(2):389–406. https://doi.org/10.1007/s43681-022-00156-6

Bietti E (2021) From Ethics Washing to Ethics Bashing: A Moral Philosophy View on Tech Ethics. J Soc Computing 2(3):266–283. https://doi.org/10.23919/JSC.2021.0031

Buhmann A, Fieseler C (2023) Deep Learning Meets Deep Democracy: Deliberative Governance and Responsible Innovation in Artificial Intelligence. Bus Ethics Q 33(1):146–179. https://doi.org/10.1017/beq.2021.42

Burgos JM, Melé D (2018) Personalism. In Encyclopedia of Business and Professional Ethics (pp. 1–6). Springer International Publishing. https://doi.org/10.1007/978-3-319-23514-1_99-1

Cheruvalath R (2018) Internet Neutrality: A Battle Between Law and Ethics. Int J Semiot Law 31(1):145–153. https://doi.org/10.1007/S11196-017-9531-Z

Colander D (2000) The death of neoclassical economics. J His Eco Thought 22(02):127–143. https://doi.org/10.1080/10427710050025330

Costa E, Ramus T (2012) The Italian Economia Aziendale and catholic social teaching: How to apply the common good principle at the managerial level. J Bus Ethics 106(1):103–116. https://doi.org/10.1007/s10551-011-1056-x

Crawford K (2021) Atlas of AI. Power, Politics, and the Planetary Costs of Artificial Intelligence. Yale University Press

das Neves, J. C. (2013) Managing Ethically Cultural Diversity: Learning from Thomas Aquinas. J Bus Ethics 116(4):769–780. https://doi.org/10.1007/S10551-013-1820-1/METRICS

das Neves, J. C. (2013) Corporate Transparency: A Perspective from Thomas Aquinas' Summa Theologiae. J Bus Ethics 113(4):639–648. https://doi.org/10.1007/S10551-013-1682-6/METRICS

de Colle S, Freeman RE, Wicks AC (2023) Toward Humanistic Business Ethics. Bus Soc. https://doi.org/10.1177/00076503231183681/ASSET/IMAGES/LARGE/10.1177_00076503231183681-FIG2.JPEG

Derry R (2012) Reclaiming Marginalized Stakeholders. J Bus Ethics 111(2):253–264. https://doi.org/10.1007/S10551-012-1205-X/METRICS

Dierksmeier C (2016) What is 'Humanistic' About Humanistic Management? Humanistic Management Journal 1(1):9–32. https://doi.org/10.1007/S41463-016-0002-6/METRICS

Fontrodona J, Sison AJG (2006) The nature of the firm, agency theory and shareholder theory: A critique from philosophical anthropology. J Bus Ethics 66(1):33–42. https://doi.org/10.1007/S10551-006-9052-2/METRICS

Fritts M, Cabrera F (2021) AI Recruitment Algorithms and the Dehumanization Problem. 23:791–801. https://doi.org/10.1007/s10676-021-09615-w

Goglin C (2023) The Ethics of Artificial Intelligence: Review of Ethical Machines: Your Concise Guide to Totally Unbiased, Transparent, and Respectful AI by R. Blackman; Ethics of Artificial Intelligence: Case Studies and Options for Addressing Ethical Challenges by B.C. Stahl, D. Schroeder, and R. Rodrigues; and AI Ethics by M. Coeckelbergh. J Bus Ethics. https://doi.org/10.1007/s10551-023-05538-2

Jensen MC (2002) Value maximization, stakeholder theory, and the corporate objective function. Bus Ethics Q 12(2):235–256. https://doi.org/10.2307/3857812

Johnson S, Acemoglu D (2023) Power and Progress: Our Thousand-Year Struggle Over Technology and Prosperity. Hachette, UK

Keleher L (2018) Integral human development. In Routledge Handbook of Development Ethics (pp. 29–34). Routledge. https://doi.org/10.4324/9781315626796-4

Kim TW, Maimone F, Pattit K, Sison AJ, Teehankee B (2021) Master and Slave: The Dialectic of Human-Artificial Intelligence Engagement. Humanistic Management J 6(3):355–371. https://doi.org/10.1007/s41463-021-00118-w

Kim TW, Scheller-Wolf A (2022) Technological Unemployment, Meaning in Life, Purpose of Business, and the Future of Stakeholders. In Business and the Ethical Implications of Technology (pp. 13–31). Springer Nature Switzerland. https://doi.org/10.1007/978-3-031-18794-0

Lindebaum D, Moser C, Ashraf M, Glaser VL (2023) Reading the Technological Society to Understand the Mechanization of Values and its Ontological Consequences. In Academy of Management Review (Vol. 48, Issue 3, pp. 575–592). Academy of Management. https://doi.org/10.5465/amr.2021.0159

Melé D (2003) The challenge of humanistic management. J Bus Ethics 44(44):77–88. https://doi.org/10.1023/a:1023298710412

Melé D (2005) Exploring the principle of subsidiarity in organizational forms. J Bus Ethics 60(3):293–305. https://doi.org/10.1007/s10551-005-0136-1

Melé D (2012) The firm as a "community of persons": A pillar of humanistic business ethos. J Bus Ethics 106(1):89–101. https://doi.org/10.1007/s10551-011-1051-2

Melé D (2015) Three Keys Concepts of Catholic Humanism for Economic Activity: Human Dignity, Human Rights and Integral Human Development. Issues in Business Ethics, pp. 43, 113–136. https://doi.org/10.1007/978-94-017-9704-7_7/COVER

Melé D (2021) Ethics at the workplace in the fourth industrial revolution: A Catholic social teaching perspective. Business Ethics, the Environment & Responsibility 30(4):772–783. https://doi.org/10.1111/BEER.12368

Melé D, Cantón CG (2014) The Homo Economicus Model. In Human Foundations of Management (pp. 9–29). Palgrave Macmillan UK. https://doi.org/10.1057/9781137462619

Mongelli L, Versari P, Rullani F, Vaccaro A (2018) Made in Carcere: Integral Human Development in Extreme Conditions. J Bus Ethics 152(4):977–995. https://doi.org/10.1007/s10551-018-3821-6

Munn L (2023) The uselessness of AI ethics. AI and Ethics 3(3):869–877. https://doi.org/10.1007/s43681-022-00209-w

Nath R, Manna R (2023) From posthumanism to ethics of artificial intelligence. AI & Soc 38(1):185–196. https://doi.org/10.1007/s00146-021-01274-1

Pirson MA, Lawrence PR (2010) Humanism in business—towards a paradigm shift? J Bus Ethics 93(4):553–565. https://doi.org/10.1007/s10551-009-0239-1

Raisch S, Krakowski S (2021) Artificial intelligence and management: The automation–augmentation paradox. Acad Manag Rev 46(1):192–210. https://doi.org/10.5465/AMR.2018.0072

Reeves C, Sinnicks M (2023) Totally Administered Heteronomy: Adorno on Work, Leisure, and Politics in the Age of Digital Capitalism. J Bus Ethics. https://doi.org/10.1007/S10551-023-05570-2

Rosanas JM (2008) Beyond economic criteria: a humanistic approach to organizational survival. J Bus Ethics 78(3):447–462. https://doi.org/10.1007/s10551-006-9341-9

Ryan M, Stahl BC (2021) Artificial intelligence ethics guidelines for developers and users: clarifying their content and normative implications. J Inf Commun Ethics Soc 19(1):1477–1996. https://doi.org/10.1108/JICES-12-2019-0138

Sandelands L (2009) The business of business is the human person: lessons from the catholic social tradition. J Bus Ethics 85(1):93–101. https://doi.org/10.1007/s10551-008-9751-y

Sayers J, Martin L, Bell E (2022) Posthuman Affirmative Business Ethics: Reimagining Human-Animal Relations Through Speculative Fiction. J Bus Ethics 178(3):597–608. https://doi.org/10.1007/s10551-021-04801-8

Schlag M, Melé D (2020) Building Institutions for the Common Good. The Practice and Purpose of Business in an Inclusive Economy. Humanistic Management Journal 5(1):1–6. https://doi.org/10.1007/s41463-020-00092-9

Spitzeck H, Pirson M, von Kimakowitz E, Dierksmeier C (2010) The humanistic management network. Zeitschrift Für Psychologie 218(4):246–248. https://doi.org/10.1027/0044-3409/a000035

Thomason B, Opie T, Livingston B, Sitzmann T (2023) "Woke" Diversity Strategies: Science or Sensationalism? Acad Manag Perspect 37(2):193–201. https://doi.org/10.5465/amp.2022.0181

Tilmes N (2022) Disability, fairness, and algorithmic bias in AI recruitment. Ethics Inf Technol 24(2):21. https://doi.org/10.1007/s10676-022-09633-2

Turilli M, Vaccaro A, Taddeo M (2012) Internet neutrality: Ethical issues in the internet environment. Philosophy and Technology 25(2):133–151. https://doi.org/10.1007/S13347-011-0039-2/TABLES/1

Vaccaro A (2023) Compliance Beyond Compliance: Managing Organizations with Integrity. McGraw Hill

van Maanen G (2022) AI Ethics, Ethics Washing, and the Need to Politicize Data Ethics. Digital Society 1(2). https://doi.org/10.1007/s44206-022-00013-3

Wagner-Tsukamoto S (2013) Economic Humanism and Western Management: Theory and Practice. World Humanism 15–29. https://doi.org/10.1057/9781137378491

Widder DG, Whittaker M (n.d.) Open (for Business): Big Tech, Concentrated Power, and the Political Economy of Open AI. https://ssrn.com/abstract=4543807

Zigarelli MA (1993) Catholic social teaching and the employment relationship: a model for managing human resources in accordance with Vatican Doctrine. J Bus Ethics 12(1):75–82. https://doi.org/10.1007/bf01845789

Contents

Part III Humanism, Anti-humanism, and Human Responsibility in AI

Editors and Contributors

About the Editors

Rosa Fioravante is a Post-Doctoral Researcher in Business Ethics, currently affiliated at CLSBE—Catholic Lisbon School of Business and Economics (Lisbon, Portugal)—and University of Urbino Carlo Bo (Urbino, Italy). She is member of the Center for Business in Society at IESE Business School (Barcelona, Spain). She lectures on business ethics and social responsibility courses at CLSBE for graduate students. She earned an M.S. degree in Philosophical Sciences from the University of Milan (Italy). She holds a Ph.D. from the University of Urbino Carlo Bo (Italy) in Business Administration within the Ph.D. program "Global Studies – International Economic Policy, Business and Governance". Her thesis focused on historical and contemporary exemplary Integral Human Development and Humanistic Management cases.

She has been a research assistant and visiting Ph.D. at the Centre for Business in Society of IESE Business School (Spain), and research and teaching Assistant at LUISS Guido Carli Business School in Rome (Italy). Her research interests focus on Humanistic Management and CSR, Human Flourishing, and the History of Economic and Political Thought. Some of her works appeared in edited Springer, Palgrave, and Routledge books, as well as peer reviewed academic journals within the Humanistic Management and Business Ethics field. She has been a Consultant for the Italian Chamber of Deputies and the Senate of the Republic (Rome, Italy) and a project manager for several Foundations and NGOs.

Antonino Vaccaro is a Professor in the Department of Business Ethics and in the Negotiation Unit at IESE Business School. He is also the Academic Director of the Center for Business in Society, a member of IESE Sustainability Leadership Institute and of IESE Artificial Intelligence and the Future of Management Initiative. His areas of specialization are Integral Human Development, Humanism, and Compliance. Since 2015, Professor Vaccaro has been a section editor of the *Journal of Business*

Ethics. He has also served as guest editor of Ethics and Information Technology and edited several Springer books.

His research has been published in leading peer-reviewed scientific journals such as the *Academy of Management Journal*, *Research Policy*, *Journal of Economic Behavior and Organization*, *Technological Forecasting and Social Change*, *Journal of Management Studies*, *Ethics and Information Technology*, *Business Ethics Quarterly*, *Journal of Business Ethics*, and *The Information Society*. His studies have been featured by outlets such as the Economist and Forbes. He has consulted on compliance and cyber-security issues for companies in North America, Europe, Latin America, and Africa.

Contributors

Vaccaro Antonino IESE Business School, Barcelona, Spain

Paula Boddington Geller Institute of Ageing and Memory, University of West London, London, UK

Simona Chiodo Politecnico di Milano, Milano, Italy

João César das Neves Catolica Lisbon School of Business and Economics, Universidade Católica Portuguesa, Lisboa, Portugal

Mario Ferrante University of Palermo—UNIPA, Palermo, Italy

Ignacio Ferrero School of Economics and Business, University of Navarra, Pamplona, Spain

Francesco Vincenzo Giarmoleo ISSA School of Applied Management, University of Navarra, Pamplona, Spain

David J. Gunkel Northern Illinois University, DeKalb, IL, USA

Marta Rocchi DCU Business School, Dublin City University, Dublin, Ireland

Alberto Romele IRMÉCCEN, Université Sorbonne Nouvelle, Paris, France

Fioravante Rosa Catolica Lisbon School of Business and Economics, Universidade Católica Portuguesa, Lisbon, Portugal

Martin Schlag University of St. Thomas, Saint Paul, MN, USA

John Tasioulas Oxford, UK

Peggy Tsai Newyork, NY, USA

Part I
Humanistic Ethics and Dehumanization in AI

Chapter 1
Humanism, Dehumanization, Integral Human Development: An Overview of Boundaries and Capabilities of Human-Centered Artificial Intelligence in Business and Organizations

Fioravante Rosa and Vaccaro Antonino

Abstract The chapter focuses on the main threats of dehumanization posed by Artificial Intelligence (AI) to Business organizations involved in its design and deployment at large. By highlighting dehumanization as an overarching ethical concern, it argues for humanistic ethics as the main suitable approach to solve everyday ethical dilemmas, arising for decision-makers faced with AI related moral possible shortcomings. It focuses on developers' social and ethical responsibilities to ensure moral design of AI by assessing moral boundaries of desirable technological innovation and its social purposes. Furthermore, it assesses personal, organizational and stakeholder relationships level practices, informed by humanistic ethics. By this way, it proposes a framework able to evaluate AI adoption in light of human flourishing and integral human development. The latter approach is identified and discussed as opposed to non-humanistic ethical streams currently informing ethics of AI debate.

Keywords Ethics of AI · Humanism and AI · Dehumanization · Ethical risks

> Your scientists were so preoccupied with whether or not they could they didn't stop to think if they should.
>
> Ian Malcolm, *Jurassic Park*

> But there is another conclusion: to laugh at logic if it runs counter to the interests of men.

F. Rosa (✉)
Catolica Lisbon School of Business and Economics, Universidade Católica Portuguesa, Lisbon, Portugal
e-mail: rosa.fioravante@uniurb.it

V. Antonino
IESE Business School, Barcelona, Spain

R. Fioravante and A. Vaccaro (eds.), *Humanism and Artificial Intelligence*, SpringerBriefs in Philosophy, https://doi.org/10.1007/978-3-031-85478-1_1

Theodor W. Adorno, *Dialectic of Enlightenment: Philosophical Fragments*

It takes something more than intelligence to act intelligently.
Fyodor Dostoyevsky, *Crime and Punishment*

1.1 Introduction

The famous statement from a 1979 IBM presentation: "A computer can never be held accountable, therefore a computer must never make a management decision", thanks to the advent of Artificial Intelligence, has become very remote or very upcoming.

Artificial Intelligence (AI) is here defined as "any kind of artificial computational system that shows intelligent behaviour, i.e., complex behaviour that is conducive to reaching goals" or systems "designed to mimic multiple human intelligences such as the capabilities to do, think, and feel [...] able to interpret external data, learn from such data, and use those learnings to achieve specific goals and tasks through flexible adaptation" (Haenlein et al. 2022). Far-reaching consequences of AI are raising a range of such extensive concerns that have been compared in magnitude to nuclear power: in the famous letter by leaders from OpenAI, Anthropic, Google DeepMind, philosophers and practitioners highly involved in AI design, it reads "Mitigating the risk of extinction from AI should be a global priority alongside other societal-scale risks such as pandemics and nuclear war." ("Pause Giant AI Experiments: An Open Letter, Future Of Life website).[1] Although threats coming from AI are, unlike those of nuclear power, at this stage highly speculative, numerous statements released by developers of both technologies are virtually indistinguishable from the others; both are asking for extensive and immediate regulation and warning the general public of foreseen potential damage to humankind and its organized social life due to its deployment[2] (Prasad et al. 2023).

Ethical dilemmas arising from AI, design, and deployment in organizations come from its actual and foreseen ability to substitute, control, and manage humans and human activities, which were previously impossible to automate (Kim et al. 2021). Business and working organizations are pivotal in enhancing or taming, worsening, or preventing AI social and ethical shortcomings (Blackman and Niño 2023), mainly depending on how they approach and deploy ethical decision-making over such dilemmas. Foundational debates in business ethics are at stake when addressing the ethics of AI, which can be grouped into two significant areas:

> First, boundaries between legal and illegal behavior are unclear and easy to exploit by virtually all stakeholders. Using technologies to control employees, promoting deceptive campaigns, and mismanaging data privacy (Ebrahimi and Matt 2023; Halpern et al. 2008) are examples of intended unethical organizational behaviors. The latter exploit grey areas, regulatory loopholes, and missing or ineffective ethical codes and principles to increase

[1] https://futureoflife.org/open-letter/pause-giant-ai-experiments/.

[2] https://www.nytimes.com/2023/06/10/upshot/artificial-intelligence-nuclear-weapons-quiz.html.

profitability and competitive standing at the expense of integrity, moral conduct, and environmental and social concerns. Other unethical stances highlighted are those tied to AI physical and social infrastructure: exploiting natural resources to satisfy AI's need for increased energy and exploiting human labor to train and interact with AI without adequate safeguarding of both its current conditions and future unfolding (Crawford 2021; Mazzi and Floridi, n.d.; van Wynsberghe 2021). Issues of intended unethical behavior are discussed in the widening field of corporate responsibility and accountability of AI (Martin 2019; Novelli et al. 2023).

Ethically challenging trade-offs in AI-driven organizations display various natures, depending on whether the organization is primarily involved in designing the technology or in adopting it. Examples of such trade-offs for developing bodies are decisions upon developing AI through an open sources model, eventually deploying extensive ethical continuous external checks over experiments, or speeding the latter to strike newer frontiers in the shortest time feasible. Disagreements on such decisions have characterized, among others, OpenAI governance throughout its fast expansion during the last years, eventually leading to mistrust in leadership and a vast debate on its organizational mission (Widder and Whittaker 2023).

Second, unethical behavior may be unintended and unforeseen by the organization. This is the case of purchasing black box technologies, thus losing control of automated operations (Berente et al. 2021). Examples of common trade-offs faced by managers involved in decisions on adopting AI seeking to obtain competitive advantage through fast implementation of technologies while dealing with a large number of compliance risks posed by such technologies due to unclear internal functioning of AI adopted (Bélisle-Pipon et al. 2023). While promoting such changes, decision-makers face many algorithmic ethical shortcomings (racial and gender biases, misalignment between human values and AI unintended outputs, among others, Floridi et al. 2018). The primary debates are authorship and property rights infringement scandals, employees' distrust, and fear of job displacement (Agrawal et al. 2019; Munn 2024; Reeves and Sinnicks 2023a). Thus, transparency is at stake in all stages of the pipeline to ensure that AI works towards human intended purposes and that all parts involved are aware of functioning and malfunctioning (Kim et al. 2022; Vaccaro and Madsen 2009).

The epochal challenge depicted has indeed elicited a vast number of contributions discussing ethical backgrounds to promote guidelines for AI development and management (Berente et al. 2021) (Attard-Frost et al. 2023). While a substantial "convergence" of the content of currently adopted ethical guidelines (Ryan and Stahl 2021) has been observed, common criticalities in their being timely and practical have been underlined (Munn 2023). Factors influencing such lack of effectiveness have been discussed: tendencies to underestimate—whether purposely or not—ethical implications of AI, related to a phenomenon that has been labeled "ethics bashing" (Bietti 2021); the ever-changing landscape of AI innovations, which requires the high capability of navigating uncertainty (Stahl et al. 2022); the inefficiency of ethical guidelines in the absence of other sources of ethical conduct, such as professional norms, clear responsibility attribution, clear mechanisms of makeup for trial and error, legal and professional accountability (Mittelstadt 2019).

This work addresses all the above-mentioned ethical challenges through the lenses of humanistic ethics and humanism in business as a cornerstone tradition of business ethics literature (Melé 2015; Pirson and Lawrence 2010). First, we highlight AI-related ethical questions and implications that broadly fall outside classic debates on the ethics of IT in business ethics literature. Indeed, similar technologically driven challenges have long been debated for other past technological advancements (Melé 2021). In a similar facet, for example, the advent of Information Computer Technologies (ICTs) has raised concerns over human rights protection in the digital world, accountability and transparency, moral duties for business users, workers' rights limitations, and the need for re actualization of labor relations (Cath and Floridi 2017; Cini 2023; Vaccaro and Madsen 2009). Nonetheless, the questions raised by AI ethics can easily fall under ethical approaches showing distinctive preferences for overcoming humans' current ontological state (Brusseau 123 C.E.; Nath and Manna 2023), which previous technological advancement did not display to such a degree. Ethical perspectives of beyond-humanism have been dwelling in the idea that technology can, through subsequent innovations, spontaneously overcome undesirable consequences it entails. By rejecting technological, moral neutrality, we argue that humanistic ethics confronting AI has to raise questions similar to applied ethics questions surrounding bioethics. Thus, promoting an "ex-ante" approach concerning human biological boundaries and the moral desirability to overcome them (Florida et al. 2021; Gill 2016; Zimmerman et al. 2023). This can replace "ex-post" approaches, focused on optimizing AI models while reducing sources of harm without questioning its purposes and desirability (Wright and Schultz 2018) (Widder and Whittaker 2023).

Second, we argue how accordingly humanistic ethics can contribute on at least three dimensions in safeguarding the human-centered application of technology: it prevents anthropological reductionism by underestimating personal human spiritual and immaterial dimensions to be enhanced by the organization as moral duty (Fontrodona and Sison 2006); it prevents devaluing human experience through values reductionism, leading to technological advancement as the sole rationale of the organization, undermining "organizational moral structure" (Lindebaum et al. 2023) (Roszkowska and Melé 2021); it promotes humanizing stakeholders' through their participation in AI decisions potentially affecting them (Hooker and Kim 2022; Sachs and Kujala 2022; Sison and Fontrodona 2013).

Third, we discuss how, among many scholars who have been focusing on the ethical shortcomings of AI deployment, only a minority has expressly framed its ethical issues in terms of risks and perils of dehumanization, both in terms of humanizing machines and automating humans (Craze 2019; Fritts and Cabrera 2021; Väyrynen and Laari-Salmela 2018; Chiodo 2022). Dehumanization can be broadly defined as a term that refers to any process, action, or belief through which individuals or groups perceive or act towards other individuals or groups as less worthy of human attributes and human treatment. As it has been summarized: "Dehumanization—the designation of the unlivable, the unintelligible, the ungrievable inhuman—is that almost unimaginable process by which human beings are rendered so radically other that their lives count for nothing." (Oliver 2011, p. 85). Such a process can be enrooted in denial of human features of the Other and the degradation of their integrity (Kaufmann et al. 2011). Main manifestations of dehumanization are enlisted as instrumental dehumanization, treatment of people as tools and ends; denial of human qualities, objectification, and stereotypical reification; moral exclusion, disregard for moral reasoning and standing of the other and therefore excluding them from moral considerations; reduction to non-human entities, offering animal-like or machine-like consideration to Otherness (Craze 2019; Haslam and Loughnan 2013). Whatever the forms were taken, "one aspect seems to be always present: dehumanization establishes difference and distance between human beings (Kronfeldner 2021, p. 9). The themes converging within this literature underscore the multifaceted nature of technological dehumanization. The standardization of human life, reduction of individuality, and the shift toward mechanized optimization speak to the extensive control technology exercises over human behavior and societal structures. This amalgamation of variables points to a systemic dehumanization effect, challenging established ethical norms and interpersonal trust while altering organizational climates and decision-making paradigms. Nonetheless, to our knowledge, humanism in business literature has provided a minority of contributions focusing specifically on dehumanization. By operationalizing such a concept, we highlight how dehumanization risks should be foreseen by addressing both dehumanizing practices created by AI use and dehumanization practices already existing in human-led decision-making but that AI can enhance or tame.

We, therefore, contribute to humanism as a framework to address AI ethical shortcomings on at least two levels: first, by looking not only at AI-driven increased opportunities and competitive advantage ends (Brynjolfsson and McAfee 2014) instead at the human ends of all economic activities and relationships changed by the advent of AI (Pirson 2022; Sandelands 2009) (Lindebaum et al. 2023b). Second, by correctly assessing dehumanization manifestation and risks (Craze 2019; Haslam and Loughnan 2013) in everyday social intercourses and organizational settings (Väyrynen and Laari-Salmela 2018).

In order to contribute to theoretical and practical advancements of humanistic ethics confronted with AI, we ask: How can Humanism serve as an ethical underpinning framework for normative and descriptive research on AI in business and organizations? How can Humanistic Ethics prevent dehumanization risks in organizations and support human-centered AI?

The remainder of the chapter is organized as follows: the first paragraph presents the main arguments summarizing shortcomings in ethical approaches to AI focused on the "ex-post" ethical guardrail, discussed as being enrooted in ethical theories aimed at surpassing humans' boundaries. The latter is critically assessed, and humanistic ethics is discussed as an alternative approach. The second paragraph proposes a discussion of AI "ex-ante" ethical intervention through the lenses of Integral Human Development as a paradigm of understanding technology as a means toward human ends, preventing AI automation from becoming the sole organizational rationale. The third paragraph discusses the notion of dehumanization as an overarching ethical concern regarding AI ethical risks; the fourth paragraph enlists the main contributions and proposes several future research paths.

1.2 Human-Centered AI Without Humanism: Beyond Technological Moral Neutrality

The first law of technology by Melvin Kranzberg in 1985 famously stated: "Technology is neither good nor bad; nor is it neutral". (Kranzberg 1986). Confronted with AI, organizations face unprecedented trade-offs between AI design and use for social positive impact purposes and AI exploitation to increase profitability and competitive standing while disregarding or underestimating possible ethical downfalls of its use (Mazzi and Floridi 2023). We here contend that two main approaches are used to face such a pressing issue: on the one hand, an "ex-post" approach, which relies on theories of technology transcending humans, based on the shared belief that subsequent innovations will mitigate the harms of precedent technological advancements (Campolo and Crawford 2020). On the other hand, an ethical stance deploying questions of applied ethics similar to bioethics, i.e., foreseeing an "ex-ante" approach: seeking to prevent ethical risks affecting human development by questioning the boundaries of morally desirable innovation. We argue that the second approach falls under humanistic ethics, while the first fall short of addressing moral guardrails and AI design and development goals throughout its pipeline (Munoko et al. 2020).

In light of the epochal challenges depicted above, criticism has been raised on developers' and big techs' observed behavior of foreseeing ethical guardrails of AI through "ex-post" measures. These measures fall under approaches using what has been called "Safe AI" and "Explainable AI": seeking to design AI by recognizing harmful impacts and minimizing them while circulating it, and building capabilities in human-AI interaction in order to facilitate human intervention to avoid harms mentioned above in the future (Harland et al. 2023). Scholars and practitioners have underlined how significant corporations involved in AI experimenting might be adopting a so-called "let us see how it goes" approach (Seele and Schultz 2022; Widder and Whittaker 2023): being caught in a tight race with competitors to deliver following AI models, developing corporations are addressing potential harms caused to humanity by such technologies while the latter are commercialized. Although deploying variable degrees of disclosure, clarifying present and possible future risks at different process stages. For example, in its fundamental format, it inserts disclaimers of non-accuracy of information delivered by Generative Artificial Intelligence with ChatGPT or a warning for fake content creation by MidJourney. Another example of an "ex-post" approach is the mechanism of Reinforced Learning Through Human Feedback (RLTHF), which is used to correct AI mistakes once the technology has been tested and circulated. Such approaches to ethical AI aim to optimize its models while reducing their harm. The latter, primarily used in current "Narrow AI" (AI designed for specific tasks), is coherent with utilitarianism and consequentialist perspectives, seeking to obtain AI efficacy as a primary objective at the expense of justifiable minor ethical shortcomings arising in the process (Tasioulas 2022).

Nonetheless, "Narrow AI" is not the only dimension engaging AI's most prominent developers. Although many perplexities (see, among others, Fjelland 2020) have been raised on the actual advent of ambitious Artificial General Intelligence (AGI), Artificial Super Intelligence (ASI), and others, projects like these are an explicit horizon for experiments of major AI developers, to the point that believing in AGI has been labeled a "religious belief" for those working at OpenAI (https://www.wired.com/story/what-openai-really-wants/). Therefore, understanding the ethical underpinnings of these organizations towards AI implications can shed light on the current ethical orientation of leaders and investors in the AI industry.

By foreseeing futuristic scenarios where machines are conscious, feeling, and capable of autonomous understanding, projects like AGI seek to imbue into machines that largely escape from human understanding itself of how the human mind works, leading to the famous observation by Michael Polanyi on "we know more than we can tell" (Fjelland 2020; Gigerenzer and Gaissmaier 2010)—dynamics of human reasoning and acting such as tacit knowledge, heuristics, intuition, and others. Through AI, ASI projects seek to achieve impossible capabilities for human intelligence in virtually all areas of human intelligence and action. Thus, building AI can "augment" human intelligence systematically for specific tasks. The latter has been addressed as the possibility for humanity to reach its worst or best wellbeing peak, depending on whether such ASI will be "hostile" or "friendly": the autonomy foreseen for such an AI would lead to a development impossible to completely forecast in terms of human-machines interactions (Gill 2016). Projects like AGI and ASI elicit ethical concerns not only on singular and punctual shortcomings of innovations but also concerning boundaries and desirability of machines' autonomy and of surpassing humankind's current state. Some current developments in AI are already pointing in such direction: questioning whether AI can be conscious, informs efforts of defining consciousness in non-humans (Lenharo 2023a, 2023b), and urges to define how human intentionality changes through interacting with a quasi-intentional technology (Zimmerman et al. 2023):

> AI, the technology using it, and the output generated by its use are long lasting and can take on a life of their own. It is not easy to predict how users' intentions will correspond to developer intentions, nor how the quasi-intention programmed into an artifact itself can be exploited or simply go wrong. The intentions of the parties and the quasi-intention of the AI itself across an artifact's timeline from conception to use may conflict or be aligned. (Zimmerman et al. 2023, p. 1004)

Furthermore, although some studies seem to confirm that AI still performs poorly, compared to humans, in conditions of unstable contexts, uncertain horizons of choices, and without proper human intervention (Gigerenzer 2022; Raisch and Krakowski 2021), developers involved in AGI and ASI projects are looking at new solutions aimed to substitute humans in highly critical decision-making processes. To do so, they must face what is now famously known as the "alignment problem." The latter compels all efforts to bestow human values (as well as considerations, emotional responses, and other variables) into algorithmic decision-making and unfolding so that the output is compatible with human objectives (Gabriel 2020) (Wright and Schultz 2018).

As these projects rely heavily on the belief that the current human ontological state can be evolved, augmented, and surpassed, they call into question ethical theories challenging human biological constraints: visions of relationships between humans and technologies that yield "beyond-human" understandings and entities. Common to such theories is the idea that by changing "what we are" and "how we are," innovations can spontaneously tame their implied harms through other subsequent innovations (Brusseau 123 C.E.). Theories of Posthumanism, for instance, reject anthropocentrism and question the human domain over technology and the surrounding environment (Braidotti 2013) (Sayers et al. 2022). With such an approach, it is possible to conceive autonomous AI as a dimension where humans are not leading technology, but rather, technology leads humans "beyond" humans (Merinda Simmons 2020). Theories of Transhumanism look into the possibility of transcending human limitations through technological progress, aiming at the tech-augmentation of the human. A typical example of transhumanistic technologies is Bio-enhancement products.

An example is Biohax International, the leader in the sector of microchips inserted in human bodies, to ensure quick and easy access to a range of facilities (home, gym, workplace, etc.) while keeping monitoring of health functions and others, which is very popular in Sweden (Giesen 2020). These beyond-humanism approaches do not hold humans as the sole locus of intentional and moral agency, as they object to human exceptionalism. By shifting the focus from the agent to the interaction, these theories underpin approaches in business ethics and organizational behavior studies that ground responsibility not in the human actor but instead in the effects of such interactions:

> A posthumanist practice theory, in denying the centrality of humans, defines the practice as an agencement of elements (humans, nonhumans, more-than-humans, discourses, bodies, rules, knowledge) that achieve agency in their being intra-acting. Intra-action refers to the mutual constitution of entangled agencies [...] This principle of 'agentivity' means that we do not study managers as individuals or collectives, managerial work, and activities, management discourse in isolation, nor managerial education or learning as separate activities rather we study the social effects of their interconnections. (Gherardi and Laasch 2022)

Procedures informed by these approaches are underpinned by the belief in desirability, sometimes even in the inevitability of blurring the lines between humanizing machines and automating humans (Chiodo 2022; Nath and Manna 2023).

Against this scenario, where, broadly taken, it can be observed that non-humanistic approaches value technological innovation as a good per se, Humanistic ethics evaluates technological advancement in light of its human benefits, taking an "ex-ante" ethical stance on AI development. Humanistic ethics is indeed first and foremost concerned, as bioethics, with human purposes and needs to be met by innovation, explicitly addressing "ex-ante" its desirability (van Maanen 2022; Yeung et al. 2019), differently than the ones mentioned above (Brusseau 2023). Concerning AI design, humanistic ethics considers both its social impact and social motives, for instance, by addressing which are welfare goals (or its harming risks) towards which move as individuals and collectives: "[AI] systems are embedded in social, political, cultural and economic worlds, shaped by humans, institutions, and imperatives which determine what they do and how they do it. [...] When applied in social contexts such as policing, the court system, health care, and education, they [AI technologies] can reproduce, optimize, and amplify existing structural inequalities" (Crawford 2021, pp. 211–212). Humanistic ethics is therefore concerned not only with the unethical byproducts of certain technologies but with their social infrastructure as the origin of their design and the target of their use. Such a perspective is highly relevant for organizational ethical programmes on AI. As Blackman has observed, business concern with ethical AI needs to be enrooted in both structure ("the way you identify and mitigate ethical risk") and content ("what you take those ethical risks to be" (Blackman 2023, p.17).

Furthermore, as it has been recalled, humanistic ethics in AI requires at least three principles to be observed:

> 1."commitment to a plurality of values", 2. "stress on the importance of the procedures we adopt, not just the outcomes they yield", 3. "centrality it accords to individual and collective participation in our understanding of human well-being and morality." (Tasioulas 2022, p. 232)

These principles reject the idea of technological, moral neutrality by investing humans in integral responsibilities—whether held by people or/and bodies (individuals, corporations, institutions)—refusing to recognize machines' responsibility as a substitute for human control and accountability over AI creations and use (Craze 2019; Johnson 2015; Melé 2021). Indeed, all three principles to be operationalized require answering to a specific "Who" is responsible and in charge of ensuring them. Just as defining moral objectives as ethical guidelines of AI, defining agency in moral responsibility in AI represents an "ex-ante" requirement to both prevent ethical risk and, at the same time, channel innovation towards desirable goals.

In the following two paragraphs, we will discuss how such an "ex-ante" approach can be operationalized in everyday ethical dilemmas and trade-offs arising in organizations faced with AI deployment.

1.3 Humanism and the Organizational Rationale: Three-Dimensional Aspects

Humanism in business within organizational studies has acquired a wide range of popularity among scholars and practitioners thanks to its ability to inform ethical decision-making processes and aim for economic sustainability as a means to human flourishing and development (Aktouf 1992; Pirson and Lawrence 2010; Rosanas 2008). In particular, Integral Human Development (IHD), as underpinning Humanistic Management literature (Pirson 2022; Schlag and Melé 2020), is a multidimensional paradigm that emphasizes the holistic development of individuals, encompassing not only economic progress but also social, cultural, and psychological well-being (Keleher 2018). Such a paradigm has been adopted to discuss how organizations can provide safe spaces to enhance IHD potential, aiming for the wellbeing of all stakeholders, including employees, customers, and the communities in which businesses operate (Sen 1999), especially marginalized groups and fragile persons (Mongelli et al. 2018). Organizations embracing the principles of IHD prioritize ethical and sustainable practices, promote diversity and inclusion, and aim to create work environments that foster people-centered, holistic development (Nussbaum 2000).

We argue that the stream of humanism in business (de Colle et al. 2023) can inform ethical AI in organizations on at least three pivotal levels: personal level, by understanding organizations' role in fostering human integral development, thus avoiding tendencies of devaluing human experience through machines' surveillance and control (Kim et al. 2021); at organizational level, by avoiding automation efficiency to become the sole *rationale* of the organization (Lindebaum et al. 2023); at society level by informing stakeholders' relationships, focusing on safeguarding humanizing stakeholders as people and groups holding intrinsic dignity, thus preventing mistreating them as mere means and passive subjectivities in automation processes (Buhmann and Fieseler 2023; Sachs and Kujala 2022).

At the individual level, humanism promotes the overcoming limitations of the neoclassical *homo oeconomicus* approach, based on the anthropological monodimensional homo maximizer (Melé and Cantón 2014), whose acting is concerned only with one's utility curve satisfaction. On the contrary, humanism and IHD emphasize the interconnectedness of various dimensions of human life and advocate for policies and practices that enable individuals to flourish in all aspects of their lives, including education, health, social inclusion, and personal fulfillment (Acevedo 2012; Burgos and Melé 2018). In this way, humanistic ethics can fully reflect the complexity of human experience to assess AI impacts in terms of its enhancement. More in general, organizations are running the risk of increasing, through their AI-led operations, the omni-pervasive use of those psychological, moral, spiritual, and cultural dimensions of human life as a means to increase technological efficiency rather than each person's wellbeing (Reeves and Sinnicks 2023b) (Melé 2021).

Indeed, it has been observed that, through extensive automation, virtually every aspect of human life, even friendships, love exchanges, and companionship, can become "mechanized and highly economized sociability" (Marszałek-Kotzur 2022). An example of such tendency is what has been called the "Gamification" of Human Resource Management, especially with regards to employees' productivity: a phenomenon through which employees are encouraged to work longer hours or achieve more production targets by using play mechanisms of game-like-competition; deploying AI in such contexts can essentially enhance gamification possibilities, thus using AI creative power to harness organizations' members' free and resting time, rather than freeing people's creative and relational dimensions from tedious and unsatisfactory tasks (Hammedi et al. 2020; Wünderlich et al. 2020).

Another example of gamification through algorithmic mediation has been described within the context of personal life as the mechanism promoted by dating apps and online dating (Abolfathi and Santamaria 2020). Although offering a pretense of efficiency in matching preferences for partners, thus yielding time-saving and expanding meeting opportunities for users, dating online and app services have faced much criticism for their algorithmic choices. Aside from bias in matching algorithms (ex., between white and non-white people, upper and lower economic status, etc.) being extensively reported, and CEOs dealing with discriminating outputs having become a Harvard Business Case in Business Ethics and Diversity topics (https://hbsp.harvard.edu/product/7977-HTM-ENG), the business model of online dating are facing other ethical shortcomings. As Gingerenzer argues, dating services overestimate AI's potential to run correctly in an area of affection bounds, which is unpredictable *par excellence* (Gigerenzer 2022). Users count on dating apps to fulfill their romantic and sexual longings. However, this need remains unaddressed mainly, thus facing a situation in which, on one side, apps are trying to maximize profit by monetization romantic and sexual needs for companionship (what has been called "the macdonaldization of romance" (Stoicescu 2020)) while users become increasingly unsatisfied with dating settings unsuited for their need. A comprehensive production of AI has warned of the risk of overestimating technological judgment while underestimating humans. This tendency has been called "enchanted determinism": the idea that algorithmic decisions can perform better in terms of objectivity and neutrality than humans, as well as the belief that algorithms themselves, in their neutrality, are responsible for their possible adverse outcomes (Campolo and Crawford 2020). Such perspective, coherent with the strands mentioned above of beyond-humanism projects, has nonetheless been sharply criticized and proven in its far-reaching limitation: extensive and persistent algorithmic bias is only one of the many issues deriving from AI's tendency to reduce complexity through proxy and rely on past occurrences to predict and inform the future (Tilmes 2022) (Tambe et al. 2019). AI systems can only work correctly towards human intended outcomes when deployed in highly stable, well-confined contexts; furthermore, algorithms perform worse than humans in all those uncertain and complex contexts where human gut feelings, intuition, and heuristics come into play in a way that remains largely to be adequately grasped by human understanding itself, remaining far from being embedded in machines (Gigerenzer 2022). While some scholars have advised a revision of the classic "freemium" model to increase dating app profits, its model could be revised through a humanistic perspective to elicit companies' ethical stances on using AI to promote more human interaction rather than relying on automated sorting and matching. This could be done by foreseeing, together with access to premium versions of the platform, free offline socialization events organized in partnership with selected NGOs and citizen activists' organizations. Such events could foresee volunteering or advocacy activities, thus enriching the user's personal experience, making time and room to participate in a cause while meeting other people with similar interests. To pair online dating services with positive social impact events could better users' experience by fulfilling more than one need: participating in volunteering or social activities can be a positive experience as such, even if the romantic or sexual encounter is not suitable to their desires, allowing adjusting algorithmic sorting with different variables than those traditionally causing racial and gender biases, while also showing commitment from the dating service to offer an online medium explicitly focused on the offline social wellbeing of users. Humanism reclaims dimensions of interpersonal rewarding intercourses, leisure, and personal passions as fundamental ingredients of mental health and personal wellbeing. Therefore, as dimensions to be reclaimed in their gratuity and spontaneity rather than subsumed by profit purposes, exploitation bears inevitable social and personal costs (Pfeffer 2018).

At the organizational level, when confronting ethical issues arising in AI-driven organizations, reasoning by analogy (Seele and Schultz 2022), it is possible to identify a reductionist approach to automation similar to the one deployed by economistic thinking (Melé 2013). Humanism has addressed the latter as the tendency to reduce the organization's scope to the sole economic profitability, regardless of human quality treatments, negative externalities, and its broader social impact (Melé 2014) (Van Der Linden and Freeman 2017). A similar tendency has been highlighted when discussing the organizational *rationale* being subsumed by mechanization: technological innovation can shrink the role of human values and their relevance to operations, strategic decision-making, and organizational change (Lindebaum et al. 2023). The economistic approach and the mechanization of values share the underpinning idea of efficiency, whether adopted from the start or increasingly present, as the sole and primary scope of organizational survival, echoing Friedman's famous motto against understanding Corporate Social Responsibility. In this way, the organization undergoes a perversion of its functioning: "By creating certain standards of measuring reality and presenting it in the form of numerical representations, man has given control over himself to algorithms, which have deprived many phenomena of their context and meaning" (Marszałek-Kotzur 2022, p. 272).

Furthermore, they share a common disregarding and denying of spiritual and intangible spheres informing organizational functioning and purpose: in its stream enrooted in Catholic Social Teaching (CST), IHD focuses on organizations as social bodies with the moral duty to acknowledge each person's spiritual, psychological, economic, and moral dimensions. It emphasizes the interconnectedness of these facets of human life. It insists on the responsibility of society, organizations, and institutions to promote conditions that enable individuals to achieve their full potential, ensuring material wellbeing and spiritual and moral growth (Pope Paul VI, Populorum Progressio 1967). In CST, IHD serves as a body of guiding principles that advocates for solidarity, justice, and the Common Good, urging to address structural injustices and inequalities while prioritizing the dignity and rights of every person, especially the marginalized and vulnerable (Pope Francis, Laudato Si' 2015; (Arnaud and Wasieleski 2014; Zigarelli 1993).

The corporation addresses such a bundle of moral duties through what has been called "organizational moral structure" (Roszkowska and Melé 2021), relying on the notion of the moral agency of the organization and its underpinning organizational moral values (Scott 2002). AI moral responsibility requires a structural adequacy of the organizational moral structure: first, through building "trans-organizational awareness" concerning AI, i.e., the need to involve all levels and structures in an ambitious reform of organizational culture aimed at eliciting members' trust towards both technology adopted and governance decisions upon them (Ammanath and Blackman 2021). Second, through careful management of AI throughout the entire organizational value chain, due to its extensive impact at a global scale: "[AI is] a manifestation of highly organized capital backed by vast systems of extraction and logistics, with supply chains that wrap around the entire planet" (Crawford 2021, pp. 18–19). AI is far from just a digital infrastructure: it rests on material infrastructures and social fabric, sustaining it through physical and natural resources (van Wynsberghe

2021) and foreseeing human labor to train and better its functioning. Responsible AI requires ethical surveillance of a particular technology deployment and an extensive consideration of its social impact throughout its pipeline. Among the main targets of responsible AI should be the organization's responsibility to avoid underestimating the potential worsening of stakeholders' conditions in already fragile or marginalized groups and focus on groups disproportionately affected by AI developing material infrastructure. This ethical challenge can be observed in so-called "AI sweatshops": organizations are reconceiving part of their global value chain by using underpaid labor to train AI learning systems.[3] This observed phenomenon poses two major ethical issues: one, more traditional, rests on fair and decent working conditions as one of the main targets of SDGs and ethical compliance (Mazzi and Floridi 2023). A second, more specifically focused AI-focused debate has sprung over processes and programs involving humans training AI through human recognition, human feedback, and humans dealing with large amounts of data to feed machine learning (among others). The phenomenon elicits vast ethical concern, to the point that some have suggested that workers take control of the process by promoting cooperatives to own the training outputs (Sriraman et al. 2020). From a humanistic perspective, the organization is not solely concerned with a narrow part of its global operations and supply chain; instead, its moral structure comprehensively extends to all of it to prevent unethical behavior in all related spheres (Aguiñaga and Leal 2023). In the same facet, organizations are bound to be responsible for both digital and material infrastructures that sustain AI. To thoroughly apply such perspective to programs and initiatives of training AI by humans, it is possible to foresee specific programs for involved workers in AI training, combining both their goal to develop AI and workers' training aimed at their upskilling and reskilling. This can mitigate the worst consequences of turning workers' activity into self-endangering: by training AI with no additional prospects, these people would face, once they succeeded in their tasks, job loss. Pairing upskilling and reskilling programs with their AI training programs would offer new prospects and new skills to workers, thus protecting their future while bettering their chances for a vocational job (Kim and Scheller-Wolf 2022). In this way, organizations can focus on the meaningfulness of tasks performed, taking the perspective of people performing them rather than evaluating tasks' usefulness per se. This approach is coherent with the preeminence accorded by CST and humanism to the so-called "subjective dimension of labor" (i.e., the role of work in people's development and social life) over its objective one (the role of capital and means of production within an organized economy) (Melé 2021).

Third, at the stakeholders' relationships level, humanism proposes treating stakeholders as people with intrinsic dignity, autonomous points of view, and personal qualities, all exceeding economic transactions at stake in organizational operations. Such a view is summarized in stakeholders' engagement perspectives aiming to humanize stakeholder relationships (Kujala et al. 2022; Sachs and Kujala 2022).

[3] https://www.washingtonpost.com/world/2023/08/28/scale-ai-remotasks-philippines-artificial-intelligence/.

Research has shown how moral standards in moral behavior decline when interactions change from humans to humans and machines (Giroux et al. 2022). This can facilitate unethical behavior in a variety of stakeholder relationships: members of the organization can increase amoral or immoral behavior when confronting machines rather than colleagues; externals, such as customers, might increase their eagerness to try to exploit machines' failures to their advantage (Kim et al. 2023). Increased unethical behavior in human–machine interaction is also observed the other way around: organizations might be tempted to adopt AI systems to control members beyond ethical boundaries (Varma et al. 2022) while using its highly deceptive power to elicit customers' desired responses (for example, to bypass customers' resistance (Garvey et al. 2023). Diffusion of such behaviors can result in an overall loss of trust in stakeholders' relationships.

A widespread example of stakeholders' backlash due to generative AI adoption is the wave of creative workers' protests, which is interesting to virtually all creative industries (global cinema, music, arts, content creation industry, etc.). The protests are two-fold: On the one hand, fear of job replacement fuels many professionals' resentment against AI, used in movie directors' activities, novelists, AI-designed people to replace actors, and even AI fake influencers replacing real people's online content creation. The foreseeing of such replacement has been highly debated: claims of creative jobs being awarded to AI might be vastly exaggerated, and other sources of financing for creative humanly-performed jobs might be foreseen as distinct from automated ones. On the other hand, protests have sprung from using creative works and artifacts by tech developers to feed AI without granting credits and compensation to artists and owners of such work. The issue is a quickly rising one due to its extent: companies have exploited the gray area of insufficient law on copyright infringement with AI; furthermore, publishers themselves are discussing ways of selling authorship rights on past catalogs in their possession to big techs to make a significant profit, facing potential legal trouble with authors, who did not sign contracts during past years which explicitly address such particular case. An even more subtle issue of authorship and source recognition is tied to Google Bard and ChatGPT's use of internet information to answer questions on their search engines without crediting media and newspaper outlets where the information was found. Such protests have taken a turn with legal suing from The New York Times to OpenAI and Microsoft for illegal use of published work to train AI.[4]

Such illegal and, if not unethical, behavior by big techs disregards human creativity and artifact value by exploiting its output without crediting the human effort and human intelligence driving it, unveiling a process of disregarding stakeholders' creativity to replace it with AI. Contrary to the process of humanizing stakeholders, treating them as an end rather than a means, in this case, stakeholders are reified and used as a means for technological progress and foreseen profit. Given the complexity of the case, in both its legal and ethical implications, organizations intending to use human creative work to feed generative AI should adopt, as a general ethical rule,

[4] https://www.nytimes.com/2023/12/27/business/media/new-york-times-open-ai-microsoft-lawsuit.html.

extensive processes of democratized stakeholder engagements: much of the strikes, protests, and lawsuits have come and will come from the impossibility for affected stakeholders to have a saying in the feeding AI process, even when (as in the case of news outlets) are critical stakeholders for the organization (in this case, big techs). This is critical to companies not wanting to face backlash, in terms of protests, boycotts, and others, by industry workers, other companies supplying human content, and consumers solidarizing with the cause of displaced artists and media outlets. By democratizing the process of human content use for AI purposes, companies propositioning generative AI technologies can promote stakeholders' protagonism in assessing and negotiating adequate compensation, foreseeing new roles of human creativity, elaborating on how to reach creativity augmentation rather than automation (Raisch and Krakowski 2021).

Humanism promotes participation as a driver of personal and organizational well-being (Fontrodona and Sison 2006; Sison and Fontrodona 2013). By following the principle of subsidiarity, which highlights the importance of upper levels being supported by freedom and adequate degrees of autonomy for lower levels, foreseeing affected stakeholders' participation can powerfully elicit their protagonism, as well as channeling their involvement in decision-making processes, ensuring accountability and transparency (Pope Benedict XVI, Caritas in Veritate 2009; Sandelands 2009). Moreover, especially within CST literature deployed in business ethics studies, pivotal importance is given to stakeholders' participation in the firm determinants of shared purposes, as well as to their achievable means to ensure, at the same time, economic and human sustainability of foreseen activities (Fontrodona and Sison 2006; Rosanas 2008). This principle is helpful in AI-driven organizational changes, as secular literature has also underlined how stakeholders' participation can enhance and support democratic accountability of AI-led processes, securing support for controversial decisions and promoting step-by-step engagement of pluralistic voices (Buhmann and Fieseler 2023; Novelli et al. 2023). Furthermore, the dimension of participation of stakeholders involved in automation processes can support humanizing businesses in engaging otherwise marginalized groups (Derry 2012; Freeman 1994) who are often disproportionately affected by its negative consequences, as well as by the development of critical infrastructures to enable the correct functioning of AI systems, all leading to further concentration of power (Crawford 2021).

1.4 AI-Driven Organizations in Enhancing or Preventing Dehumanization: An Overarching Ethical Concern

By adopting a humanistic perspective, it is possible to analyze all previously mentioned ethical shortcomings linked to AI as potential threats of dehumanization, varying in urgency and impact. Business Ethics literature has underlined how dehumanization, once discussed only in extreme contexts of war and violence, can also be traced in everyday social intercourses and organizational settings (Väyrynen and

Laari-Salmela 2018) (Carroll and Hannan 2018). Furthermore, ethics of AI literature has discussed how AI irresponsible design and deployment can insert dehumanization practices, which hold dire consequences for internal and external stakeholders (Fritts and Cabrera, 2021) (Hooker and Kim 2022). We here contend that dehumanization is an overarching ethical concern and should be understood by looking at dehumanization perils from technologies themselves and human-led dehumanization processes of dehumanization, which technologies can enhance or help in taming.

In particular, two main aspects of dehumanization are at stake in organizations designing and deploying AI: first, humanizing machines, thus relying on their ability to perform human-like activities with increased efficiency, by underestimating trade-offs arising from losing other human components (for example, critical thinking in decision making, empathy in diagnosis, knowledge of processes, etc.). This may lead to human de-responsabilization. We observed that organizations are reasonably widely tempted to adopt AI to speed production, optimize internal processes, and support stakeholder relations (*par excellence* with customers). AI represents a formidable driver of competitive advantage (Kemp 2023). Furthermore, reasons for "motivated blindness" can underpin the underestimation of ethical AI implications: when decision-making is delegated to non-humans, it offers the possibility to reify the blame by bestowing it upon the machine, and it puts a filtering distance between the executor and those affected by the executive decision (Detert et al. 2008). The second dehumanizing risk is the mechanization of humans, a process through which humans are understood as fungible in organizational dynamics, thus being subjected to devices' work optimization rather than subjecting technological advancements to human needs. Such process of mechanization of people leads to progressive instrumentalization of humans, defined as:

> [...] people are viewed as objects or automata, as they are denied those features that define human nature: individuality, interpersonal warmth, cognitive openness, and agency. When these features are denied to people, they are seen as being machinelike, replaceable ("fungibility"), and they are treated in an emotionally distant manner or denied an emotional connection altogether. They might be seen as lacking self-determination or incapable of making autonomous decisions. Those persons who view others in such a manner refuse to acknowledge any of their attempts at self-actualization or cognitive openness (referring to flexibility and mental curiosity as a part of human nature). (Väyrynen and Laari-Salmela 2018, pp. 96–97)

This has already been observed in paradoxes such as humans being given fatiguing and repetitive tasks that are managed by algorithms: this is the case, among others, of platform work of rider food delivery and other Gig economy contexts (Crawford 2021; Craze 2019; James 2023).

Hiring algorithm deployment has observed an example of a straightforward process of dehumanization through AI (Fritts and Cabrera, 2021). The phenomenon has reached such an extent that Amazon's hiring program through AI has been put to a stop after years of significant investments and development due to its recurring bias in hiring disproportionately men over women.[5] Companies facing this issue

---

[5] https://www.reuters.com/article/idUSKCN1MK0AG/.

focus on bettering the algorithms, thus deploying trust in algorithms' capabilities to make better decisions than humans. This is consistent with focusing on speeding up the process of curricula screening. This approach can be understood as a case of "enchanted determinism" (Campolo and Crawford 2020): relying on machines' decisions in the hope that they will be more neutral than humans'. From a humanistic perspective, this approach underestimates the weight that corporate culture, intertwined with values, has on recruitment processes and, more in general, on human quality treatment (Melé 2014). Indeed, deploying humanistic ethics would suggest that companies focus on reasons underpinning the sources of biases and focus on fixing their organizational culture, which results unfit for specific groups and people. Suppose the technology shows sexist behavior by the organization, for instance, by disproportionately hiring males instead of females. In that case, this can be used as a red flag to address why, in previous years, the organization has been built revolving around males as employees. By looking into organizational culture, workplace fit for women, and organizational stances on gender issues, the organization can start a comprehensive reform program towards equal opportunities enhancement. While the current approach focuses on fixing the algorithm, which is desirable, the humanistic approach would suggest further acknowledging the role of the organization within a scenario of structural inequality (for example, fewer women in STEM, therefore less presence of women's CVs in the database), and use it to promote equality with counterbalancing measures. Rather than bestowing hiring responsibility upon AI, the organization can keep complete control over the process by ethically intervening off and on the algorithm: first, "off-AI", by enquiring into women's roles and points of view in the organization, surveying their most felt difficulties in gaining experiences and titles required by the organization. Coherently, carefully scrutinize AI vendors who have assessed such variables in designing their technology. Second, "on-AI" uses the gathered information to correct and intervene in the algorithm with additional checks, such as oversampling some groups and using different weights on critical variables. Third, cross-checking trial results of selection with relevant social imbalances for gender inclusion: for example, given the gender pay gap, is the algorithm selecting more women in roles with less compensation? Or, given the rate of return to work after childbirth, is the algorithm including women within an age cohort when pregnancies usually occur? Fourth, "on-AI" adjust the algorithm to the information drawn from the cross-check between organizational internal imbalances and societal gender issues. This discriminatory algorithm can be used for non-discriminatory purposes, thus keeping human responsibility and control over AI decision-making, escaping scenarios of overestimating AI's neutrality. This is how a humanistic perspective focused on inclusion can guardrail both de-responsibilization and instrumentalization processes tied to AI use.

A second primary source of human responsibilization and instrumentalization is tied to cases of AI dehumanization risks related not to intrinsic unethical features of the algorithm (as in the hiring process just presented) but to human dehumanizing behavior adopted in AI use. The latter can be enhanced or tamed by AI. A significant case of such dehumanization is one of the girl reported to have been sexually assaulted in the metaverse, now under scrutiny by the UK police, as well as other similar cases.[6] As experiences in the metaverse, through avatars and augmented reality, can elicit similar neural and physical responses to real-life experiences, virtual sexual assaults are now debated as a widespread potential source of dehumanizing consequences. Sexual assault is indeed one of the most cruel and widespread forms of dehumanization. While authorities are still progressing on policies to punish and manage virtual crime in augmented reality ecosystems, organizations are responsible for building them by targeting their safety for all social groups.

This is one of those cases in which companies, even those highly concerned with accountability and transparency on ethical AI use, might be far behind in figuring out how to hold accountable users' behavior and tackling humans' increased tendency in virtual ecosystems to be aggressive. From humanistic ethics, sexual assault is a case of disregarding human dignity in all its multifaced, physical, psychological, and moral dimensions, and all such dimensions should be granted protection in virtual spaces as well as in physical ones. The case of metaverse sexual assault gets away from AI regulations based on ethical AI, as they do not depend directly on how the digital ecosystem is built but on the behavior adopted by human users within such an ecosystem.

This source of dehumanization needs to be addressed by current ethics AI approaches revolving around principles and guidelines derived from them (Mittelstadt 2019; Munn 2023; Pruss 2023). Indeed, companies are trying to tame unethical AI deployment by listing principles and values and seeking ethicists' counseling about how to operationalize such lists. Cases like the "metaverse rape" point to the need to overcome the "principle approach" to reach better policies to prevent humans' misuse of technology. Humanistic ethics, in this regard, elicit questions such as: Which virtues should the ecosystem promote? Which are the main drivers of violent behavior connected with virtual behavior, and, consequently, how can the ecosystem be adapted to prevent them? An "off-AI / on-AI" ethical strategy is needed to address these variables, first, by developing "off-AI," a critical assessment of violent behavior in non-virtual situations which may be similar to the virtual ecosystem developed; second, by intervening in the "on-AI" design process to isolate possible devices used to violent purposes. Third, go back to "off-AI" to cross-check the safety of digital ecosystems by setting trials and experiments focusing on those critical variables and gathering more fragile groups' feedback on their perceived safety and feeling at ease. Lastly, provide "on-AI" processes of personal accountability, i.e., by verifying users' identity and having users agree on codes of conduct and others. Alternatively, training people to use the metaverse with designed ethical boundaries and educational games to elicit respectful behavior might be a way to increase the chances of positive reinforcement of correct behavior for people who showed aggressive patterns in the past.

[6] https://nypost.com/2024/01/13/tech/i-was-gang-raped-in-the-metaverse-my-trauma-is-very-real/.

https://www.businessinsider.com/police-investigate-digital-gang-rape-teen-vr-metaverse-horizon-worlds-2024-1?r=USandIR=T.

These are only two examples of how the grey area of ethical AI can be exploited to enhance current social imbalances and risks of dehumanization or try to use it by looking at taming their sources.

1.5 Concluding Remarks and Future Paths of Research

We here summarize the main contributions and possible practical implications of the chapter:

> First, we discuss how technological moral neutrality, *i.e., the belief that technological advancement is positive progress* per se *without further moral connotation, informs the* ethical underpinning of major AI projects. By discussing the case of Artificial General Intelligence, Artificial Super Intelligence, and similar projects, we highlight how ethical AI developers can adopt theories of beyond-humanism approaches (posthumanism, transhumanism, etc.) to justify their quest to promote AI surpassing human boundaries. Humanistic ethics can help guardrail AI-related ethical design by, first and foremost, asking why particular technologies are developed and who benefits from their outputs. In this regard, we contribute to the field of ethics of AI by looking into its shortcomings by adopting a bioethics perspective, as the closest applied ethics field to AI ethics, by focusing on how humanistic ethics can help in operationalizing such view in the context of business organizations (Mazzi and Floridi, n.d.; Zimmerman et al. 2023).

This perspective significantly impacts CEOs and big tech companies, as top managers and policymakers will increasingly be confronted with decisions on the strategic aims of AI mega-projects. Also, conflicts on such views have been the source of major internal companies' disagreement among top managers in the past (see the case of OpenAI), therefore signaling the need for robust ethical enrooting of decision-making upon AI design goals.

Second, we discuss how humanistic ethics can prevent unethical behavior and enhance human flourishing in at least three dimensions. At the individual level, we highlight how AI can turn emotional dimensions of human life (such as love and friendship) into commercialized dimensions through algorithmic management. We propose to adopt pervasive partnerships with NGOs and civil society organizations to counterbalance this tendency by offering spaces to preserve the gratuity of multifaceted dimensions of a rewarding human social life. At the organizational level, we identify the risk of automation becoming the primary organizational rationale, thus disregarding values and their roles in underpinning the organizational moral structure. We, therefore, propose to address unethical AI use throughout all pipelines and global value chains, taking responsibility for AI in all its infrastructure and avoiding human rights harms being sacrificed to its fast-paced development. Last, in stakeholders' relationships, AI can risk losing trust and incurring protests and boycotts by looking at AI's impact in disregarding humanizing stakeholders. Therefore, we propose democratizing stakeholders' engagement to foresee collaborative governance of AI major transitions in all industries, especially those subjected to extensive workforce reskilling and layoffs. In this way, we contribute to the literature on business ethics facing AI disruption by developing a three-dimensional model aimed at preventing AI from becoming the "master" of humans (den Hond and Moser 2023; Kim et al. 2021), preserving humanistic relationships between internals and externals (Derry 2012; Kim and Scheller-Wolf 2022; Sachs and Kujala 2022); helping organizations in focusing on counterbalancing AI potential for competitive advantage with clear targets of human integral development and wellbeing (Melé 2015, 2021; Vaccaro 2023).

This perspective is precious to practitioners faced with difficult decisions on deploying ethical decision-making without incurring ethical digital washing (Bietti 2021; Seele and Schultz 2022; Yeung et al. 2019). Indeed, we show how humanistic ethics can address the three dimensions altogether by informing organizational culture so that organizational practices can be coherent with one another without running the risk of investing resources in ineffective principles-list and general values statements, challenging to be operationalized (Attard-Frost et al. 2023; Munn 2023; Ryan and Stahl 2021; van Maanen 2022).

Lastly, we contribute to the literature on AI and dehumanization in organizations by highlighting how human de-responsibilization and instrumentalization processes can be tamed by correctly assessing dehumanization risks and foreseeing "on/off AI" processes. The latter aims to prevent dehumanization from inherent unethical bias, other undesirable features of deployed algorithms, and unethical use by humans of AI. By looking into actual cases of hiring AI discrimination and sexual assaults in virtual realities, we contribute to highlighting organizational moral responsibility to use AI towards equitable and fair human treatment of all involved groups (Craze 2019; Fritts and Cabrera, 2021; Kronfeldner 2021; Väyrynen and Laari-Salmela 2018).

References

Abolfathi N, Santamaria S (2020) Dating disruption-how Tinder gamified an industry. MIT Sloan Manag Rev 61(3):7–11

Acevedo A (2012) Personalist business ethics and humanistic management: insights from Jacques Maritain. J Bus Ethics 105(2):197–219. https://doi.org/10.1007/s10551-011-0959-x

Agrawal A, Gans J, Goldfarb A (2019) The economics of artificial intelligence: an agenda. https://www.nber.org/books-and-chapters/economics-artificial-intelligence-agenda

Aguiñaga E, Leal AR (n.d.) Supply chain management. Humanistic management and circular economy: fostering industry innovation and decent work through responsible consumption and production through partnership. https://doi.org/10.4324/9780429351117

Aktouf O (1992) Management and theories of organizations in the 1990s: Toward a critical radical humanism? Acad Manag Rev 17(3):407–431. https://doi.org/10.2307/258717

Ammanath B, Blackman R (2021, July) Everyone in your organization needs to understand AI ethics. Harvard Business Review. https://hbr.org/2021/07/everyone-in-your-organization-needs-to-understand-ai-ethics

Arnaud S, Wasieleski DM (2014) Corporate humanistic responsibility: social performance through managerial discretion of the HRM. J Bus Ethics 120(3):313–334. https://doi.org/10.1007/s10551-013-1652-z

Attard-Frost B, De los Ríos, A., and Walters, D. R. (2023) The ethics of AI business practices: a review of 47 AI ethics guidelines. AI Ethics 3(2):389–406. https://doi.org/10.1007/s43681-022-00156-6

Bélisle-Pipon JC, Monteferrante E, Roy MC, Couture V (2023) Artificial intelligence ethics has a black box problem. AI & Soc 38(4):1507–1522. https://doi.org/10.1007/S00146-021-01380-0/FIGURES/6

Berente N, Gu B, Recker J, Santhanam R (n.d.) Special issue: managing AI. Managing artificial intelligence 1.https://doi.org/10.25300/MISQ/2021/16274

Berente N, Gu B, Recker J, Santhanam R (2021) Managing artificial intelligence. MIS Q 45(3)

Bietti E (2021) From ethics washing to ethics bashing: a moral philosophy view on tech ethics. J. Soc. Comput. 2(3): 266–283. https://doi.org/10.23919/JSC.2021.0031

Blackman R, Niño C (2023) How to avoid the ethical nightmares of emerging technology

Blackmann R (2023) Ethical machines your concise guide to totally unbiased, transparent, and respectful AI. Harvard Business Review Press

Braidotti R (2013) The posthuman. (Polity Press)

Brusseau J (123 C.E.) Discover artificial intelligence mapping AI avant-gardes in time: Posthumanism, transhumanism, genhumanism. Discov Artif Intell 3, 32. https://doi.org/10.1007/s44163-023-00080-6

Brusseau J (2023) Mapping AI avant-gardes in time: posthumanism, transhumanism, genhumanism. Discover Artificial Intelligence 3(1):32. https://doi.org/10.1007/s44163-023-00080-6

Brynjolfsson E, McAfee A (2014) The second machine age: Work, progress, and prosperity in a time of brilliant technologies. WW Norton and Company

Buhmann A, Fieseler C (2023) Deep learning meets deep democracy: deliberative governance and responsible innovation in artificial intelligence. Bus Ethics Q 33(1):146–179. https://doi.org/10.1017/beq.2021.42

Burgos JM, Melé D (2018) Personalism. In Encyclopedia of business and professional ethics (pp 1–6). Springer International Publishing. https://doi.org/10.1007/978-3-319-23514-1_99-1

Campolo A, Crawford K (2020) Enchanted determinism: power without responsibility in artificial intelligence. Engaging science, technology, and society, pp 6, 1–19. https://doi.org/10.17351/ESTS2020.277

Carroll GR, Hannan MT (2018) The demography of corporations and industries. Princeton University Press

Cath C, Floridi L (2017) The design of the internet's architecture by the Internet Engineering Task Force (IETF) and human rights. Sci Eng Ethics 23(2):449–468. https://doi.org/10.1007/s11948-016-9793-y

Chiodo S (2022) Human autonomy, technological automation (and reverse). 37, 39–48. https://doi.org/10.1007/s00146-021-01149-5

Cini L (2023) How algorithms are reshaping the exploitation of labour-power: insights into the process of labour invisibilization in the platform economy. Theory Soc 52(5):885–911. https://doi.org/10.1007/S11186-023-09520-9

Crawford K (2021) Atlas of AI. Power, politics, and the planetary costs of artificial intelligence. Yale University Press

Craze G (2019) Corporate social responsibility and dehumanization. Philosophy of Management 18(1):43–53. https://doi.org/10.1007/s40926-018-0085-2

de Colle S, Freeman RE, Wicks AC (2023) Toward humanistic business ethics. Bus Soc. https://doi.org/10.1177/00076503231183681/ASSET/IMAGES/LARGE/10.1177_00076503231183681-FIG2.JPEG

den Hond F, Moser C (2023) Useful servant or dangerous master? technology in business and society debates. Bus Soc 62(1):87–116. https://doi.org/10.1177/00076503211068029

Derry R (2012) Reclaiming marginalized stakeholders. J Bus Ethics 111(2):253–264. https://doi.org/10.1007/S10551-012-1205-X/METRICS

Detert JR, Treviño LK, Sweitzer VL (2008) Moral disengagement in ethical decision making: a study of antecedents and outcomes. J Appl Psychol 93(2):374.

Ebrahimi S, Matt C (2023) Not seeing the (moral) forest for the trees? How task complexity and employees' expertise affect moral disengagement with discriminatory data analytics recommendations Journal of Information Technology. https://doi.org/10.1177/02683962231181148

Fjelland R (2020) Why general artificial intelligence will not be realized. Humanities and Social Sciences Communications 7(1):10. https://doi.org/10.1057/s41599-020-0494-4

Floridi L, Cowls J, Beltrametti M, Chatila R, Chazerand P, Dignum V, Luetge C, Madelin R, Pagallo U, Rossi F, Schafer B, Valcke P, Vayena E (2018) AI4People—An ethical framework for a good AI society: opportunities, risks, principles, and recommendations. Mind Mach 28(4):689–707. https://doi.org/10.1007/s11023-018-9482-5

Floridi L, Cowls J, Beltrametti M, Chatila R, Chazerand P, Dignum V, Luetge C, Madelin R, Pagallo U, Rossi F, Schafer B, Valcke P, Vayena E (2021) An ethical framework for a good AI society: opportunities, risks, principles, and recommendations (pp. 19–39). https://doi.org/10.1007/978-3-030-81907-1_3

Fontrodona J, Sison AJG (2006) The nature of the firm, agency theory and shareholder theory: A critique from philosophical anthropology. J Bus Ethics 66(1):33–42. https://doi.org/10.1007/S10551-006-9052-2/METRICS

Freeman RE (1994) The politics of stakeholder theory. Bus Ethics Q 4(4):409–421. https://doi.org/10.2307/3857340

Fritts M (2021) And Cabrera, · Frank. AI recruitment algorithms and the dehumanization problem. 23:791–801. https://doi.org/10.1007/s10676-021-09615-w

Gabriel I (2020) Artificial intelligence, values, and alignment. Mind Mach 30(3):411–437. https://doi.org/10.1007/s11023-020-09539-2

Garvey AM, Kim T, Duhachek A (2023) Bad news? Send an AI. Good News? Send a J Mark 87(1): 10–25. https://doi.org/10.1177/00222429211066972

Gherardi S, Laasch O (2022) Responsible management-as-practice: mobilizing a posthumanist approach. J Bus Ethics 181(2):269–281. https://doi.org/10.1007/s10551-021-04945-7

Giesen KG (2020) The transhumanist ideology and the international political economy of the fourth industrial revolution. 143–156. https://doi.org/10.1007/978-3-658-30512-3_9.

Gigerenzer G (2022) How to stay smart in a smart world: why human intelligence still beats algorithms. MIT Press.

Gigerenzer G, Gaissmaier W (2010). Heuristic decision making. https://doi.org/10.1146/Annurev-Psych-120709-145346,62,451-482.10.1146/ANNUREV-PSYCH-120709-145346

Gill KS (2016) Artificial super intelligence: beyond rhetoric. AI & Soc 31(2):137–143. https://doi.org/10.1007/s00146-016-0651-x

Giroux M, Kim J, Lee JC, Park J (2022) Artificial intelligence and declined guilt: retailing morality comparison between human and AI. J Bus Ethics 178(4):1027–1041. https://doi.org/10.1007/s10551-022-05056-7

Haenlein M, Huang MH, Kaplan A (2022) Guest editorial: Business ethics in the era of artificial intelligence. J Bus Ethics 178(4): 867–869.

Halpern D, Reville PJ, Grunewald D (2008) Management and legal issues regarding electronic surveillance of employees in the workplace. J Bus Ethics 80(2):175–180. https://doi.org/10.1007/S10551-007-9449-6

Hammedi W, Leclercq T, Poncin I, Alkire L, Nasr N (2020) Uncovering the dark side of gamification at work: Impacts on engagement and well-being ☆. https://doi.org/10.1016/j.jbusres.2020.08.032

Harland H, Dazeley R, Nakisa B, Cruz F, Vamplew P (2023) AI apology: interactive multi-objective reinforcement learning for human-aligned AI. Neural Comput Appl 35(23):16917–16930. https://doi.org/10.1007/s00521-023-08586-x

Haslam N, Loughnan S (2013). Dehumanization and Infrahumanization. https://doi.org/10.1146/annurev-psych-010213-115045

Hooker J, Kim TW (2022) Humanizing business in the age of artificial intelligence. In Dion M, Freeman RE, Dmytriyev SD (eds) Humanizing business. issues in business ethics, vol 53. Springer, Cham (pp 601–613). https://doi.org/10.1007/978-3-030-72204-3_40

James A (2023) Platform work-lives in the gig economy: Recentering work–family research. Gend Work Organ. https://doi.org/10.1111/GWAO.13087

Johnson DG (2015) Technology with no human responsibility? In Journal of business ethics (Vol. 127, Issue 4, pp. 707–715). Kluwer Academic Publishers. https://doi.org/10.1007/s10551-014-2180-1

Kaufmann P, Kuch H, Neuhäuser C, Webster E (2011) Humiliation, degradation, dehumanization: human dignity violated. 265

Keleher L (2018) Integral human development. In Routledge handbook of development ethics (pp. 29–34). Routledge. https://doi.org/10.4324/9781315626796-4

Kemp A (2023) Competitive advantage through artificial intelligence: toward a theory of situated AI. Acad Manag Rev. https://doi.org/10.5465/amr.2020.0205

Kim T, Lee H, Kim MY, Kim S, Duhachek A (2023). AI increases unethical consumer behavior due to reduced anticipatory guilt. https://doi.org/10.1007/s11747-021-00832-9

Kim TW, Maimone F, Pattit K, Sison AJ, Teehankee B (2021) Master and slave: the dialectic of human-artificial intelligence engagement. Humanistic Management Journal 6(3):355–371. https://doi.org/10.1007/s41463-021-00118-w

Kim TW, Routledge BR (2022) Why a right to an explanation of algorithmic decision-making should exist: a trust-based approach. Bus Ethics Q 32(1):75–102. https://doi.org/10.1017/beq.2021.3

Kim TW, Scheller-Wolf A (2022) Technological unemployment, meaning in life, purpose of business, and the future of stakeholders. In Business and the ethical implications of technology (pp. 13–31). Springer Nature Switzerland. https://doi.org/10.1007/978-3-031-18794-0_2

Kronfeldner M (2021) Introduction: mapping dehumanization studies. In The Routledge handbook of dehumanization (pp. 1–36). Routledge

Kujala J, Sachs S, Leinonen H, Heikkinen A, Laude D (2022) Stakeholder engagement: past, present, and future. Bus Soc 61(5):1136–1196. https://doi.org/10.1177/00076503211066595

Lenharo M (2023) AI consciousness: scientists say we urgently need answers. Nature. https://doi.org/10.1038/d41586-023-04047-6

Lenharo M (2023b) If AI becomes conscious: Here's how researchers will know. Nature. https://doi.org/10.1038/d41586-023-02684-5

Lindebaum D, Moser C, Ashraf M, Glaser VL (2023a) Reading the technological society to understand the mechanization of values and its ontological consequences. In Academy of management review (Vol. 48, Issue 3, pp. 575–592). Academy of Management. https://doi.org/10.5465/amr.2021.0159

Marszałek-Kotzur I (2022) Cognitive technologies—are we in danger of humanizing machines and dehumanizing humans? Management Systems in Production Engineering 30(3):269–275. https://doi.org/10.2478/MSPE-2022-0034

Martin K (2019) Ethical implications and accountability of algorithms. J Bus Ethics 160(4):835–850. https://doi.org/10.1007/S10551-018-3921-3/FIGURES/4

Mazzi F, Floridi L (n.d.) Philosophical studies series the ethics of artificial intelligence for the sustainable development goals

Mazzi F, Floridi L (2023) Introduction: understanding the ethics of artificial intelligence for the sustainable development goals. In The ethics of artificial intelligence for the sustainable development goals (pp. 3–7). Cham: Springer International Publishing

Melé D (2013) Antecedents and current situation of humanistic management. Afr J Bus Ethics 7(2):10–19. https://doi.org/10.4103/1817-7417.123079

Melé D (2014) "Human quality treatment": five organizational levels. J Bus Ethics 120(4):457–471. https://doi.org/10.1007/s10551-013-1999-1

Melé, D. (2015). Three keys concepts of catholic humanism for economic activity: human dignity, human rights and integral human development. Issues in business ethics, pp. *43*, 113–136. https://doi.org/10.1007/978-94-017-9704-7_7/COVER

Melé D (2021) Ethics at the workplace in the fourth industrial revolution: A Catholic social teaching perspective. Business Ethics, the Environment and Responsibility 30(4):772–783. https://doi.org/10.1111/BEER.12368

Melé D, Cantón CG (2014) The homo economicus model. In Human foundations of management (pp 9–29). Palgrave Macmillan UK. https://doi.org/10.1057/9781137462619_2

Kranzberg M (1986) Technology and history: Kranzberg's laws. Technol Cult 27:3

Merinda Simmons K (2020) Religious studies for cyborgs: Cognitive science and social theory after humanism. Method and Theory in the Study of Religion 32(3):276–287. https://doi.org/10.1163/15700682-12341484

Mittelstadt B (2019) Principles alone cannot guarantee ethical AI. Nat Mach Intell 1(11): 501–507. https://doi.org/10.1038/s42256-019-0114-4

Mongelli L, Versari P, Rullani F, Vaccaro A (2018) Made in carcere: integral human development in extreme conditions. J Bus Ethics 152(4):977–995. https://doi.org/10.1007/s10551-018-3821-6

Munn L (2023) The uselessness of AI ethics. AI and Ethics 3(3):869–877. https://doi.org/10.1007/s43681-022-00209-w

Munn L (2024) Digital labor, platforms, and AI. Introduction to digital humanism, pp 557–569. https://doi.org/10.1007/978-3-031-45304-5_35

Munoko I, Brown-Liburd HL, Vasarhelyi M (2020) The ethical implications of using artificial intelligence in auditing. J Bus Ethics 167(2):209–234. https://doi.org/10.1007/S10551-019-04407-1/TABLES/6

Nath R, Manna R (2023) From posthumanism to ethics of artificial intelligence. AI & Soc 38(1):185–196. https://doi.org/10.1007/s00146-021-01274-1

Novelli C, Taddeo M, Floridi L (2023) Accountability in artificial intelligence: What it is and how it works. AI & Soc. https://doi.org/10.1007/s00146-023-01635-y

Nussbaum MC (2000) Women and human development: the capabilities approach (Vol. 3). Cambridge University Press.

Oliver S (2011) Dehumanization: perceiving the body as (in)human. Library of ethics and applied philosophy, pp 24, 85–97. https://doi.org/10.1007/978-90-481-9661-6_7/COVER

Pfeffer J (2018) Dying for a paycheck: How modern management harms employee health and company performance—And what we can do about it. https://philpapers.org/rec/PFEDFA

Pirson MA (2022) The role of humanistic management in humanizing business. Issues in Business Ethics 53:489–502. https://doi.org/10.1007/978-3-030-72204-3_34

Pirson MA, Lawrence PR (2010) Humanism in business—towards a paradigm shift? J Bus Ethics 93(4):553–565. https://doi.org/10.1007/s10551-009-0239-1

Prasad Philbrick I, Wright-Piersanti T (2023, July 10) A.I. or nuclear weapons: can you tell these quotes apart? The New York Times

Pruss D (2023) Ghosting the machine: judicial resistance to a recidivism risk assessment instrument. In Proceedings of the 2023 ACM conference on fairness, accountability, and transparency (pp. 312–323).

Raisch S, Krakowski S (2021) Artificial intelligence and management: The automation–augmentation paradox. Acad Manag Rev 46(1):192–210. https://doi.org/10.5465/AMR.2018.0072

Reeves C, Sinnicks M (2023a) Totally administered heteronomy: Adorno on work, leisure, and politics in the age of digital capitalism. J Bus Ethics. https://doi.org/10.1007/S10551-023-05570-2

Rosanas JM (2008) Beyond economic criteria: a humanistic approach to organizational survival. J Bus Ethics 78(3):447–462. https://doi.org/10.1007/s10551-006-9341-9

Roszkowska P, Melé D (2021) Organizational factors in the individual ethical behaviour. The notion of the "organizational moral structure." HumIstic Manag J 6(2): 187–209. https://doi.org/10.1007/s41463-020-00080-z

Ryan M, Stahl BC (2021) Artificial intelligence ethics guidelines for developers and users: clarifying their content and normative implications. J Inf Commun Ethics Soc 19(1):1477–1996. https://doi.org/10.1108/JICES-12-2019-0138

Sachs S, Kujala J (2022) Stakeholder engagement in humanizing business. In Issues in business ethics (Vol. 53, pp. 559–572). Springer Science and Business Media B.V. https://doi.org/10.1007/978-3-030-72204-3_37

Sandelands L (2009) The business of business is the human person: lessons from the catholic social tradition. J Bus Ethics 85(1):93–101 https://doi.org/10.1007/s10551-008-9751-y

Sayers J, Martin L, Bell E (2022) Posthuman affirmative business ethics: reimagining human-animal relations through speculative fiction. J Bus Ethics 178(3):597–608. https://doi.org/10.1007/s10551-021-04801-8

Schlag M, Melé D (2020) Building institutions for the common good. the practice and purpose of business in an inclusive economy. HumIstic Manag J 5(1): 1–6. https://doi.org/10.1007/s41463-020-00092-9

Scott ED (2002) Organizational moral values. In Quarterly (Vol. 12, Issue 1)

Seele P, Schultz MD (2022) From greenwashing to machinewashing: a model and future directions derived from reasoning by analogy. J Bus Ethics 178(4):1063–1089. https://doi.org/10.1007/s10551-022-05054-9

Sen A (1999) On ethics and economics. OUP Catalogue.

Sison AJG, Fontrodona J (2013) Participating in the common good of the firm. J Bus Ethics 113(4):611–625. https://doi.org/10.1007/S10551-013-1684-4/METRICS

Sriram V, Jenkinson C, Peters M (2020) Carers' experience of using assistive technology for dementia care at home: a qualitative study. BMJ Open 10(3):e034460.

Sriraman A, Bragg J, Kulkarni A (n.d.) Worker-owned cooperative models for training artificial intelligence. https://doi.org/10.1145/3022198.3026356

Stahl BC, Antoniou J, Ryan M, Macnish K, Jiya T (2022) Organisational responses to the ethical issues of artificial intelligence. AI & Soc 37(1):23–37. https://doi.org/10.1007/s00146-021-01148-6

Stoicescu M (2020) Social impact of online dating platforms. A case study on Tinder. 2020 19th RoEduNet Conference: Networking in Education and Research (RoEduNet), 1–6. https://doi.org/10.1109/RoEduNet51892.2020.9324854

Tambe P, Cappelli P, Yakubovich V (2019) Artificial intelligence in human resources management: challenges and a path forward. Calif Manage Rev 61(4):15–42. https://doi.org/10.1177/0008125619867910

Tasioulas J (2022) Artificial intelligence, humanistic ethics. Daedalus 151(2):232–243. https://doi.org/10.1162/DAED_A_01912

Tilmes N (2022) Disability, fairness, and algorithmic bias in AI recruitment. Ethics Inf Technol 24(2):21. https://doi.org/10.1007/s10676-022-09633-2

To Make a Profit, Dating Apps Must Leverage Data Differently. (n.d.). Retrieved January 13, 2024, from https://hbr.org/2022/01/to-make-a-profit-dating-apps-must-leverage-data-differently

Vaccaro A (2023) Compliance beyond compliance: managing organizations with integrity. McGraw Hill

Vaccaro A, Madsen P (2009) Corporate dynamic transparency: the new ICT-driven ethics? Ethics Inf Technol 11(2):113–122. https://doi.org/10.1007/s10676-009-9190-1

Van Der Linden B, Edward Freeman R (2017) Profit and other values: thick evaluation in decision making. Bus Ethics Q 27(3):353–379. https://doi.org/10.1017/beq.2017.1

van Maanen G (2022) AI ethics, ethics washing, and the need to politicize data ethics. Digit Soc 1(2). https://doi.org/10.1007/s44206-022-00013-3

van Wynsberghe A (2021) Sustainable AI: AI for sustainability and the sustainability of AI. AI and Ethics 1(3):213–218. https://doi.org/10.1007/s43681-021-00043-6

Varma A, Dawkins C, Chaudhuri K (2022) Human Resource Management Review 33 (2023) 100923 Artificial intelligence and people management: A critical assessment through the ethical lens. https://doi.org/10.1016/j.hrmr.2022.100923

Väyrynen T, Laari-Salmela S (2018) Men, mammals, or machines? dehumanization embedded in organizational practices. J Bus Ethics 147(1):95–113. https://doi.org/10.1007/s10551-015-2947-z

Widder DG, Whittaker M (2023) Open (for Business): Big tech, concentrated power, and the political economy of open AI. https://ssrn.com/abstract=4543807

Wright SA, Schultz AE (2018) The rising tide of artificial intelligence and business automation: Developing an ethical framework. Bus Horiz 61(6):823–832. https://doi.org/10.1016/j.bushor.2018.07.001

Wünderlich NV, Gustafsson A, Hamari J, Parvinen P, Haff A (2020) The great game of business: Advancing knowledge on gamification in business contexts. J Bus Res 106:273–276. https://doi.org/10.1016/j.jbusres.2019.10.062

Yeung K, Howes A, Pogrebna G (2019) Forthcoming AI governance by human rights-centred design, deliberation and oversight: an end to ethics washing. Oxford University Press. https://ec.europa.eu/digital-single-market/en/news/communication-artificial-intelligence-europe.

Zigarelli MA (1993) Catholic social teaching and the employment relationship: a model for managing human resources in accordance with Vatican Doctrine. J Bus Ethics 12(1):75–82. https://doi.org/10.1007/bf01845789

Zimmerman A, Janhonen J, Saadeh, · Michael, Castelyn, C., and Saxén, H. (2023) Values in AI: bioethics and the intentions of machines and people. AI and Ethics 3:1003–1012. https://doi.org/10.1007/s43681-022-00242-9

Chapter 2
21st-Century Alienation: From Engineered Humans to Predicted Humans

Simona Chiodo

Abstract Emerging technologies seem to bring out unprecedented forms of human alienation, from the general issue of what we may define as engineered humans to the particular issue of what we may define as predicted humans. First, I shall reflect upon the way in which our language increasingly changes when we address our relationship with emerging technologies. More precisely, the change of our language shows a kind of optimisation that is taken to the extreme, starting with the optimisation of humans' performances: the more engineered humans are (in that they identify their purpose not with feeling good, for instance, but with performing in faster and more profitable ways), the better they are (in that they measure themselves not against typically human values, such as feeling good, for instance, but against typically engineering values, such as efficiency). But a remarkable paradox emerges: the more humans work on optimising themselves, the more they (paradoxically) work on moving optimisation from themselves, i.e. their capabilities as autonomous humans (starting with self-perception and self-mastery), to technologies, i.e. ways of engineering, specifically automating, themselves. Second, I shall reflect upon the technological prediction of humans' future as what may be thought of as the most extreme way to engineer them. Even though the cradle of Western culture, from scripture to mythology, continuously stresses that knowledge can be dangerous, specifically for humans, the history of Western culture coincides with the increasing effort to make knowledge the primary objective of human activities, from philosophy itself to science and technology. More precisely, the more technology develops, the more its primary objective is knowing our future, i.e. predicting our future, from our bodies' performances to our minds' performances. Are humans still free to determine their own future even surprisingly, i.e. against all odds?

Keywords Alienation · Engineered humans · Predicted humans

S. Chiodo (✉)
Politecnico di Milano, Milano, Italy
e-mail: simona.chiodo@polimi.it

R. Fioravante and A. Vaccaro (eds.), *Humanism and Artificial Intelligence*, SpringerBriefs in Philosophy, https://doi.org/10.1007/978-3-031-85478-1_2

2.1 Introduction

Emerging technologies seem to bring out unprecedented forms of human alienation, from the general issue of what we may define as engineered humans to the particular issue of what we may define as predicted humans.

In Sects. 2.2, 2.3, and 2.4, I shall reflect upon the way in which our language increasingly changes when we address our relationship with emerging technologies, starting with the exemplary case of human digital twins. More precisely, the change of our language shows a kind of optimisation that is taken to the extreme, starting with the optimisation of humans' performances: the more engineered humans are (in that they identify their purpose not with feeling good, for instance, but with performing in faster and more profitable ways), the better they are (in that they measure themselves not against typically human values, such as feeling good, for instance, but against typically engineering values, such as efficiency). But a remarkable paradox emerges: the more humans work on optimising themselves, the more they (paradoxically) work on moving optimisation from themselves, i.e. their capabilities as autonomous humans (starting with self-perception and self-mastery), to technologies, i.e. ways of engineering, specifically automating, themselves.

In Sects. 2.5, 2.6 and 2.7, I shall reflect upon the technological prediction of humans' future as what may be thought of as the most extreme way to engineer them (again, starting with the exemplary case of human digital twins). Even though the cradle of Western culture, from scripture to mythology, continuously stresses that knowledge can be dangerous, specifically for humans, the history of Western culture coincides with the increasing effort to make knowledge the primary objective of human activities, from philosophy itself to science and technology. More precisely, the more technology develops, the more its primary objective is knowing our future, i.e. predicting our future, from our bodies' performances to our minds' performances. Are humans still free to determine their own future even surprisingly, i.e. against all odds?

2.2 The Exemplary Case of Human Digital Twins

The general phenomenon of the engineering of humans and the particular phenomenon of the prediction of their future through emerging technologies may be addressed by focusing on human digital twins as a kind of tip of the iceberg. Human digital twins bring out something that increasingly characterises the relationship between humans and emerging technologies.

A digital twin is defined by three essentials (see at least Glaessgen and Stargel 2012 and Grieves 2014)[1]: a physical object (which may be both inorganic and

[1] As far as literature reviews are concerned, see at least Negri et al. (2017), Jones et al. (2020), Van der Valk et al. (2020), Liu et al. (2021), Mylonas et al. (2021), Botín-Sanabria et al. (2022) and Fuller et al. (2022).

organic), a technological, specifically digital, object and a constantly mutual relationship between them, which means that, if the former changes, the latter also changes, and vice versa. If the physical object is organic, specifically human, we move from the digital twin in general to the human digital twin in particular. The former is meant to optimisation and efficiency, from manufacturing (where it is used to monitor and predict physical objects' performances in faster and cheaper ways)[2] to smart cities (where it is used to plan and predict more efficient urban scenarios, starting with energy saving).[3] The latter is also meant to optimisation and efficiency, especially in healthcare, where it is used to predict and make decisions on drugs, surgery and life expectancy.[4] More precisely, human digital twins are increasingly used in personalised healthcare: "Recently, medical technologies have moved from a traditional 'one-size-fits-most' model towards the customisation of mass medicine. Therefore, PDT [personal digital twins] could be used for customised short-term and long-term treatment by customising medications for individuals based on their current vital organs status, anatomy, unique genetic makeup, behaviour, daily routines, etc." (Sahal et al. 2022, p. 23). It is no coincidence that the words "customisation", "customised" and "customising" are continuously repeated. The current discourse on healthcare increasingly prioritises personalisation over generalisation—and stressing personalisation also means stressing the shift from patients to clients.

For instance, the authors of the article quoted above continuously replace the notion of patient with the notion of client and even write "clients (i.e. patients)" (Sahal et al. 2022, p. 9), which means that the current discourse on healthcare is increasingly characterised by the following shifts: first, the shift from patients to clients and, second, the shift from doctors to entrepreneurs. Thus, for instance, according to the authors of the article quoted above, "healthcare providers and stakeholders [...] maximise their business by making personalised decisions and recommendations for their clients" (Sahal et al. 2022, p. 11) and, according to other authors, "the [human] digital twin will act as an accelerator for the contemporary switch of focus from treatment to prevention, meaning that the main function of the data will be to avoid contact with the physician rather than improve this contact" (Popa et al. 2021, p. 10). We may summarise as follows: personalising means not only the possible advantage of bettering healthcare but also the possible disadvantage of worsening the doctor-patient relationship, in that, if doctors become entrepreneurs and patients become clients, first, profit risks winning over care ("healthcare providers and stakeholders [...] maximise their business") and, second, paradoxically enough, impersonal relationships risk winning over personal (and empathetic) relationships ("to avoid contact with the physician rather than improve this contact"). Why? Because there seems to be something even more attractive, which both doctors as entrepreneurs and patients

[2] See at least Holler, Uebernickel and Brenner (2016), Kritzinger et al. (2018), Qi and Tao (2018) and Lu et al. (2020).

[3] See at least Mohammadi and Taylor (2017), Allam and Jones (2021), Deng et al. (2021) and Shahat et al. (2021). And see at least Ford and Wolf (2020), Fana et al. (2021) and Allam et al. (2022) on disaster management in particular.

[4] See at least Bruynseels, Santoni de Sio and van den Hoven (2018), Gahlot et al. (2019), Kamel Boulos and Zhang (2021), Popa et al. (2021), Okegbile et al. (2022) and Sahal et al. (2022).

as clients seem to share: optimisation. On the one hand, doctors as entrepreneurs strive to optimise their performances, from care to profit. On the other hand, even though patients as clients worsen at least two things, in that they pay more money for paradoxically less personal (and empathetic) relationships with their doctors as entrepreneurs, they equally strive to optimise their performances—more precisely, patients as clients equally strive to optimise their performances as high-performing humans, from their bodies to their minds.

2.3 High-Performing Humans

According to the authors of the article quoted above, human digital twins in healthcare "can help people improve their personal productivity development and increase their health longevity by following efficient self-care routines in their daily life" (Sahal et al. 2022, p. 11). If we consider other publications on human digital twins, specifically the best representatives (about two dozen) of several publications reviewed (about two hundred) by relying on Web of Science's and Scopus' databases, we realise that optimisation as high-performing humans is key. Several authors stress that optimisation results from capitalism.[5] From a philosophical perspective, we may try to add something more by starting with the following question: why, for the sake of optimisation, are we willing to pay more money for paradoxically less personal (and empathetic) relationships with our doctors as entrepreneurs?

In the publications analysed, the notion of optimisation, together with the notion of efficiency, continuously emerges. For instance, in Barricelli et al. (2020) there are fourteen occurrences of the noun "optimisation" and seven occurrences of the variously conjugated verb "optimise" and in Shahat et al. (2021) there are three occurrences of the noun "optimisation" and six occurrences of the variously conjugated verb "optimise". The notion of optimisation leads to other notions, starting with "the use of words like [...] 'increase efficiency', 'anomaly', 'deviation', 'undesired', and 'correct'" (Korenhof et al. 2021, p. 1756), and, again, "'better management and control', 'diagnostics', 'health management', to 'increase lifespan and success', etcetera" (Korenhof, Blok and Kloppenburg 2021, p. 1765). The notion of efficiency frequently emerges. For instance, in Shahat et al. (2021) there are nine occurrences of the noun "efficiency" and three occurrences of the adjective "efficient". If we read the dictionary definition of the word "optimisation", we are directed to the business dictionary, where we learn that "optimisation" means "the process of making something as good or effective as possible".[6] And, if we read the dictionary definition of the word "efficiency", we learn that "efficiency" means "good use of time

[5] See at least Crary (2013) and Sadowski (2020).

[6] See https://dictionary.cambridge.org/dictionary/english/optimization (accessed in December 2022).

and energy, without wasting any".[7] Thus, the words "optimisation" and "efficiency" identify a specific kind of improvement, which does not have to do, for instance, with the kind of improvement that is masterfully represented by Homer's *Odyssey*, from which, through Odysseus' almost endless journey, we learn that improving may mean the opposite of "effective" and "good use of time and energy, without wasting any" (see also the critical perspective developed by Fioravante and Vaccaro 2025). Conversely, the words "optimisation" and "efficiency" identify a specific kind of improvement that has to do with "as good or effective as possible" "without wasting" "time and energy"—the words "optimisation" and "efficiency" identify the kind of improvement that characterises engineering.

When we consider the application areas of human digital twins, we realise that optimisation and efficiency emerge as the ways in which humans can become high-performing especially when it comes to money-making (also as the ultimate result of humans as workers), human minds' performances (especially decision-making) and human bodies' performances (especially health).

As far as money-making is concerned, digital twins are important in organisational processes: "digital replication of organisational processes can determine the most efficient way to conduct business", which "allows for performance improvement" (Ukko et al. 2022, p. 257 and 254). On the one hand, "performance improvement" means money-saving: for instance, a digital twin is a "fast and inexpensive experimentation" (Ford and Wolf 2020, p. 2) that "allows people to save costs by determining the most efficient ways to conduct business" (Ukko et al. 2022, p. 254. See also "performance improvement" as "cutting costs": Anshari et al. 2022, p. 7 and Ukko et al. 2022, p. 257). On the other hand, "performance improvement" means money-making: for instance, "healthcare industry is adopting emerging technologies such as IoT [internet of things], AI [artificial intelligence], and DTs [digital twins] to improve business" (Sahal et al. 2022, p. 15). And finance even shows that, when it comes to making decisions to make money, digital twins can be the best advisors: "Making better and faster decisions that can be executed flawlessly is critical for delivering superior and long-term business value to organisations. DT [Digital twins] could perhaps be the key to making intelligent decisions in this new reality" (Anshari et al. 2022, p. 4), which leads us to human minds' performances (especially decision-making).

As far as human minds' performances (especially decision-making) are concerned, digital twins are important to pursue a technologically "optimis[ed] efficiency [...] increas[ing] the prospect of efficiency [itself] in many frontiers such as decision making" (Allam et al. 2022, p. 10 and 13), where speaking of "good use of time and energy, without wasting any", means not only that "time" is something to accelerate (for instance, "allowing for real-time predictions, among others", Allam et al. 2022, p. 13) but also that "time" is something to cut (for instance, "it is possible to use digital replication to see how quickly an organisation could respond to a decision. Thus, there is huge potential to develop organisational agility through fast and

[7] See https://dictionary.cambridge.org/dictionary/english-italian/efficiency (accessed in December 2022).

intelligent decisions based on real-time data", Ukko et al. 2022, p. 254. "[R]eal-time data available from [...] technologies can reduce the time to obtain data and improve decisions by providing additional information as [...] management leaders respond to conditions that often change quickly, requiring quick responses", Ford and Wolf 2020, pp. 1–2).

As far as human bodies' performances (especially health) are concerned, digital twins are important to pursue optimisation and efficiency both when health is a personal matter (for instance, when digital twins "optimise the performance of patient-specific treatment plans", Okegbile et al. 2022, p. 1) and when health is a professional matter (for instance, when a digital twin "produces understandable suggestions which can be used by trainers to trigger optimisation actions in the athletes' behaviour", Barricelli et al. 2020, p. 26, 637. See also Bruynseels et al. 2018).[8] We may focus on a specific case as an exemplary case to start reflecting upon the application areas of human digital twins from a philosophical perspective: the exemplary case of human sleep. Interestingly enough, human sleep has moved from being thought of as a kind of empty time (before Freud's revolution) to being thought of as something crucial to understand (after Freud's revolution) to being thought of as something crucial to optimise, precisely in our technological era. For instance, "a novel and more radical feature emerged [...] within the category of sleep management functions. The Sleep Cycle monitoring apps incorporated a range of management functions, often set manually to enable personalised and customised reminders or sounds relating to going to sleep or waking up (e.g., customisable alarm sounds, manually set sleep/wake time, sleep aid sounds, bedtime reminder). A significant extension of sleep management functions, however, is the algorithmically determined 'smart wake up' feature [...] [that] extends from assisting with sleep management to automating sleep–wake rhythms. Going beyond measurement, these apps offer a more direct 'intervention' into the timing of the user's wake up at the most optimal point within the phases of the sleep cycle. [...] [T]he 'smartness' of the app indicates a shift from disciplinary self-mastery to a more distributed and adaptive form of delegated monitoring and optimised intervention. [...] If the sleep trackers are concerned with tracking the cyclical times of the day, our circadian biorhythms, the 'smart wake up' feature attempts to divine and/or produce a precise moment in optimising sleeping and waking rhythms" (O'Neill and Nansen 2019: no page number. See also Williams, Coveney and Gabe 2013, Baron et al. 2017 and Lyall 2021). There are at least two philosophical issues upon which to reflect. First, the issue of the engineering of humans. Even human sleep, which has been thought of as a kind of empty time for millennia, becomes something crucial to optimise as something engineered through "management functions", "monitoring apps", "personalised and customised reminders or sounds" (i.e. "customisable alarm sounds, manually set sleep/wake time, sleep aid sounds, bedtime reminder"), "delegated monitoring and optimised intervention". Thus, human sleep becomes "algorithmically determined" as something engineered—human sleep becomes "automat[ed]" as something engineered. Second, the issue of humans' shift from (human) autonomy

[8] More generally, see at least Littlefield (2018) and Reagle (2019).

to (technological) automation, which is introduced by the first issue itself. More precisely, on the one hand, (human) autonomy seems to be pursued as the capability to "optimis[e] sleeping and waking rhythms" to perform better both as human minds and as human bodies. But, on the other hand, the capability to "optimis[e] sleeping and waking rhythms" is not human at all. Conversely, the (human) capability of "self-mastery" is replaced by (technological) "delegated monitoring and optimised intervention"—the human capability of "self-mastery", which may even be the core of human autonomy as Kant's "will's own lawgiving" (Kant 1785, p. 4, 450), is replaced by technological automation. Even more precisely, a remarkable paradox emerges: the more humans work on optimising themselves, the more they (paradoxically) work on moving optimisation from themselves, i.e. their capabilities as autonomous humans, to technologies, i.e. ways of engineering, specifically automating, themselves. Metaphorically speaking, it is as if humans want to improve their running speed by taking the bus.

As other kinds of technological automation show, the dissolution of the human capability of self-mastery also means the dissolution of the human capability of self-perception as what underpins the human capability of self-mastery itself. For instance, the phenomenon of the quantified self[9] shows, again, a remarkable paradox. Even though self-trackers want to optimise themselves, starting with their bodies' performances, they dissolve self-perception as what underpins their bodies' performances by replacing it with wearable technologies that make self-perception (which is, by definition, autonomous) dissolve in technological automation. For instance, the following cases are instructive. According to the first testimony, "[w]e (the apps and I) had co-constructed a digital model of myself, and here I was, managing myself, it seems, by proxy. The feedback from that digital model often took precedence over how I physically felt. When I didn't eat 'enough' protein I felt weaker, and when I had too much sugar I felt fatter. These were delayed reactions; a re-reading of my body from the model. I've yet to decide: is this model pushing me closer in contact or further away from myself and my world?" (Williams 2013, p. 3). According to the second testimony, the self-tracker even decides to stop self-tracking, in that "I had stopped trusting myself / letting the numbers drown out / my intuition / my instincts[.] / Each day / my self-worth was tied to the data[.] / One pound heavier this morning? / You're fat. / 2 g too much fat ingested? / You're out of control. / Skipped a day of running? / You're lazy" (Carmichael 2010: no page number). According to the third testimony, "when I see the numbers from Basis contradict my positive assessment of my rest, my sense of having rested well is suddenly undermined as if those Basis numbers somehow have the power to make me doubt my own experience".[10] There are at least two philosophical issues upon which to reflect: not only the explicit dissolution of self-perception (which is, by definition, autonomous) in technological automation but also the implicit dissolution of epistemic accuracy in epistemic inaccuracy. Thus, on the one hand, we address, again, the paradoxical shift from the optimisation of humans through exercising their autonomous capabilities

[9] See https://quantifiedself.com/ (accessed in December 2022).

[10] See https://quantifiedself.com/show-and-tell/?project=756 (accessed in December 2022).

to the optimisation of humans through replacing their autonomous capabilities with technological automation—which means the paradoxical shift from the optimisation of humans to the engineering of humans. On the other hand, we address the equally paradoxical shift from the kind of epistemic accuracy resulting from experts (i.e. doctors, who are capable of reading data against the background of medical knowledge and general health condition) to the kind of epistemic inaccuracy resulting from non-experts (i.e. self-trackers, who are not capable of reading data against the background of medical knowledge and general health condition).[11]

Thus, even more urgently, the philosophical question we should try to answer is the following: why are we willing to put ourselves in paradoxical positions, in which we trade our autonomy, i.e. true optimisation of our own capabilities, for technological automation, i.e. false optimisation of our own capabilities? More precisely, why are we willing to trade our autonomy as what has been thought of as the core of our identity for millennia (starting with humans who are asked to bear the epistemological and ethical burdens of dramatic individual decisions, from Sophocles' to Shakespeare's to Pirandello's protagonists), for technological automation[12]?

2.4 Engineered Humans

The possible answer to the question asked above may result from a further reflection upon the meaning of the shift from autonomous humans to automated, i.e. engineered, humans.

According to Bruynseels et al. de Sio and van den Hoven (2018), human digital twins "provide a conceptual instrument to analyse the impact of these novel engineering practices on core concepts in current debates on healthcare, like health, disease, preventative care, and enhancement. One can analyse these healthcare concepts in analogy with engineering concepts of 'normal functioning', 'malfunctioning', 'predictive maintenance', 'performance optimisation', and the 'implementation of new functionality'" (Bruynseels et al. 2018, p. 2. See also the critical perspective developed by Brusoni and Vaccaro 2017 and Haenlein, Huang and Kaplan 2022: the issue goes far beyond healthcare).[13] We may continue by saying that speaking of the shift from autonomous humans to automated, i.e. engineered, humans means, for instance, using the words quoted above "normal functioning" and "malfunctioning" instead of the words "feeling good" and "not feeling good", using the words quoted

[11] As far as the shift from experts to non-experts is concerned, see at least, for an instructive sociological perspective, Eyal (2019).

[12] I extensively worked on the issue of trading human autonomy for technological automation in Chiodo (2022, 2023a, 2023b and 2024).

[13] Kamel Boulos and Zhang (2021) also attribute to Bruynseels et al. (2018) the "observ[ation of] close similarities between healthcare practices driven by data and modern engineering approaches driven by digital twins. They noted that the latter applies digital twins for predictive management and maintenance of complex systems, such as identifying faulty parts and simulating intervention outcomes" (Kamel Boulos and Zhang 2021, p. 6).

above "predictive maintenance" instead of the word "care", using the words quoted above "performance optimisation" instead of the words "patient recovery" and using the words quoted above "implementation of new functionality" instead of the words "personal development". Again, why? Why are we willing to replace, for instance, the idea of "care" with the idea of "predictive maintenance"?

It is not credible that we exclusively obtain a disadvantage, i.e. the dissolution of our autonomy in technological automation. We should also, and especially, obtain an advantage, which should explain the reason why we increasingly trade our autonomy for technological automation. A clue is given by the words quoted above: "is this model pushing me closer in contact or further away from my self and my world?". We may reason as follows: if it is true that we increasingly use "model[s] pushing" us "further away from" ourselves, starting with our own capabilities, as we have seen in several cases, it is also true that what we may want is precisely to be "push[ed]" "further away from" ourselves, starting with our own capabilities—more precisely, what we may want is precisely to be "push[ed]" "further away from" what may be thought of as our distinguishing capability for millennia, i.e. our autonomy as our distinguishing capability to bear the epistemological and ethical burdens of our dramatic individual decisions.

Thus, do we increasingly design and use technology as the best replacement of our autonomy (i.e. our bearing the epistemological and ethical burdens of our dramatic individual decisions) with technological automation? The cases reviewed above lead us to answer yes, from the case of money-making (where "better and faster decisions" are moved from us to technology) to the case of human minds' performances (where "decision making" is moved from us to technology) to the case of human bodies' performances (where, when we are patients, our self-perception and self-mastery underpinning our decisions are increasingly replaced by data resulting from technology and, when we are doctors, our personal and empathetic doctor-patient relationship underpinning our decisions is increasingly replaced by data resulting from technology)—we increasingly design and use technology, i.e. technological automation, as the best saboteur of our autonomy as our increasingly unbearable burden of making individual decisions that, especially in dramatic circumstances, are asked to be epistemologically true and ethically right.

As Kant masterfully teaches us, our autonomy is precisely the reason why we are epistemologically and ethically responsible for our individual decisions. Our autonomy is not only, advantageously, "the ground of the dignity of human nature and of every rational nature" (Kant 1785, p. 4, 436) but also, disadvantageously, what makes us "culpable and deserving of punishment" (Kant 1788, p. 5, 100) whenever our individual decisions, and consequent individual actions, turn out to be epistemologically false and ethically wrong. Contemporary philosophy even takes Kant's masterful work on the notion of autonomy to the extreme (see at least Dworkin 1988, Frankfurt 1988, Ekstrom 1993, Friedman 2003 e Bratman 2007). And our autonomy even becomes our most unbearable burden: contemporary Western culture is characterised more than ever by the idea according to which, first, being successful means being individually successful and, second, being individually successful means being individually capable of making decisions and doing actions that turn out to be epistemologically true and ethically right—we are asked more than ever to individually optimise our decisions and actions.

My proposal is to read our current way of designing and using technology as our desperate attempt to move, sometimes consciously and sometimes unconsciously, our autonomy as our most unbearable burden from ourselves to technology—my proposal is to read our current way of designing and using technology as our desperate attempt to move from autonomy, which means bearing the burden of individual responsibility, to automation, which means making the burden of individual responsibility dissolve in our own engineering.

2.5 "Where Ignorance is Bliss, 'tis Folly to Be Wise"

As I shall argue in what follows, we may think of the technological prediction of our future as the most extreme way of automating, i.e. engineering, ourselves.

As we have seen, human digital twins are a kind of tip of the iceberg, from prediction when it comes to money-making to prediction when it comes to human minds' performances to prediction when it comes to human bodies' performances (especially when it comes to health, where the use of human digital twins "computes trustable predictions of the physical twins' conditions", Barricelli et al. 2020, p. 26, 637, in that human digital twins predict not only "responses to surgical interventions", Sahal et al. 2022, p. 12, but also "the future state of an individual's health to allow the activation of efficient preventive measures", Okegbile et al. 2022, p. 1). More generally, algorithms increasingly predict our future in detail, from our birth and health to our disease and death through our families, work, passions and whatever, in addition to our salary, insurance, mortgage and even shopping from what food to eat at noon to what book to read at midnight. Contemporary Western culture seems to forget the idea according to which ignorance may be better than knowledge, at least sometimes, as modern Western culture does not forget: "Where ignorance is bliss,'tis folly to be wise" (Gray 1747: vv. 99–100).

The idea that Gray does not forget arises from ancient culture: both mythology and philosophy work on the idea that even the scripture brings out, according to which "the Lord God commanded the man, 'You are free to eat from any tree in the garden; but you must not eat from the tree of the knowledge of good and evil, for when you eat from it you will certainly die'" (Gen. 2, 16–17). As far mythology is concerned, for instance, Tiresias goes blind after having seen Athena, i.e. the goddess of knowledge, naked, i.e. revealed: "Only Tiresias, on whose cheek the down was just darkening, still ranged with his hounds the holy place. And, athirst beyond telling, he came unto the flowing fountain, wretched man! And unwillingly saw that which is not lawful to be seen. And Athena was angered, yet said to him: 'What god, o son of Everes, led thee on this grievous way? Hence shalt thou never more take back thine eyes!'" (Call. H. 5, 75–81). And Cassandra suffers from her power of prediction: "Alas, alas, the sorrow of my ill-starred doom! For it is my own affliction, crowning the cup, that I bewail. Ah, to what end did you bring me here, unhappy as I am? For nothing except to die—and not alone" (Aesch. Ag. 1136–1139). As far as philosophy is concerned, for instance, Plato explains that Socrates' ignorance makes him the wisest, in that it is the condition for knowledge: "I [Socrates] am wiser than this man [considered the wisest]; for neither of us really knows anything fine and good, but this man thinks he knows something when he does not, whereas I, as I do not know anything, do not think I do either" (Plat. Apol. 21 d). Moving from ancient philosophy to modern philosophy, for instance, Descartes thinks of doubting as the condition for knowing: "I observed that this truth, I think, therefore I am (*cogito ergo sum*), was so certain and of such evidence that no ground of doubt, however extravagant, could be alleged" (Descartes 1637, p. IV). And Kant decides to start his masterful philosophical work by identifying reason's limits: "Human reason has the peculiar fate in one species of its cognitions that it is burdened with questions which it cannot dismiss, since they are given to it as problems by the nature of reason itself, but which it also cannot answer, since they transcend every capacity of human reason" (Kant 1781, p. A VII). And moving from modern philosophy to contemporary philosophy, for instance, Wittgenstein defines the task of philosophy as the identification of knowledge's limits: "Philosophy sets limits to […] what can be thought; and, in doing so, to what cannot be thought. It must set limits to what cannot be thought by working outwards through what can be thought" (Wittgenstein 1921, pp. 4.113–4.114).[14]

Yet, contemporary Western culture is characterised by a paradoxical contradiction. On the one hand, the legacy of past millennia is taken up. On the other hand, emerging technologies are even obsessed with the prediction of humans' future.

As an exemplary case of the first issue (i.e. taking up the legacy of past millennia), empirical research[15] proves that we do not want our future to be predicted, in that, precisely as in the case of Cassandra, we do not want the kind of "endless pain, suffering, and regret" (Gigerenzer and Garcia-Retamero 2017, p. 179) that the power of prediction may mean: we want "to avoid the negative emotions that may arise from foreknowledge of negative events [and] to maintain the positive emotions of surprise and suspense" (Gigerenzer and Garcia-Retamero 2017, p. 181). The empirical research is based on answers to ten questions. The first half of the questions is about negative events ("Would you want to know today (a) when your partner will die? (b) From what cause your partner will die? (c) When you will die? (d) From what cause you will die? And (e) Whether your marriage will eventually end in divorce or not?" (Gigerenzer and Garcia-Retamero 2017, p. 186). And the second half of the questions is about positive events ("Would you like to know whether there is life after death? […] Would you want to know the sex of your child before birth? Would you want to know in advance what you are getting for Christmas?

[14] As far as the current philosophical debate is concerned, see at least Le Morvan (2011) and Peels (2010 and 2011).

[15] It is defined as "the first representative nationwide studies to estimate the prevalence and predictability of deliberate ignorance for a sample of 10 events" (Gigerenzer and Garcia-Retamero 2017, p. 179).

[...] Would you want to know from the friend how it [a recording of a soccer game] ended (as opposed to asking not to tell)? [...] Would you have the sapphire [bought in a far-away country for a large sum] tested to be sure whether it is genuine or not?" (Gigerenzer and Garcia-Retamero 2017, p. 186). The result of the empirical research is that the percentage of participants who do not want to know when it comes to negative events is 88.3% on average[16] and, interestingly enough, even the percentage of participants who do not want to know when it comes to positive events is more than half, i.e. 56.4% on average.[17] Thus, it seems that the legacy of past millennia wins over the prediction of humans' future: in most cases, humans do not want their future to be predicted—but then why are emerging technologies even obsessed with the prediction of humans' future, to the point that "[r]esearchers report having identified biomarkers that help in predicting when a person will die and from what cause" (Gigerenzer and Garcia-Retamero 2017, p. 179. See also Cawthon et al. 2003)"?

2.6 Predicted Humans

Again, human digital twins are a kind of tip of the iceberg. For instance, in addition to the cases we have seen, the general idea is that "human skills [are] boosted by DTs' [digital twins'] analyses, predictions, and recommendations" (Barricelli et al.: 167,657), in that, again through the analogy between humans and engineering, "[t]his real-time system modification leads to dramatic improvements, e.g., in the manufacturing field as well as in medical-system engineering, since the prediction capability allows planning repairs or maintenance, thus preventing disruptions and potentially costly breakdowns" (Barricelli, Casiraghi and Fogli: 167,657).

Human scientists start critically reflecting upon the consequences of using human digital twins to predict humans' future. For instance, there is a risk of replacing a present characterised by health with nothing but a possible future characterised by disease, which means replacing the idea of healthy humans with the idea of humans who are always patients, i.e. clients: "The subject is healthy according to current healthcare practices, but her digital twin indicates a certain likelihood of developing a disease later on, therefore making that the person 'is not ok'" (Bruynseels, Santoni de Sio and van den Hoven 2018, p. 6). Thus, the human digital twin "of a person will not be merely instrumental in better decisions in healthcare interventions, but will also be part of that person's identity" (Bruynseels et al. 2018, p. 6), which means that "the mere fact that other people or institutions think that you are going to be sick or weak or short-lived may make you sick, weak or short-lived" (Bruynseels et al. 2018, p. 8).

[16] According to the authors, the key reason is "to avoid the negative feeling of regret after having learned that an undesirable event is going to happen" (Gigerenzer and Garcia-Retamero 2017, p. 183).

[17] According to the authors, the key reason is "to maintain the positive feeling of surprise and suspense" (Gigerenzer and Garcia-Retamero 2017, p. 183).

Even more dramatically, "the digital twin simulating my cardiovascular system may one day 'knock on my door' in order to warn me of an imminent severe heart disease" (Braun 2021, p. 397) and "this will change my life completely because besides the possibility of offering me opportunities to ward off the physical manifestation of disease, the digital twin will be exercising power over me and my life" (Braun 2021, p. 397).

Before reflecting upon the meaning of "exercising power over me and my life", it is worth adding that emerging technologies' obsession with the prediction of humans' future extends far beyond human digital twins. The use of predictive algorithms grows exponentially, from families, work and passions to salary, insurance, mortgage and even shopping. For instance, we increasingly use hiring algorithms. But, according to an article published in the "Harvard business review", they frequently happen to make "highly superficial predictions: they predict not who will be successful in the role, but who is most likely to click on that job ad" (Bogen 2019: no page number), which also means leading "job ads to be delivered in a way that reinforces gender and racial stereotypes" (Bogen 2019: no page number). And if the question is why we increasingly use hiring algorithms even though we know that their predictions frequently happen to be not only wrong but also unfair, the answer is the following: the reason why, "[t]oday, this initial big cut of candidates is often made 'automatically', by an algorithm" (Persson 2016, p. 1), is that "[t]his is a technological feat that simplifies the life of a recruiter tremendously, and really can be seen as a necessary advancement to meet the conditions of hundreds and thousands of applicants for single positions, in today's job market" (Persson 2016, p. 1). Most clearly, the reason why we move from autonomous decisions to automated decisions is that automation "simplifies the life of a recruiter tremendously"—again, automation means moving unbearable burdens from ourselves to technology by making them dissolve in our own engineering, starting with the engineering of our own decisions. But why are we willing to engineer even our future, if it is true that it means "exercising power over me and my life"?

Let us use the legacy of past millennia to try to answer. Sophocles may teach us, first, what it means to predict our future by using the most reliable tools we have at our disposal, to the point that we even engineer our future, and, second, why, paradoxically enough, we actually engineer our future even though we do not want it to be predicted.

Interestingly enough, Oedipus shares Tiresias' destiny of going blind after having known. In the case of Oedipus, reliably knowing means being predicted by Phoebus: "I went to Delphi [...] and Phoebus [...] set forth other things, full of sorrow and terror and woe: that I was fated to defile my mother's bed, that I would reveal to men a brood which they could not endure to behold, and that I would slay the father that sired me. When I heard this, I turned in flight from the land of Corinth, from then on thinking of it only by its position under the stars, to some spot where I should never see fulfilment of the infamies foretold in my evil fate. And on my way I came to the land in which you say that this prince perished" (Soph. OT 787–800). Thus, the reason why Oedipus makes Phoebus' prediction happen is precisely that he desperately tries not to make it happen after having known. Knowing, specifically predicting, is precisely the cause of Oedipus' tragedy: "Alas, how terrible it is to have wisdom when it does not benefit those who have it" (Soph. OT 316–317). And Oedipus goes blind not by being punished by the goddess of knowledge, as in the case of Tiresias, but even by punishing himself: "Light, may I now look on you for the last time" (Soph. OT 1183), which means that he decides to do without his sight, i.e. the symbol of knowledge, after having understood that it may cause humans' tragedy, especially in the case of the prediction of their future.

If we use Sophocles' Oedipus to reflect upon what it means to predict our future by using the most reliable tools we have at our disposal, to the point that we even engineer our future, we may reason as follows. Let us imagine being Oedipus. What do we do if we know that our future will be "full of sorrow and terror and woe" after having been predicted by using the most reliable tools we have at our disposal, i.e. predictive technologies, in our case, from predictive algorithms to human digital twins? We may imagine answering as follows:

1. we may follow Oedipus' example, which means that we may desperately try not to make the prediction come true (in the case of Oedipus, by turning "to some spot where I should never see fulfilment of the infamies foretold in my evil fate").
2. We may follow the opposite example, which means that we may desperately fall into fatalism by thinking that whatever we do will result in "sorrow and terror and woe".
3. We may follow an extreme variant of Oedipus' example, which means that we may desperately try not to make the prediction come true by committing suicide.
4. We may follow an extreme variant of the opposite example, which means that we may desperately fall into self-deceptive fatalism by thinking that the prediction cannot in any way influence our emotions, thoughts, decisions and actions.

The four answers may have further variants, but it is not credible that the latter can totally diverge from the former. If it makes sense, we may take a further step by stressing what the four answers share:

1. we can always use the word "desperately" to describe our condition, in that, if it is true that the prediction results from the most reliable tools we have at our disposal (i.e. Phoebus in the case of Oedipus and predictive technologies in our case), it is also true that we can do nothing but seriously consider the prediction, which means going through a desperate time in any case.
2. We can always describe our condition as a kind of cause and effect relationship, in that, if it is true that the prediction results from the most reliable tools we have at our disposal (i.e. Phoebus in the case of Oedipus and predictive technologies in our case), it is also true that we can do nothing but make our emotions, thoughts, decisions and actions be influenced by the prediction, to the point that the latter causes the former as its effects. In the case of Oedipus, it is precisely the prediction what causes that "I came to the land in which you say that this prince perished". In our case, it is precisely the prediction what causes, for instance, "that the person 'is not ok'", "that person's identity", to the point that "this will change my life completely" by "exercising power over me and my life", and being discriminated by "gender and racial stereotypes".

The issue of our condition as a kind of cause and effect relationship is key. Even though, from magic to science, the attempt to predict the future has always been crucial, we should distinguish between, for instance, the weather forecast and "when a person will die and from what cause". Predicting "when a person will die and from what cause", together with several other details of one's future, means entering what makes one a human being—predicting one's future in the ways described above means entering one's autonomy as one's possibility and capability to imagine and plan one's future. And, if one cannot imagine and plan one's future, one's automation and engineering is taken to the extreme. When one can imagine and plan one's future, one can be autonomous even though one's imaginations and plans will not come true (for instance, if I imagine and plan to write a novel, I exercise my autonomy by imagining and planning it, even though, for internal and external causes, I will not write it). But, when one cannot imagine and plan one's future, one cannot be autonomous at all, in that one is deprived not only of one's autonomous actions but also, and especially, of one's autonomous emotions, thoughts and decisions—one is deprived of what makes one a human being, in that one engineers oneself by moving from being the cause of effects to being the effect of causes.

Whenever we, as humans, imagine and plan our future, we can be autonomous starting with our possibility and capability to make sense of our present, even though, for internal and external causes, our imaginations and plans will not come true—we can be autonomous by making sense of our present, no matter what our future will be. Conversely, if, according to the most reliable tools we have at our disposal, we are predicted to die next year, our autonomy as our possibility and capability to imagine and plan not only who we will be in the future but also who we are in the present dramatically decreases. And the key reason why our autonomy dramatically decreases is that we are deprived of imagining and planning our future as what plays a key role in making sense of our present—imagining and planning our future identity plays a key role in making sense of our present identity.

But then, if even doctors are asked to consider the case in which patients do not want to know, why do we increasingly automate, i.e. engineer, the prediction of our future? And why do we increasingly fall into the paradox described above, which means that, on the one hand, we do not want to be predicted and, on the other hand, we actually engineer our future by automating predictions that dramatically decrease our autonomy?

2.7 Burdened Humans

According to my proposal (i.e. reading our current way of designing and using technology as our desperate attempt to move from autonomy, which means bearing the burden of individual responsibility, to automation, which means making the burden of individual responsibility dissolve in our own engineering), the possible answer to the questions asked above may be the following: we are burdened by our autonomy to the extent that we even make its dissolution in technological automation win over "the negative emotions that may arise from foreknowledge of negative events"—we are burdened by our autonomy to the extent that we even trade our individual responsibility for imagining and planning our future for its dissolution in technological automation.

If we go back to Kant's masterful work on the notion of autonomy, we understand that speaking of autonomy means speaking of "the will's own lawgiving" not only as what makes humans "culpable and deserving of punishment", as we have seen, but also as what makes humans move from being an "*automaton*" (Kant 1788, p. 5, 97)[18] to being "free" (Kant 1785, p. 4, 450). Surprisingly enough, Kant uses the word "*automaton*", which is the etymological root of the word "automation" (and he even uses it at least a century and a half before its contemporary ubiquitous use).[19] More precisely, in the case of humans, being an "*automaton*" means the following condition: "if the freedom of our will were none other than [...] psychological and comparative but not also transcendental, i.e. absolute [...], then it would at bottom be nothing better than the freedom of a turnspit, which, when once it is wound up, also accomplishes its movements of itself" (Kant 1788, p. 5, 97). Thus, being an "*automaton*" means being driven by something "psychological and comparative", i.e. heteronomous conditions (for instance, when the will of an individual is driven by being afraid of disobeying the will of another individual). Conversely, being autonomous, together with being "free", means being driven by something "transcendental, i.e. absolute", i.e. autonomous conditions (for instance, when the will of an individual is driven by their "will's own lawgiving", even though they are afraid of disobeying the will of another individual).

If we use Kant's work to reflect upon our technological era, specifically our trade of our autonomy for technological automation, the following question may arise: why should we want to move from being "free", which is something that clearly values us, to being an "*automaton*", which is something that clearly devalues us? More precisely, why should we want to move from being "free" to having nothing but "the freedom of a turnspit, which, when once it is wound up, also accomplishes its movements of itself"? According to my proposal, the possible answer to the questions asked above may be the following: precisely because we want, sometimes consciously and sometimes unconsciously, to trade our autonomous "freedom", which is exceedingly heavier to bear, for "the freedom of a turnspit", which is exceedingly lighter to bear—precisely because we want, paradoxically enough, to free ourselves from the kind of "freedom" that results from our autonomy, in that, especially in years characterised by extreme individualism and competitiveness, speaking of autonomous

[18] More precisely, an "*automaton*" "*spirituale*, when it is driven by representations" (Kant 1788, p. 5, 97), as partly divergent from the analogous "*automaton materiale*, when the machine is driven by matter" (Kant 1788, p. 5, 97). In the first case, we have to do with humans and, in the second case, we have to do with machines.

[19] Since 1947, when Ford Motor Company decided to "set up an 'automation department'. [...] [The] new unit hoped to increase the use of existing technologies—hydraulic, electromechanical, and pneumatic—to speed up operations and enhance productivity on the assembly line" (Rifkin 1955, p. 66).

"freedom" means speaking of unbearable burdens that, first, are desperately individual and, second, are something we desperately try to measure up to, frequently without succeeding at all.

Thus, "the freedom of a turnspit, which, when once it is wound up, also accomplishes its movements of itself", may be read as our perfect way to free ourselves through technology. Whenever we automate, i.e. engineer, our decisions and actions, from using predictive algorithms to using human digital twins, we actually trade our human identity for the identity of "a turnspit" characterised by the cause and effect relationship. On the one hand, "it is wound up", which identifies its cause as heteronomous. On the other hand, it "accomplishes its movements of itself", which identifies its being nothing but an effect of a heteronomous cause, even though it may seem to move by itself. Analogously, whenever we automate, i.e. engineer, our decisions and actions, on the one hand, we are driven by heteronomous causes (for instance, when our actions are caused by algorithms as black boxes). On the other hand, we are nothing but effects of heteronomous causes, even though we may seem to exercise our autonomous "freedom", in that we do not stop acting—we are nothing but automated, i.e. engineered, effects of heteronomous causes. Could Kant have thought of something more devaluing for our identity as human identity?

Yet, again, we should consider that the reason for the kind of self-sabotage described above may be even touching: especially in years characterised by extreme individualism and competitiveness, our autonomy even becomes our most unbearable burden, in that it is, first, desperately individual and, second, something we desperately try to measure up to, frequently without succeeding at all.

If it makes sense, the automation, i.e. the engineering, of our future through technological predictions, from predictive algorithms to human digital twins, may be read not only as the most extreme way to engineer ourselves but also, and especially, as our perfect way to free ourselves from our most unbearable burden, i.e. our autonomy at its greatest extent—all in all, what may be more unbearable than our individual responsibility for imagining and planning our future as the kind of success in which we frequently will not succeed at all even though we desperately try to measure up to it? Thus, automating, i.e. engineering, our future through technological predictions may be read as our perfect way to trade our challenging existence for the far less challenging existence of "a turnspit", whose future "is wound up". Whenever we let technology predict our future, we trade our challenging individual responsibility sometimes for others' responsibility and sometimes, and especially, for something that cannot have responsibility at all—whenever we let technology predict our future, we trade our challenging capability to determine our future even surprisingly, i.e. against all odds, for far less challenging predetermined odds.

2.8 Conclusion

We may summarise by saying that we have reflected upon an unprecedented form of alienation, specifically a 21st-century form of alienation.

According to the SEP definition, alienation arises from the convergence of the following three essentials: "there has to be a separation; the separation has to be problematic; and it has to obtain between a subject and object that properly belong together".[20] We may think of ourselves and our future as "a subject and object that properly belong together", but which are "problematic[ally]" "separat[ed]". According to Jaeggi, there is no alienation when there is "something like self-determination and being the author of one's own life" (Jaeggi 2014, p. 39), i.e. when "one is present in one's actions, steers one's life instead of being driven by it, independently appropriates social roles and is able to identify with one's desires, and is involved in the world" (Jaeggi 2014, p. 155). Conversely, there is alienation when there is "an inadequate power and a lack of presence in what one does, a failure to identify with one's own actions and desires and to take part in one's own life" (Jaeggi 2014, p. 155). As we have seen, whenever our actions are the effects of emerging technologies as their causes, we are not "present in" our actions. For instance, whenever "[t]he feedback from that digital model" takes "precedence over how I physically felt", I am not "present in" "how I physically felt". Whenever "the numbers drown out / my intuition / my instincts", I am not "present in" "my intuition / my instinct". Whenever "the numbers from Basis contradict my positive assessment of my rest", I am not "present in" "my rest"—more generally, I am not "present in" "my own experience".

The examples listed above show alienation as being alienated from one's present actions, which is not an unprecedented form of alienation, even though the kinds of technologies used are novel. Conversely, what may be thought of as an unprecedented form of alienation, specifically a 21st-century form of alienation, is the exponential growth of the following phenomenon: designing and using technology as one's perfect way to free oneself from one's autonomy at its greatest extent, which even becomes one's most unbearable burden—again, one's most unbearable burden as one's individual responsibility for imagining and planning one's future, which is precisely the background against which one's present in particular, and especially one's identity in general, makes sense in a culture driven by the idea of individually succeeding. Thus, on the one hand, we desperately strive to engineer ourselves to measure up to our future as the proof of our individual success and, on the other hand, we desperately, and even touchingly, strive to engineer our future to sabotage what may also turn out to be the proof of our individual failure—we are even willing to alienate ourselves from our future, which is the condition for being human as being even against all odds, to sabotage what may also turn out to be the proof of our individual failure: all in all, "a turnspit", whose future "is wound up", cannot actually fail.

[20] See https://plato.stanford.edu/entries/alienation/ (accessed in December 2022).

References

Aeschylus (1926) Agamemnon. H.W. Smyth (ed). Harvard University Press, Cambridge

Allam Z, Bibri SE, Jones DS, Chabaud D, Moreno C (2022) Unpacking the "15-minute city" via 6G, IoT, and digital twins. Towards a new narrative for increasing urban efficiency, resilience, and sustainability. Sensors 22(1369):1–17

Allam Z, Jones DS (2021) Future (post-COVID) digital, smart and sustainable cities in the wake of 6G. Digital twins, immersive realities and new urban economies. Land Use Policy 101:1–13

Anshari M, Almunawar MN, Masri M (2022) Digital twin. Financial technology's next frontier of robo-advisor. J Risk Financ Manag 15(163):1–9

Baron K, Abbott S, Jao N, Manalo N, Mullen R (2017) Orthosomnia. Are some patients taking the quantified self too far? J Clin Sleep Med 2(13):351–354

Barricelli BR, Casiraghi E, Gliozzo J, Petrini A, Valtolina S (2020) Human digital twin for fitness management. IEEE access 8: 26637–26664

Bogen M (2019) All the ways hiring algorithms can introduce bias. Harv Bus Rev , May 6, no page numbers

Botín-Sanabria DM, Mihaita A-S, Peimbert-García RE, Ramírez-Moreno MA, Ramírez-Mendoza RA, de J. Lozoya-Santos, J (2022) Digital twin technology challenges and applications. A comprehensive review. Remote Sens 14(1335):1–25

Bratman ME (2007) Structures of agency. Oxford University Press, Oxford, Essays

Braun M (2021) Represent Me, please! Towards an ethics of digital twins in medicine. J Med Ethics 47:394–400

Brusoni S, Vaccaro A (2017) Ethics, technology and organizational innovation. J Bus Ethics 143:223–226

Bruynseels K, Santoni de Sio F, van den Hoven J (2018) Digital twins in health care. Ethical implications of an emerging engineering paradigm. Front Genet 9:1–11

Callimachus (1921) Hymn to Athena. Ed. by A.W. Mair. Heinemann-G.P. Putnam's sons, London-New York

Carmichael A (2010) Why I stopped tracking, https://quantifiedself.com/blog/why-i-stopped-tracking/

Cawthon R, Smith K, O'Brien E. et al. (2003) Association between telomere length in blood and mortality in people aged 60 years or older. Lancet 361:393–395

Chiodo S (2022) Human autonomy, technological automation (and reverse). AI & Society. J Knowl, Cult Commun 1(37):39–48

Chiodo S (2023a) Technology and the overturning of human autonomy. Springer, Cham

Chiodo, S. (2023b). Trading human autonomy for technological automation. In S. Lindgren (ed) Handbook of critical studies of artificial intelligence. Edward Elgar Publishers, Cheltenham

Chiodo S (2024) Predicted humans. Emerging technologies and the burden of sensemaking. Routledge-Taylor & Francis Group, Abingdon-New York

Crary J (2013) 24/7. Terminal capitalism and the ends of sleep. Verso, London-Brooklyn-New York

Deng T, Zhang K, Shen Z-J (2021) A systematic review of a digital twin city. A new pattern of urban governance toward smart cities. J Manag Sci Eng 6:125–134

Descartes R (1637, 1912) A discourse on method. Ed. by J. Veitch. J.M. Dent and Sons, London

Dworkin G (1988) The theory and practice of autonomy. Cambridge University Press, Cambridge

Ekstrom LW (1993) A coherence theory of autonomy. Philos Phenomenol Res 53:599–616

Eyal G (2019) The crisis of expertise. Polity Press, Cambridge-Medford

Fana C, Zhanga C, Yahjab A, Mostafavi A (2021) Disaster city digital twin. A vision for integrating artificial and human intelligence for disaster management. Int J Inf Manag 56:1–10

Fioravante R, Vaccaro A (2025) Humanism, dehumanisation, integral human development. An overview of boundaries and capabilities of human-centered artificial intelligence in business and organisation. In R. Fioravante, A. Vaccaro A., eds., Humanism and artificial intelligence, Springer, Cham

Ford DN, Wolf CM (2020) Smart cities with digital twin systems for disaster management. J Manag Eng 4(36):1–10
Frankfurt HG (ed) (1988) The importance of what we care about. Cambridge University Press, Cambridge
Friedman M (2003) Autonomy, gender, politics. Oxford University Press, Oxford
Frischmann B, Selinger E (2018) Re-engineering humanity. Cambridge University Press, Cambridge-New York
Fuller A, Fan Z, Day C, Barlow C (2020) Digital twin. Enabling technologies, challenges and open research. IEEE access 8:108952–108971
Gahlot S, Reddy SRN, Kumar D (2019) Review of smart health monitoring approaches with survey analysis and proposed framework. IEEE Internet Things J 2(6):2116–2127
Gigerenzer G, Garcia-Retamero R (2017) Cassandra's regret. The psychology of not wanting to know. Psychol Rev 2(124):179–196
Glaessgen E, Stargel D (2012) The digital twin paradigm for future NASA and US Air Force vehicles. In "53rd AIAA/ASME/ASCE/AHS/ASC structures, structural dynamics and materials conference", American Institute of Aeronautics and Astronautics, 1–14
Gray T (1747) Ode on a distant prospect of Eton College. Dodsley, London
Grieves M (2014) Digital twin. Manufacturing excellence through virtual factory replication, NASA, Washington
Haenlein M, Huang MH, Kaplan A (2022) Business ethics in the era of artificial intelligence. J Bus Ethics 4(178):867–869
Holler M, Uebernickel F, Brenner W (2016) Digital twin concepts in manufacturing industries. A literature review and avenues for further research. Proceedings of the 18th international conference on industrial engineering, 1–9
Homer (1998) Odyssey. Translation by A.T. Murray revised by G.E. Dimock. Harvard University Press, Cambridge
Jaeggi R (2014) Alienation. Columbia University Press, New York
Jones D, Snider C, Nassehi A, Yon J, Hicks B (2020) Characterising the digital twin. A systematic literature review. CIRP J Manuf Sci Technol 29:36–52
Kamel Boulos MN, Zhang P (2021) Digital twins. From personalised medicine to precision public health. J Pers Med 11(745):1–12
Kant I (1781, 1988) Critique of pure reason. Ed. by P. Guyer and A. Wood. Cambridge University Press, Cambridge-New York
Kant I (1785, 1998) Groundwork of the metaphysics of morals. Ed. by M.J. Gregor. Cambridge University Press, Cambridge
Kant I (1788, 1996) Critique of practical reason. Ed. by M.J. Gregor, introduction by A. Wood. Cambridge University Press, Cambridge
Korenhof P, Blok V, Kloppenburg S (2021) Steering representations. Towards a critical understanding of digital twins. Philos Technol 34:1751–1773
Kritzinger W, Karner M, Traar G, Henjes J, Sihn W (2018) Digital twin in manufacturing. A categorical literature review and classification. IFAC papers on line 11(51):1016–1022
Le Morvan P (2011) On ignorance. A reply to peels. Philosophia 2(39): 335–344
Le Morvan P (2021) Knowledge, ignorance and true belief. theoria 1(77):32–41
Leopold D (2022) Alienation. In Stanford encyclopaedia of philosophy, October 6, https://plato.stanford.edu/entries/alienation/
Littlefield MM (2018) Instrumental intimacy. Johns Hopkins University Press, Baltimore, EEG wearables and neuroscientific control
Liu M, Fang S, Dong H, Xu C (2021) Review of digital twin about concepts, technologies, and industrial applications. J Manuf Syst 58:346–361
Lu Y, Liu C, Wang KI-K, Huang H, Xu X (2020) Digital twin-driven smart manufacturing. Connotation, reference model, applications and research issues. Robot Comput-Integr Manuf 61:1–14
Lyall B (2021) The ambivalent assemblages of sleep optimization. Rev Commun 2(21):144–160

Mohammadi N, Taylor JE (2017) Smart city digital twins. 2017 IEEE symposium series on computational intelligence, 1–5

Mylonas G, Kalogeras A, Kalogeras G, Anagnostopoulos C, Alexakos C, Muñoz L (2021) Digital twins from smart manufacturing to smart cities. A survey. "IEEE access" 9, 143222–143249

Negri E, Fumagalli L, Macchi M (2017) A review of the roles of digital twin in CPS-based production systems. Procedia Manuf 11:939–948

O'Neill C, Nansen B (2019) Sleep mode. Mobile apps and the optimisation of sleep-wake rhythms. First Monday 6(24):no page numbers

Okegbile SD, Cai J, Yi C, Niyato D (2022) Human digital twin for personalised healthcare. Vision, architecture and future directions. IEEE network:1–7

Peels R (2010) What is ignorance? philosophia 1(38):57–67

Peels R (2011) Ignorance is lack of true belief. A rejoinder to Le Morvan Philosophia 2(39):345–355

Persson A (2016) Implicit bias in predictive data profiling within recruitments. In A. Lehmann, et al., eds., Privacy and identity management. Facing up to next steps. Springer, Cham, 212–230

Pirandello L (1925, 1992) One, no one and one hundred thousand. Ed. by W. Weaver. Sprul Editions, New York

Plato (1966) Apology. Ed. by H.N. Fowler. Harvard University Press-Heinemann, Cambridge-London

Popa E.O., van Hilten M, Oosterkamp E, Bogaardt M-J (2021) The use of digital twins in healthcare. Socio-ethical benefits and socio-ethical risks. Life Sci, Soc Policy 6(17):1–25

Qi Q, Tao F (2018) Digital twin and big data towards smart manufacturing and industry 4.0. 360-degree comparison. IEEE Access 6:3585–3593.

Reagle JM (2019) Hacking life. The MIT Press, Cambridge, Systematised living and its discontents

Rifkin J (1995) The end of work. The decline of the global labour force and the dawn of the post-market era. Putnam Publishing Group, New York

Sadowski J (2020) Too smart. How digital capitalism is extracting data, controlling our lives, and taking over the world. The MIT Press, Cambridge

Sahal R, Alsamhi SH., Brown KN (2022) Personal digital twin. A close look into the present and a step towards the future of personalised healthcare industry. Sensors 22(5918):1–35

Shahat E, Hyun CT, Yeom C (2021) City digital twin potentials. A review and research agenda. Sustainability 13:1–20

Shakespeare W (1998) 1998. Hamlet. Oxford University Press, Oxford-New York

Sophocles (1887) Oedipus Tyrannus (OT). R. Jebb (ed). Cambridge University Press, Cambridge

The holy bible (1983). New York International Bible Society, East Brunswick

Ukko J, Saunila M, Nasiri M, Rantala T, Holopainen M (2022) Digital twins' impact on organisational control. Perspectives on formal vs social control. Inf Technol People 8(35):253–272

Van der Valk H, Hase H, Moller F, Arbter M, Henning JL, Otto B (2020) A taxonomy of digital twins. Am Conf Inf Syst 26:1–10

Williams K (2013) The weight of things lost. Self-knowledge and personal informatics. CHI, 1–4

Williams S, Coveney C, Gabe J (2013) Medicalisation or customisation? Sleep, enterprise and enhancement in the 24/7 society. Soc Sci Med 79:40–47

Wittgenstein L (1921, 1963) Tractatus logico-philosophicus. D. Pears and B. McGuinness (eds). Routledge & Kegan Paul, London

Simona Chiodo is a full professor of philosophy at Politecnico di Milano. She is doing research in epistemology, specifically on the relationship between reality and ideality, in philosophy of technology, focusing on understanding the philosophical meaning of current technologies, and in aesthetics, specifically on the notion of beauty. Among her recent publications, the monographs Predicted humans. Emerging technologies and the burden of sensemaking (Routledge, 2024) and Technology and the overturning of human autonomy (Springer, 2023). She was visiting professor at the University of Cambridge and the University of Edinburgh. She was visiting scholar at the University of Pittsburgh. She was academic visitor at Massachusetts Institute of Technology,

Chalmers University of Technology, ETH Zurich, TU Delft and Xi'an University of Architecture and Technology. She spent research stays at Harvard University. She is vice-dean of the School of Architecture, Urban Planning and Construction Engineering of Politecnico di Milano, co-founder of META (Social Sciences and Humanities for Science and Technology at Politecnico di Milano) and member of the IDEA League Ethics Working Group.

Chapter 3
Artificial Intelligence, Humanistic Ethics

John Tasioulas

Abstract Ethics is concerned with what it is to live a flourishing life and what it is we morally owe to others. The optimizing mindset prevalent among computer scientists and economists, among other powerful actors, has led to an approach focused on maximizing the fulfilment of human preferences, an approach that has acquired considerable influence in the ethics of AI. But this preference-based utilitarianism is open to serious objections. This essay sketches an alternative, "humanistic" ethics for AI that is sensitive to aspects of human engagement with the ethical often missed by the dominant approach. Three elements of this humanistic approach are outlined: its commitment to a plurality of values, its stress on the importance of the procedures we adopt, not just the outcomes they yield, and the centrality it accords to individual and collective participation in our understanding of human well-being and morality. The essay concludes with thoughts on how the prospect of artificial general intelligence bears on this humanistic outlook.

Keywords Humanistic ethics · Humanism and AI · Ethical frameworks · Ethics of AI

Ethics is, first and foremost, a domain of ordinary human thought, not a specialist academic discipline. It presupposes the existence of human choices that can be appraised by reference to a distinctive range of values. The delimitation of this range, among other values such as aesthetic or religious values, is philosophically controversial. But on a fairly standard reading, two very general, interlocking questions lie at the heart of ethics: What is it to live a good or flourishing life? And what is it that we owe to others, notably fellow human beings, but also nonhuman animals or even inanimate nature? The first question brings us into the territory of individual well-being; the second into that of morality, especially the obligations we owe to others and the rights they hold against us. Philosophers expound theories of well-being and morality and their interrelations, but all of us, in living our lives, constantly make

J. Tasioulas (✉)
Oxford, UK
e-mail: aiethics@philosophy.ox.ac.uk

R. Fioravante and A. Vaccaro (eds.), *Humanism and Artificial Intelligence*, SpringerBriefs in Philosophy, https://doi.org/10.1007/978-3-031-85478-1_3

choices that reflect answers to these questions, however inchoate or unconscious they may be.

Engagement with ethics is inescapable in decision-making about artificial intelligence.[1] The choices we make regarding the development and deployment of AI-based technologies are ultimately intelligible only in terms of the fallible pursuit of ethical values such as the acquisition of knowledge and control or the promotion of health, justice, and security. Moreover, all forms of "regulation" that might be proposed for AI, whether voluntary self-regulation in deciding whether to use a social robot as a caregiver, or the social and legal norms that should govern the manufacturing and use of such robots, ultimately implicate choices that reflect judgments about ethical values and their prioritization.

A clear-eyed appreciation of the pervasive significance of ethics for AI is sometimes obscured by an odd contraction that the idea of ethics is liable to undergo in this domain. So, for example, Kate Crawford, author and founder of the AI Now Institute, urges us to "focus less on ethics and more on power" because "AI is invariably designed to amplify and reproduce the forms of power it has been deployed to optimize Crawford (2021)." But what would the recommended focus on power entail? For Crawford, it means interrogating the institutional power structures in which AI is embedded by reference to ideas of equality, justice, and democracy. But the irony is that these three ideas are either themselves core ethical values or, in the case of democracy, need to be explicated and defended in terms of such values.

Nonetheless, Crawford's injunction usefully prompts reflection on the various ways the idea of ethics has been unduly diminished in recent discussions about AI, no doubt partly a result of the prominent role of big tech players in shaping the field of "AI ethics" to limit the threat it poses to their commercial ambitions. Consider three ways the diminishment of ethics is typically effected.

Content. The content of ethical standards is often interpreted as exclusively a matter of fairness, which is primarily taken to be a relational concern with how some people are treated compared with others. Illustrations of AI-based technology that raise fairness concerns include facial recognition technology that systematically disadvantages darker-skinned people or automated resume screening tools that are biased against women because the respective algorithms were trained on data sets that are demographically unrepresentative or that reflect historically sexist hiring practices. "Algorithmic unfairness" is a vitally important matter, especially when it exacerbates the condition of members of already unjustly disadvantaged groups. But this should not obscure the fact that ethics also encompasses nonrelational concerns such as whether, for example, facial recognition technology should be deployed at all in light of privacy rights or whether it is disrespectful to job applicants in general to rank their resumes by means of an automated process.

Scope of application. Ethics is sometimes construed as narrowly individualistic in focus: that is, as being concerned with guiding individuals' personal conduct, rather than also bearing on the larger institutional and social settings in which their decisions are made and enacted[2]. In reality, however, almost all key ethical values, such as justice and charity, have profound implications for institutions and patterns of social organization. Plato's *Republic*, after all, sought to understand justice in the individual soul by considering it "writ large" in the polity. Admittedly, some philosophers treat political justice as radically discontinuous from justice in the soul. The most influential proponent of the discontinuity thesis in recent decades is John Rawls, who contends that pervasive reasonable disagreement on ethical truth disqualifies beliefs about such truths from figuring as premises in political justification Rawls (1993). This is a sophisticated controversy, which cannot be addressed here, save to note that this kind of move will always face the response that the phenomenon of reasonable disagreement, and the need for respect that it highlights, is itself yet a further topic for ethical appraisal, and hence cannot displace the need to take a stand on ethical truth Tasioulas (2022).

Means of enforcement. There is a widespread assumption that ethics relates to norms that are not properly enforceable-for example, through legal mechanisms-but instead are backed up primarily by the sanction of individual conscience and informal public opinion. But the general restriction of ethics to "soft" forms of regulation in this way is arbitrary. The very question whether to enact a law or other regulatory norm and, if so, how best to implement and enforce it, is one on which ethical values such as justice and personal autonomy have a significant bearing. Indeed, there is a long-standing tradition, cutting across ideological boundaries, that identifies justice precisely with those moral rights that should in principle receive social and legal enforcement.

In short, we should reclaim a broad and foundational understanding of ethics in the AI domain, one that potentially encompasses deliberation about any form of regulation, from personal self-regulation to legal regulation, and which potentially has radical implications for the reordering of social power.

Given its inescapability, ethical thought is hardly absent from current discussions around AI. However, these discussions often suffer from a tendency either to leave inexplicit their operative ethical assumptions or else to rely upon them uncritically even when they are made explicit. We can go even further and identify a dominant, or at least a prominent, approach to ethics that is widely congenial to powerful scientific, economic, and governmental actors in the AI field.

Like anyone else, AI scientists are prone to the illusion that the intellectual methods at their disposal have a far greater problem-solving purchase than is warranted. This is a phenomenon that Plato diagnosed in relation to the technical experts of his day, artisans such as cobblers and shipbuilders. The mindset of scientists working in AI tends to be data-driven, it places great emphasis on optimization as the core operation of rationality, and it prioritizes formal and quantitative techniques. Given this intellectual orientation, it is little wonder that an eminent AI scientist, like Stuart Russell, in his recent book *Human Compatible: AI and the Problem of Control*, is drawn to preference-based utilitarianism as his overarching ethical standpoint[3].

Russell's book takes the familiar worry that AI—in the form of an artificial general intelligence (AGI) that surpasses human intellectual capabilities-will eventually spiral out of control, unconstrained by human morality, with disastrous consequences. But what is human morality? Russell appears to take it as axiomatic that the morally right thing to do is whatever will maximize the fulfilment of human preferences Russell (2019). In terms of our two core concerns of ethics, the fulfilment of human preferences is taken to encompass well-being, and the fundamental moral injunction is to maximize overall well-being thus conceived. So ethics is reduced to an exercise in prediction and optimization: which act or policy is likely to lead to the optimal fulfilment of human preferences?

But this view of ethics is notoriously open to multiple serious-I believe, fatal-objections. Its concern with aggregating preferences threatens to override important rights that erect strong barriers to what can be done to individuals. Why not feed a few Christians to the lions if their preferences to stay alive are outweighed by the preferences of a sufficiently large number of blood-thirsty Roman spectators? And that is even before we observe that many preferences are infected with racism, sexism, or other prejudices; that they may reflect false or incomplete information; or that they may be psychological adaptations to oppressive circumstances. Ethics operates in the crucial space of reflection on what our preferences should be, a vital consideration that makes a belated appearance in the last few pages of Russell's book.[4] It cannot take those preferences as ultimate determinants of value.

There are moral philosophers who defend versions of preference utilitarianism that are patched-up to address these difficulties. But the idea that preference utilitarianism is a highly contestable moral theory does not really register in Russell's book, which conforms with my suspicion that it approximates to a default position among leading actors in the AI field.

The same broad approach is heavily influential among leading economic and governmental actors. This is perhaps less obvious, since the doctrine is standardly modified by positing wealth-maximization as the more readily measurable proxy for preference satisfaction. Hence the tendency of GDP to hijack governmental decision-making around economically consequential technologies, with the resultant sidelining of values that are not readily catered to by the market, such as public goods like access to justice and health care or the preservation of a sustainable environment. Hence, also, the legitimation of profit maximization by corporations as the most effective institutional means to societal wealth maximization. Of course, many who adopt such an approach have never heard of utilitarianism or, if they have, may explicitly reject it. But one revealing indication of the dominance of an ideology is the way that people who disavow it can nonetheless remain in its intellectual grip.

A key priority for those working in the field of AI ethics is to elaborate an ethical approach that transcends the limitations and distortions of this dominant ethical paradigm. In my view, such a humanistic ethics-one that encompasses aspects of human engagement with the ethical that are not adequately captured by the methods of natural science and mainstream economics, but that are the traditional concern of the arts and humanities-would possess at least the following three, interrelated features (the three Ps).

Pluralism. The approach would emphasize the plurality of values, both in terms of the elements of human well-being (such as achievement, understanding, friendship, and play) and the core components of morality (such as justice, fairness, charity, and the common good). This pluralism of values abandons the comforting notion that the key to the ethics of AI will be found in a single master concept, such as trustworthiness or human rights. How could human rights be the comprehensive ethical framework for AI when, for example, AI has a serious environmental impact beyond its bearing on anthropocentric concerns? And what of those important values to which we do not have a right, such as mercy or solidarity? Nor can trustworthiness be the master value. Being parasitic on compliance with more basic values, trustworthiness cannot itself displace those values.

Beyond the pluralism of values is their incommensurability. We are often confronted with practical problems that implicate an array of values that pull in different directions. In such cases, although some decisions will be superior to others, there may be no single decision that is optimal: in choosing an occupation, teaching may be a better field for me than surgery, but we cannot assume there is a single profession that is, all things considered, best, rather than a limited array of eligible alternatives that are no worse than the others. This incommensurability calls into question the availability of some optimizing function that determines the single option that is, all things considered, most beneficial or morally right, the quest for which has animated a lot of utilitarian thinking in ethics.

It is worth observing that confidence about the deployment of AI to minimize "noise" in human judgment-the unwanted variability, for example, in hiring decisions by employers or sentencing by judges-displayed in the important new work of Daniel Kahneman, Olivier Sibony, and Cass Sunstein, sometimes involves an implicit reductionism about the values at stake that downplays the scope for incommensurability[5]. For example, the authors treat bail decisions fundamentally as predictions of the likelihood that the accused will abscond or reoffend, sidelining considerations such as the gravity of the offense with which they have been charged or the impact of detention on the accused's dependents.[6] But such decisions typically address multi-value problems, and there is no guarantee that there is a single best way of reconciling the competing values in each case. This means not only that algorithms will need to be more sophisticated to balance multiple salient values in reaching a correct decision, but that much of what looks like noise may be acceptable variability of judgments *within* the range of rationally eligible alternatives.

Procedures, not only outcomes. Of course, we want AI to achieve valuable social goals, such as improving access to education, justice, and health care in an effective and efficient way. The COVID-19 pandemic has cast into sharp relief the question of what outcomes AI is being used to pursue: for example, is it enabling physicians to diagnose and triage patients faster and more effectively, or is it primarily engaged in profit-making activities, like vacuuming up people's attention online, that have little or no redeeming social value?[7]. The second feature of a humanistic approach to ethics emphasizes that what we rightly care about is not just the value of the outcomes that AI applications can be used to deliver, but the procedures through which it does so.

If, for example, important practical decisions exhibit the phenomenon of incommensurability, then we may have good reason to ensure that they are assigned to humans, rather than to automated processes, to preserve a valuable form of autonomy for humans as they express and develop their tastes and characters in choosing from divergent, but rationally eligible, pathways in life. Of course, there is the further question of how to balance such autonomy against demands for consistency (or "noiselessness"), especially in public decision-making. Should we tolerate significant divergence in sentencing across judges, or should the demands for "horizontal equity" prevail, ensuring that like cases are treated alike? Proponents of the latter view often recommend the use of algorithms to guide or replace human decision-making. This itself is a difficult question of striking a balance between competing considerations in our legal culture, with no *ex ante* guarantee that one solution will emerge as superior overall.

But the case for according ultimate decision-making authority to humans can also be made even if we suppose that a single correct answer is always available. Take, for example, the use of AI in cancer diagnosis and its use in the sentencing of criminals. Intuitively, the two cases seem to exhibit a difference in the comparative valuing of the soundness of the eventual decision or diagnosis and the process through which it is reached. When it comes to cancer, generating the most accurate diagnosis may be all-important, it being largely a matter of indifference whether this is generated by an AI diagnostic tool or the exercise of human judgment. In criminal sentencing, however, being sentenced by a robot judge-even if the sentence is likely to be less biased or less "noisy" than one rendered by a human counterpart-appears to sacrifice important values, such as the ideal of reciprocity among fellow citizens that is central to the rule of law Tasioulas (2020).

This last point is familiar, of course, in relation to such process values as transparency, procedural fairness, and explainability. Even if the procedure followed by the judicial algorithm can be made transparent, there is a serious question-given, for example, the vast discrepancy between machine learning and ordinary human reasoning processes-whether it affords an explanation of the right kind, an explanation that a criminal defendant can grasp as offering intelligible reasons for the decision to imprison him. But the point goes beyond the important issue of explainability. How does it feel to contemplate the prospect of a world in which judgments that bear on our deepest interests and moral standing have, at least as their proximate decision-makers, autonomous machines that do not have a share in human solidarity and cannot be held accountable for their decisions in the way that a human judge can?

Participation. The third feature relates to the importance of participation in the process of decision-making with respect to AI, whether as an individual or as part of a group of self-governing democratic citizens. At the level of individual well-being, this takes the focus away from theories that equate human well-being with an end state such as pleasure or preference-satisfaction. These end states could in principle be brought about through a process in which the person who enjoys them is passive: for example, by the government putting a happiness drug into the water supply. Contrary to this passive view, it would stress that successful engagement with valuable pursuits is at the core of human well-being Raz (1986).

If the conception of human well-being that emerges is deeply participatory, then this bears heavily on the delegation of decision-making power to AI applications. One of the most important sites of participation in constructing a good life, in modern societies, is the workplace Gheaus and Herzog (2016). According to a McKinsey study, around 30% of all work activities in 60% of occupations could one day be automated Manyika and Sneader (2018). Can we accept the idea that the large-scale elimination of job opportunities can be compensated for by the benefits that automation makes available? The answer partly depends on whether the participatory self-fulfilment of work can, any time soon and for the vast majority of those rendered jobless, be feasibly replaced by other activities, such as art, friendship, play, or religion. If it cannot, addressing the problem with a mechanism like a universal basic income, which involves the passive receipt of a benefit, will hardly suffice. Instead, much greater attention will need to be paid to how AI can be integrated into productive practices in ways that do not so much replace human work as enhance its quality, making it more productive, fulfilling, and challenging, while also less dangerous, repetitive, and lacking in meaning[8].

Similarly, we value citizen participation as part of collective democratic self-government. And we do so not just because of the instrumental benefits of democratic decision-making in generating superior decisions by harnessing cognitive diversity, but also because of the way in which participatory decision-making processes affirm the status of citizens as free and equal members of the community[9]. This is an essential plank in the defense against the tendency of AI technology to be co-opted by technocratic modes of decision-making that erode democratic values by seeking to convert matters of political judgment into questions of technical expertise[10].

At present, much of the culture in which AI is embedded is distinctly technocratic, with decisions about the "values" encoded in AI applications being taken by corporate, bureaucratic, or political elites, often largely insulated from meaningful democratic control. Indeed, a small group of tech giants accounts for the lion's share of investment in AI research, dictating its overall direction and setting the prevalent moral tone. Meanwhile, AI-enabled social media risks eroding the quality of public deliberation that a genuine democracy needs, such as by promoting the spread of disinformation, aggravating political polarization, or using bots in astroturfing campaigns. Similarly, the use of AI as part of corporate and governmental efforts to monitor and manipulate individuals undermines privacy and threatens the exercise of basic liberties, effectively discouraging citizen participation in democratic politics[11].

As with workplace participation, we need to reflect seriously on how AI and digital technology more generally can enable, rather than hinder and distort, democratic participation[12]. This is especially urgent given the declining faith in democracy across the globe in recent years, including in long-established democracies such as the United Kingdom and the United States. Indeed, the disillusionment is such that, in a recent poll, 51% of Europeans favored replacing at least some of their parliamentarians with AI[13]. There is still time to salvage the democratic ideal that an essential part of civic dignity is participation in self-government.

An additional complexity here concerns how these two modes of participation—in the workplace and in politics-are connected. It is obvious that active participation in the two domains is mutually reinforcing in important ways. Thus, powers of reason and sociability that are developed in a participatory workplace, and that foster a sense of equal civic dignity, can be brought to bear in democratic deliberation about political questions, just as democratic control over the impact of new technologies on the workplace can help preserve and enhance its vital role as a site of genuine human fulfilment[14].

I have mainly focused on narrow AI, conceived as AI-powered technology that can perform limited tasks (such as facial recognition or medical diagnosis) that typically require intelligence when performed by humans. This is partly because serious doubt surrounds the likelihood of artificial general intelligence emerging within any realistically foreseeable time frame, partly because the operative notion of "intelligence" in discussions of AGI is problematic,[15] and partly because a focus on AGI often distracts us from the more immediate questions of narrow AI[16].

With these caveats in place, however, one can admit that thought experiments about AGI can help bring into focus two questions fundamental to any humanistic ethic: What is the ultimate source of human dignity, understood as the inherent value attaching to each and every human being? And how can we relate human dignity to the value inhering in nonhuman beings? Toward the end of Kazuo Ishiguro's novel *Klara and the Sun*, the eponymous narrator, an "Artificial Friend," speculates that human dignity-the "human heart" that "makes each of us special and individual"-has its source not in something within us, but in the love of others for us Ishiguro (2021). But a threat of circularity looms for this boot-strapping humanism, for how can the love of others endow us with value unless those others already have value? Moreover, if the source of human dignity is contingent on the varying attitudes of others, how can it apply equally to every human being? Are the unloved bereft of the "human heart"?

Questions like these explain the tendency among some to interpret the inherent value of each individual human being as arising from the special love that a supremely good transcendent being-God, represented by the sun, in Ishiguro's novel, which the solar-powered Klara treats as a kind of life-sustaining divinity-has for each human being in equal measure Wolterstorff (2008). But invoking a divine being to underwrite human dignity leads us into obvious metaphysical and ethical quagmires, which in turn raise the difficult question of whether the inherent worth of human beings can be explicated within a broadly naturalistic framework Wiggins (2008). Supposing that it can be, this is compatible with a distinct kind of dignity also inhering in other beings, such as nonhuman animals.

We are still struggling to integrate the value of nonhuman animals within our ethical thought. Doing so requires overcoming the baleful influence of longstanding practices in which animals are treated either as possessing merely instrumental value in relation to human ends, or at best intrinsic value that is conditional on their role in human life. The dream of AGI, should it ever become a reality, will generate an even more acute version of this problem, given the prominent role that our rational capacities play in elevating human dignity above the dignity of other beings known to us [[17]]. For the foreseeable future, however, our focus must be on properly integrating AI technology into a culture that respects and advances the dignity and well-being of humans, and the nonhuman animals with whom we share the world, rather than on the highly speculative endeavor of integrating the dignity of intelligent machines into our existing ethical framework.

Author's Note This essay began life as a blog post for the Ada Lovelace Institute, "The Role of the Arts and Humanities in Thinking about Artificial Intelligence (AI)." I am grateful to the Institute for permitting me to reuse some material here. I have benefited from comments on previous drafts from Dominic Burbidge, Hélène Landemore, Seth Lazar, Ted Lechterman, James Manyika, Adrian Vermuele, Carina Prunkl, Divya Siddarth, Carissa Veliz, Glen Weyl, Mike Woolridge, and John Zerilli. I regret that I have not been able to pursue many of their very stimulating comments within the confines of this short essay.

Notes

1. I shall assume a very broad understanding of AI as essentially the use of machines to perform tasks that characteristically require intelligence when performed by humans. My focus will primarily be on "narrow" AI applications, such as facial recognition, surveillance, and risk-assessment, rather than artificial general intelligence, though I say something about the latter toward the very end.
2. Some of these issues are compellingly developed by Joshua Cohen in "Don't Shoot the Algorithm" (unpublished manuscript).
3. The "effective altruism" movement, which has significant allegiance among tech elites, is arguably one expression of this depoliticized and, in its effect, ultimately conservative view of ethics. See Amia Srinivasan, "Stop the Robot Apocalypse," *London Review of Books* 37 (18) (2015).
4. I am here identifying an influential mode of thought that Russell's book epitomizes. It should be emphasized, however, that there have always been scientists in this domain who have urged the importance of a multidisciplinary approach with an important humanistic dimension, such as in Joseph Weizenbaum, *Computer Power and Human Reason: From Judgment to Calculation* (San Francisco: Freeman & Co, 1976); and, more recently, in Nigel Shadbolt and Roger Hampson, *The Digital Ape: How to Live (in Peace) with Smart Machines* (London: Scribe, 2018).
5. Ibid., 255.
6. Ibid., chap. 10.
7. For a discussion of studies showing that AI predictive tools made no real difference in diagnosing and triaging COVID-19 patients, and in some cases, may have been harmful, see William Douglas Heaven, "Hundreds of AI Tools Have Been Built to Catch Covid, None of Them Helped," *MIT Technology Review*, July 30, 2021, https://www.technologyreview.com/2021/07/30/1030329/machine-learning-ai-failed-covid-hospital-diagnosis-pandemic/.
8. For an exploration of this theme, see Frank Pasquale, *New Laws of Robotics: Defending Human Expertise in the Age of AI* (Cambridge, Mass.: Harvard University Press, 2020).
9. For a powerful recent defense of democracy along these lines, see Josiah Ober, *Demopolis: Democracy Before Liberalism in Theory and Practice* (Cambridge: Cambridge University Press, 2017).
10. For a candid statement, by a Silicon Valley billionaire, of the need to harness the libertarian promise of technology to an antidemocratic ethos, see Peter Thiel, "The Education of a Libertarian," *Cato Unbound: A Journal of Debate*, April 13, 2009, https://www.cato-unbound.org/2009/04/13/peter-thiel/education-libertarian
11. For a helpfully wide-ranging discussion of some of these issues, see Joshua Cohen and Archon Fung, "Democracy and the *Digital Public Sphere," in Digital Technology and Democratic Theory*, ed. Lucy Bernholz, Hélène Landemore, and Rob Reich (Chicago: University of Chicago Press, 2021).
12. For some positive thinking along these lines, see Hélène Landemore, "Open Democracy and Digital Technologies," in *Digital Technology and Democratic Theory*. For useful discussions of digitally enhanced democracy in pioneering countries such as Estonia and

Taiwan, see Hans Kundani, *The Future of Democracy in Europe: Technology and the Evolution of Representation* (London: Chatham House, 2020), https://www.chathamhouse.org/sites/default/files/CHHJ7131-Democracy-Technology-RP-INTS-200228.pdf; and Divya S (2021) Taiwan: Grassroots digital democracy that works. New York, Radical Exchange, https://www.radicalxchange.org/media/papers/Taiwan_Grassroots_Digital_Democracy_That_Works_V1_DIGITAL_pdf

13. "More Than Half of Europeans Want to Replace Lawmakers with AI, Study Finds," CNBC, May 27, 2021, https://www.cnbc.com/2021/05/27/europeans-want-to-replace-lawmakers-with-ai.html. For an interesting discussion of "algocracy" ("rule by algorithm"), see Ted Lechterman, "Will AI Make Democracy Obsolete?" *Public Ethics*, August 4, 2021, https://www.publicethics.org/post/will-ai-make-democracy-obsolete. It is worth noting that proposals for algocracy often assume that the point of politics is to aggregate human preferences, in line with the preference-based utilitarianism discussed above.
14. For a perceptive discussion of the way AI threatens to disrupt the economic underpinnings of democracy, see Daron Acemoglu, *Redesigning AI: Work, Democracy, and Justice in the Age of Automation* (Boston: Boston Review Forum, 2021).
15. Like many others, Stuart Russell adopts an impoverished conception of intelligence as competence in means-ends reasoning according to which the choice of ends is made extraneous to the operations of intelligence. On this view, a machine that annihilated humanity in order to maximize the number of paper clips in existence can qualify as superintelligent. Ibid., 167. For a wide-ranging and perceptive discussion of problems with the idea of "intelligence" invoked in discussions of AGI, see Divya Siddarth, Daron Acemoglu, Danielle Allen, et al., "How AI Fails Us" (Cambridge, Mass.: Edmond J. Safra Center for Ethics, 2021).
16. Some of these concerns are discussed in John Tasioulas, "First Steps Towards an Ethics of Robots and Artificial Intelligence," Journal of Practical Ethics 7 (1) (2019): 61–95, http://www.jpe.ox.ac.uk/papers/first-steps-towards-an-ethics-of-robots-and-artificial-intelligence/.
17. See, for example, John Tasioulas, "Human Dignity and the Foundations of Human Rights" in *Understanding Human Dignity*, ed. Christopher McCrudden (Oxford: Oxford University Press, 2013), 293–314; and Jeremy Waldron, *One Another's Equals: The Basis of Human Equality* (Cambridge, Mass.: Harvard University Press, 2017).

References

Crawford K (2021) Atlas of AI: Power, politics, and the planetary costs of artificial intelligence. Yale University Press, New Haven and London, p 224

Gheaus A, Herzog L (2016) The goods of work (Other Than Money!). J Soc Philos 47(1):70–89

Ishiguro K (2021) Klara and the Sun. London, Faber, pp 218, 306

Kahneman D, Sibony O, Sunstein CR (2021) Noise: A flaw in human judgment. William Collins, London

Manyika J, Sneader K, AI, automation, and the future of work: ten things to solve for. McKinsey Global Institute Executive Briefing, June 1, 2018, https://www.mckinsey.com/featured-insights/future-of-work/ai-automation-and-the-future-of-work-ten-things-to-solve-for

Rawls J (1993) Political liberalism. New York: Columbia University Press). For an attempt to pursue the radical discontinuity thesis in relation to AI, see Iason G (2020) Artificial intelligence, values, and alignment. Minds Mach 30(3):411

Raz J (1986) The morality of freedom. Oxford, Oxford University Press, chap. 12

Russell S (2019) Human compatible: AI and the problem of control. London, Allen Lane, p 178

Russell S, Compatible H (2019) AI and the problem of control. Allen Lane, London, p 178

Srinivasan A (2015) Stop the robot apocalypse. London Review of Books 37(18)

Tasioulas J (2020) The rule of law. In: Tasioulas J (ed) The cambridge companion to the philosophy of law. Cambridge University Press, Cambridge, pp 131–133

Tasioulas J (2022) The liberalism of love. In: Brooks T (ed) Political emotions: towards a decent public sphere. London, Palgrave Macmillan.
Wiggins D (2008) Solidarity and the root of the ethical. The Lindley Lecture, University of Kansas, Lawrence
Wolterstorff N (2008) Justice: Rights and wrongs. Princeton University Press, Princeton, N.J., pp 352–361

Part II
Humanism, Law, and Spirituality in AI

Chapter 4
Algorethics: On the Relationship Among Artificial Intelligence, Law and Religion

Mario Ferrante

Abstract With the development of the digital age, artificial intelligence is increasingly present and pervasive in every aspect of daily life, both personal and social, affecting decision-making processes and stressing the already complicated relationship between science, law and religion. Hence the need to build an "algoretic," understood as ethical reflection about the use of algorithms, in order to avoid their indiscriminate and potentially discriminatory use perhaps to the detriment of the frail and marginalized. Artificial intelligence can, in fact, be distorted through specific commercial and political interests with the risk of focusing algorithms on utility and profit through selection bias or distortion/corruption in data collection and coding prejudices. The analysis of the ethical and moral implications of artificial intelligence is also a challenge and an opportunity for religions, as evidenced by the recent signing (January 2023) of the "Rome Call for AI Ethics" at the Vatican by representatives of the three Abrahamic religions. In this field, religions have the opportunity and obligation to engage their teaching, voice and authority regarding the philosophical and anthropological challenges related to artificial intelligence that loom large in their impact on present rights and future opportunities. Indeed, the confrontation with a form of intelligence that is not human, or even biological, raises essential questions for metaphysics, epistemology, ethics, and political theory. The experience and expertise of religions in all these fields constitute invaluable assets to be used to assist society in adapting artificial intelligence or adapting to it. Religions are, therefore, called upon to listen, reflect and engage by proposing an ethical and spiritual framework within which to metabolize the enormous social impact that algorithm-based technological evolution will have on the universal community in the coming decades. By reasoning on these issues, one hopes to avert the risk of a role reversal typical of the Hegelian dialectic, that is, a subversion of servant-master (in our case algorithm-man) roles based on the servant's acquired self-awareness (perhaps through the mechanism of machine learning), with an existential-type reversal, by virtue of which the servant, through acquired self-awareness, becomes free and the master becomes a servant.

Keywords Artificial intelligence · Faith · Law · Religion · Ethic

---

M. Ferrante (✉)
University of Palermo—UNIPA, Palermo, Italy
e-mail: mario.ferrante@unipa.it

R. Fioravante and A. Vaccaro (eds.), *Humanism and Artificial Intelligence*,
SpringerBriefs in Philosophy, https://doi.org/10.1007/978-3-031-85478-1_4

I would trade all my technology for an afternoon with Socrates.
Steve Jobs, *Newsweek*, 29 October 2001

4.1 Outline of the Relationship Between Law, Religion, and Artificial Intelligence

The obligatory starting point for understanding the relationship between artificial intelligence (hereafter also AI), religion and law can only be man, who finds himself in the middle (the so-called 'incentre') of a hypothetical triangle whose shape (equilateral, isosceles, acutangular, etc.) has yet to be defined, since it is not easy, at least at the moment, to determine the exact dimensions (and therefore the importance) of each of its three sides in relation to the existence of the human being. Historically, in fact, man has always had a compelling need to make use of 'only' two of the sides of our imaginary triangle, namely religion and law, to lead his life, while, on the contrary, the (induced) need to have recourse to artificial intelligence has only recently asserted itself (reasoning with Epicurus, one could define AI as a 'non-natural and unnecessary need') (Epicurus, third century B.C.).

Religion also differs from law in that it responds to an innate need, firstly individual, and then also social and collective, while law asserts itself mainly—even if not exhaustively (each person has his or her own rules of life, sometimes conflicting with the social ones, as in the case of conscientious objection)—in its social dimension, necessary for the structuring of common living, according to the well-known adage that '*ubi societas ibi ius*'.

In many cases, historically, there is also a relationship of reciprocal osmosis between religion and law, with an overlapping of religious rules that are transformed into juridical precepts, as happens especially in societies where religion becomes the founding political factor of the State (think, for example, of theocracies like Iran).

However, what religion and law have in common is the fact that they are the result of what has been defined as the 'meditating thought' as opposed to the 'calculating thought' of modern AI (Romano 2018; Quintarelli 2020; Longo e Scorza 2020; Marmo 2020; Cabitza e Floridi 2021; Pierani e Scialdone 2021, Barone 2021).

The irruption in time and history of AI seems to be able to upset the very structure of the human being rooted since the dawn of time on the two coordinates outlined above of religion and law, which, on closer inspection, have indicated the cardinal points on which to trace the existential routes not only of individual men but of the entire societies they have constituted. AI, in fact, with the affirmation of algorithmic procedures, introduces the risk of 'an absolutization of calculating thought', raising various ethical, legal, and even religious concerns, due to the potential threats to certain basic rights of individuals and groups, caused by the tendency of such systems to be opaque and biased (Domingos 2016; Benanti 2018a; Boden 2019).

4.2 Artificial Intelligence and Religion: A Possible Dialogue?

In the complex equation between religion and artificial intelligence, there is a significant unknown factor, namely the risk of altering the very concept of man as it has been outlined since Greek philosophical thought and then developed up to the present day, leading to what has been very effectively defined by many as 'transhumanism' or 'new humanism', with a transition from '*homo sapiens sapien*s' to the so-called '*homo technologicus*'.

In fact, ever since Socratic thought, the concept of man that has been established is that of "*ζῷον λόγος ἔχων*", i.e., the living being (*zoon*) that has (*echon*) speech (*logon*). It is for this reason, again according to Socrates, that man is also '*ζώον πολιτικόν*' (political animal), i.e. in need of relating in a communitarian form with his fellow human beings.

The Socratic reference to the biological datum that characterizes the human being (re-evaluated by Darwinist theories, beyond Heidegger's critique of the zoological definition of man), contrasts not only ideally but ontologically with the character, typical of the divine, of being devoid of the biological aspect (the *zoon*) and of being, on the contrary, pure "*λόγος*". On this point, it must be remembered that, according to the Gospel of John, "in the beginning was the Word ("*λόγος*") and the Word was with God, and God was the Word…". A literal interpretation of the quoted text shows, therefore, that a proper and qualifying element of the divinity is its being pure "Word" ("*λόγος*"), i.e., devoid of the biological substratum that characterizes the human being and historicizes it, thus rendering it mortal.

AI therefore presents a characteristic that places it in a dangerous relationship of otherness in comparison with man, in that it presents itself as pure "*λόγος*", untied from a physical support (certainly biological), placing itself in a relationship of ontological superiority with respect to the human being, inevitably conditioned by the limits connected to physicality with the abandonment of the anthropological datum. Recalling Cartesian dualism, one can say that the algorithm presents itself as pure '*res cogitans*', i.e., devoid of physical reality ('*res extensa*') (Nicolosi 1987).

In other words, with AI there is a sort of 'biological purification' with consequent abstraction of the '*λόγος*' that makes it an intangible and incorporeal entity, potentially comparable to the divine 'Word'.

Indeed, on closer inspection, AI lends itself to being considered by the average man not only as a new Prometheus (let us not forget that the epithet of Prometheus is 'he who reflects first', precisely to emphasize his intelligence), but as a modern form of religion in which the new god to be worshipped is represented by the algorithm, which, in common feeling, shares with the deities traditional some important characteristics (the so-called "incommunicable attributes) typical of divinity, such as: immortality (it has no corruptible body); ubiquity (the algorithm can operate anywhere and simultaneously); omniscience (it is able to provide answers to almost anything); infinity (both in relation to time and space); independence (given that it can autonomously increase its skills and knowledge using so-called ‘self-learning’); etc. (Duffer 2017).

Moreover, it would be a god that does not require any particular ontological proof (at most, one could analogically have recourse to the so-called “Fourth way *ex gradu perfectionis*” of St. Thomas)(Aquinas 1967), as it can be easily contacted by anyone and at any time, thus overcoming the traditional limits of unknowability and incommunicability with the divine and giving life to a new “algorithmic theology” and thus proving wrong the agnostic thinkers like Dworkin who theorized a “religion without God” (Dworkin 2013). This would give rise to a ‘religion without revelation’ (Huxley 1975) founded on a technological transcendence, aimed at resolving the conflict between science and faith, albeit with conclusions far removed from those advocated by St John Paul II in his famous Encyclical “*Fides et ratio*” (Saint John Paul II, in his 1998 Encyclical ‘*Fides et ratio*’, states that: “Faith and reason are like the two wings with which the human spirit rises towards the contemplation of truth”).

Again, the algorithm presents itself as a new entity that is approached to obtain those answers that, in antiquity, were usually requested from the oracles that were an integral part of the religious culture of the time (consider the famous Oracle of Delphi). We are, therefore, in the presence of a modern ‘oracular culture’ where the new ‘oracular places’ are the search engines capable of providing, by processing data, answers to almost all the questions of everyday life (it is striking, in this respect, that one of the largest database companies is called ‘*Oracle*’) (Benanti 2018b).

However, the algorithm is characterized by a renewed ‘oracular style’ that is certainly less cryptic in its final externalization compared to the language of the ancient oracles who merely hinted at the answer (the oracle at Delphi, Heraclitus said, does not speak but signifies), leaving man to grasp the meaning behind their, often, obscure words (the oracular responses were deliberately ambiguous—‘sibylline’, in fact—and lent themselves to various possible interpretations, such as the well-known ‘*ibis redibis non morieris in bello*’), but which is just as obscure, at least for the man in the street, as to how it is processed, i.e. with respect to the processing of the data from which it is taken to give the requested response.

The approach is, therefore, similarly religious and makes of the algorithm a novel oracle that reveals truths of life (St. Francis’s ‘*Deus mihi dixit*’. *Verba S. Francisci*: “dixit mihi Dominus, quod volebat, quod ego essem unus novellus pazzus in hoc mundo”, *Doc. Ant. Franc.*, I, Firenze 1901), realizing, at least in appearance, the mythological model of the claim to encompass the infinite in the finite, proposing a new instance of salvation founded on an eschatological renewal of humanity based not on what is to come but on what is already in being, that is to say, an ‘algorithmic *parousia*’ (a sort of ‘realized eschatology’). In other words, the advent of AI would literally give life to a modern and salvific ‘*Deus ex machina*’ (*ἀπὸ μηχανῆς θεός ‘apò mēchanḗs theós’*), this time with an even eschatological function since it would save the human being by emending him from his material imperfections and leading him towards a new ‘digital paradise’ (As reminded by Harari “in spite of what radical Islam and Christian fundamentalism preach, the most interesting place in the world from a religious perspective is not the Islamic State or the Bible Belt, but Silicon Valley. It is there that hi-tech gurus are distilling for us bold new cults that have little to do with God and much to do with technology. Promising all the ancient rewards—happiness, peace, prosperity, and even eternal life—but here on earth and with the help of technology, rather than after death and with the help of heavenly creature"; Fuccillo 2023; Harari 2016; Santoro et al. 2024).

It is, of course, a considerable danger for traditional religions (in some cases already in crisis in terms of faithfulness) which risk, if not being supplanted, then certainly being further weakened by the new algorithmic/technological cult that is highly performing, especially since it is conveyed in what we have defined as the new 'oracular places of worship' constituted by search engines and, in general, by all the electronic apparatuses on which our lives are increasingly dependent (Helland 2000; Karaflogka 2002, 2006; Vecoli 2010, 2013).

However, beyond the dreaded dangers, there are also some potential advantages for traditional religions that are not insignificant (Spadaro 2001; Comodo, Poli 2002; Araldi, Scifo 2002; Ciotola 2010). It should be considered, for instance, that in a society in which we are witnessing a constant and progressive process of secularization (Ferrari and Ferrari 2010; Ricca 2023; Rodríguez Blanco 2024), a shrewd use of AI could constitute a powerful tool to bring about a new computer evangelization (the analysis of the ethical and moral implications of artificial intelligence also represents a challenge and an opportunity for religions, as is demonstrated by the recent signing (January 2023) of the 'Rome Call for AI Ethics' in the Vatican by representatives of the three Abrahamic religions (Ventura 2021). In this field, religions have the opportunity and the obligation to engage their teaching, their voice and their authority regarding the philosophical and anthropological challenges related to artificial intelligence. Pointing to a new algorethics, the signatories committed to request the development of an artificial intelligence that serves every person and humanity as a whole; that respects the dignity of the human person, so that every individual can benefit from the advances of technology; and that does not have as its sole goal greater profit or the gradual replacement of people in the workplace).

It is no coincidence, in fact, that traditional religions are trying to equip themselves to proselytize also through new technologies, using, for example, the now well-known 'religious apps' for believers, i.e., applications with religious content for smartphones or tablets to pray or consult the sacred texts of the various religions. With the immediate outcome of the emergence of a curious but interesting blend of faith, spirit, and technology, giving rise—in turn—to an unprecedented digitalization of religiosity, or a 'digital religion', albeit without the concomitant critical long-term repercussions of a potentially risky 'process of dematerialization of places of worship' (Decimo 2021; Spadaro, Twomey 2020; D'Arienzo 2019; Guzzo 2020).

However, about 'negative externalities', the debate in the area of social sciences seems to focus—understandably—on the 'disruptive' fallout, especially with regard to the resilience of basic paradigms.

In particular, it is pointed out that AI was born out of an act of '*ὕβρις*' (hybris), of man's arrogance, who, envious of his Creator (*Genesis* 1:26), wanted, in turn, to give life to an intelligent entity molded (at least intellectually, although with robots this is also attempted physically) in a first approximation, in his own image and likeness (*imago hominis* instead of *imago Dei*): ending up, however, by giving birth, in fact, to a new "golden calf" (*Exodus* 32:4) whose cult risks compromising humanism itself, giving rise to a form of iconolatry, triggering modern forms of heresy caused by the "metaphysical fragility" of the human being. (Tirosh-Samuelson 2012).

It seems, therefore, that the traditional religious paradigm is being overturned, according to which it is the Creator who is to be praised and not the creature who is merely to be appreciated as the work of the Creator and a testament to his wise power. Never as today, therefore, do Dostoevsky's words seem to echo: "Man cannot live without kneeling before something. If man rejects God, he kneels before an idol. We are all idolaters, not atheists' (Dostoevsky 1875).

In other words, in addition to the aforementioned risk of a "transhumanism", the risk of a "transteism" also seems tangible, consisting of a rethinking of the divine in a technological key, i.e., adopting conceptual categories that appear more consistent with the thinking of modern man than traditional theological proposals. On closer inspection, this is not a simplistic 'change of God', but a transformation of the world aimed at overcoming the theistic image of God as a transcendent and otherworldly being ('*ratio ultima rerum*') with anthropomorphic and patriarchal features. In this way, far from giving rise to a form of technological secularization, the transition is made from a theistic theology to a new form of religion, paradoxically coherent with the sciences, transteist and trans-religious, operating a lucid deconstruction (à la Derrida) of the traditional religious system (Tirosh-Samuelson 2012).

Thus, the Enlightenment's request to go beyond religions as we know them, with their myths and dogmas, their doctrines and mechanisms of submission and control, seems to have been fulfilled, but ends up by relying, as we will say below, just as fideistically on AI.

4.3 Algorithm and Law: Oxymoron or Synesthesia?

A theme closely connected to the pseudo-religious value of AI is that of the extreme trust that is apodictically placed in algorithms.

Even with a purely secular view of AI that disregards, therefore, its aforementioned potential religious implications, the fact remains of the absolute and fideistic trustworthiness generally acknowledged to it. Indeed, among the advantages commonly attributed to artificial intelligence is that it operates without interruption and without downtime, facilitating decision-making and, above all, reducing the risks of human error.

This consideration of AI gives rise to the temptation to operate a sort of 'cognitive delegation' (not without risks and dangerous drifts), i.e., the attribution of a decision-making function to the algorithm, which is considered more reliable, rational, and impartial than the human being in taking decisions, often very important ones, with speed and efficiency, but with the underlying risk of giving rise to a sort of 'algorithmocracy'.

On closer inspection, therefore, the fortunes of AI are also based on a certain 'anthropological pessimism' based on a negative pragmatic judgement of the human being, which contrasts with a marked 'technological optimism' about the reliability of algorithms. It is, moreover, a pessimism of a humanist type based on a destructive and almost clastic character, closed to any hope of redemption (as seen in the philosophy of Sartre and, in general, in existentialist doctrines) that differs from Christian pessimism, of a constructive type, i.e., tending towards perfection always *in itinere* and, above all, towards a hope of final redemption.

However, it should be pointed out immediately that the ideal vision of AI as a perfect entity capable of predicting and governing human behavior, giving rise—in the specific sphere of legal decisions—to a form of predictive justice capable of realizing not only the justice of the concrete case, but also the deflative efficacy of litigation, does not entirely respond to the reality of the facts (De La Oliva Santos 2019). Indeed, precisely in the legal field, it must be noted how the presumed asepticity and impartiality of the algorithm based on the utopia of a rationality undisturbed by emotional and personal factors (the so-called 'subjectivism of the judge'), always and in any case capable of making the fairest and most impartial decisions, is by no means capable of overcoming traditional legal anthropocentrism.

Indeed, only apparently does the algorithm applied to law, especially in the function of judging, seem to recall the suggestive image of the 'machine judge' evoking the Enlightenment myth of the judging body as a mere and anodyne '*bouche de la loi*' of Montesquieu who looked at the judge as an inanimate being who must (to the exclusion of any nomopoietic action) reconstruct with logical asepticity the concrete case in point (Di Prima 2013), leading it back to that abstractly posed by the norm (converting the words of the law into the words of the judgement), using a mere syllogism, and eliminating, in this way, the role played by affectivity (understood as the combination of emotions and feelings) in the decision-making process and guaranteeing, in this way, the certainty of the law and averting the possible drifts of unlimited interpretation (Montesquieu 1748). On the contrary, one must bear in mind the inalienability of man in legal judgement, i.e. of the so-called 'human coefficient' resulting from the aforementioned 'meditating thought' that is absolutely necessary given the impossibility of reducing human thought to a mere (albeit complex and articulated) processing of data (Fioravante, Vaccaro 2025).

Relying solely on 'calculating thought' brings with it the risk of completely abandoning one of the cardinal principles on which judging legal reasoning is historically based (the '*ius dicere*'), encapsulated in the famous saying '*da mihi facta, dabo tibi ius*', to move on to a not very reassuring '*da mihi data, dabo tibi ius*' which, on closer inspection, is based on a sort of 'calculability of law' and on the predictability of human conduct. In fact, it is claimed, through data processing, to be able to profile human behavior in the abstract and with certainty, the multifaceted and unpredictable nature of which does not lend itself well to being profiled in an algorithmic key, since there is an ineradicable human space of qualitative difference with respect to the analysis made by the algorithm, which is why it is not 'ex data' but only '*ex facto oritur ius*'.

Moreover, this way, there is the risk of reducing the judicial function, especially in the penal sphere, to the mere application of the normative dictate, by means of a cold Aristotelian judicial syllogism of a 'categorical' type (unlike the human one that is more of a 'dialectical' or 'modal' type) based on the rigid implementation of the norm, without any interpretation, in which the major premise is the general law; the minor one the action whose conformity must be assessed exclusively in relation to the law itself; while the conclusion is the acquittal or conviction.

Making the judge a mere syllogizing machine, far from guaranteeing just justice, risks, on the contrary, either realizing a diallel ('*circulus in probando*') or, worse, concretizing the risk dreaded in the famous proverb '*summum ius summa iniuria*'. In this regard, the observation prevails that a mere computational/algorithmic evaluation with a semiosis of fixed content would deny the very evolutionary nature of the law (the so-called "living law") that is based on the inescapable need for constant hermeneutic activity, given the potential heterogenesis of purposes in the apparent invariance of the normative text. There is, in fact, an undeniable multiplier relationship between text, facts, principles and hermeneutic relationship: a multilevel system based on a triangulation between principles, interpreter and laws springs from the interpretative activity, where the latter looks to the former as well as to the law; and their evaluation by the jurist is basic and prescinds from a merely computational automatic judgement (the so-called 'robotic decision') (Carleo 2019).

Not to mention the difficulties connected with the algorithmic approach to equity as a criterion of judgement to implement the need to adapt the rules of law to the particular case, in order to mitigate the severity of positive law (as per the well-known definition given by Ostiense '*Aequitas est iustitia dulcore misericordiae temperata*' (Ostiense).

On closer inspection, there are sectors of human action (including the legal sector) in which there is a need for a relationship of inverse proportionality between the coefficient of humanity required by the type of activity and the use of AI, in order to avoid the risk of a depersonalization of human relations (so-called 'social dequalification'), so as to avoid a return, this time systemic and unavoidable, to the slavish application of the law, with the risks already mentioned by another Latin proverb '*dura lex sed lex*'. In short, incalculability can and must be compensated for with hermeneutics since equity cannot be sacrificed on the altar of an alleged computational efficiency.

Not to speak, beyond the function of judging, the equally delicate role played by lawyers as cultural mediators, i.e., as an interface between the legal system of which they are also part and civil society, a role that requires legal sensitivity and intuition that certainly cannot be summarized algorithmically. It is a role, that of lawyers, that unfolds in the courtroom, in the dialogical interaction between the parties and between them and the judge, that is, in establishing those interpersonal and creative relationships—on which the semantic context of the judicial adversarial process is based—that cannot be replaced by executive and depersonalized algebraic connections.

Never before has Blaise Pascal's distinction between '*esprit de geometrie*' (which deals with the external, apparent or abstract aspects of mathematics and makes use of demonstration) and '*esprit de finesse*' (which deals with man and is based on the heart, feeling and instinct rather than reason) seemed to be as relevant as it is today (Pascal 1670). In other words, with such a distinction, in addition to emphasizing the limits of Cartesian mathematics, we wish to underline the complexity of the human being, pointing out that there are two ways to understand what surrounds us and ourselves: the geometric, i.e. demonstrative, way, which has its seat in reason (*raison*) and the intuitive way, i.e. the ability to grasp the essential, which has its seat in the heart (*coeur*). In the light of this distinction, one can understand the irreducibility of the human being and his interpretative/evaluative capacity to a mere processing of serialized data operated through cold algorithmic procedures, as well as the polysemanticity of words within the univocity of numbers.

In the light of the above, it does not seem possible, at least at present, to prefigure—at least in the legal sphere—the infliction by science of yet another narcissistic wound to man, after that inflicted by Copernicus with the heliocentric theory; that inflicted by Darwin, with the evolutionary theory; by Einstein with his studies on relativity; and, in particular, by Freud, with psychic determinism, according to which all mental processes are not spontaneous, but determined by unconscious mental complexes, with the consequent denial of free will.

On the contrary, precisely with reference to Freudian determinism, according to which nothing happens by chance or in an arbitrary accidental manner, a new algorithmic determinism seems to be proposed in which human behavior is considered predictable on the basis of the mere '*id quod plerumque accidit*', assessed on the basis of the profiling of available data, with the risk of falling into undue and dangerous generalizations and making 'categorical faults' fall on the individuals who belong to those categories, giving rise to paradoxical IT clichés and new forms of digital discrimination, as we will discuss below (Garapon e Lassègue 2021).

4.4 Redefinition of the Principle of Non-Discrimination in the Dialogue Between Law and Technology: From Discrimination of the Physical Body to Discrimination of the Digital One?

Among the elements of absolute novelty in the dialogical relationship between law and artificial intelligence, linked to the decision-making role assumed by algorithms in loco personarum, it is necessary to emphasize the urgency of redefining the principle of non-discrimination, which no longer only concerns the physical body but also the digital body which has become, following the algorithmic revolution, a sort of alter ego of the human being. Indeed, it seems possible that profiles of unreasonable discrimination by algorithms may emerge, not to mention the difficulty of focusing, in terms of accountability, on the relative responsibilities, not only ethical but also legal, of the decisions made by AI.

This is an entirely new situation that poses undeniable legal challenges for the protection of the digital profile from multiple points of view (criminal, labour law, etc.) (Nicotra e Varone 2019; Trezza 2020; Taddei Elmi 2020; Ruffolo 2020; Alpa 2020; Santosuosso 2020; Bassoli 2022).

A practical example is the famous Loomis case (an African-American man), in which a district court in the US state of Wisconsin, using an algorithm called 'COMPAS' (Correctional Offender Management Profiling for Alternative Sanctions), decided not to grant probation, believing that the defendant should be considered a high risk of reoffending, to the point that he could not be effectively and safely reintegrated into the social community. This conclusion had been formulated by the algorithm based on the available data—disregarding the direct assessment of the defendant—on the mere statistical assumption of so-called 'risk scores' according to which a black person is more likely to reoffend than a white person. The decision was challenged and appealed on the grounds that it violated the right to be sentenced to a personalized punishment (data were judged and not the person of the defendant) and that it was based on an improper use of racially biased gender data in the determination of the sentence with a clear violation of the principle of equality and non-discrimination. In its judgment, the Wisconsin Supreme Court, while upholding the appealed decision, stated that, although the algorithm could be used by the court as an 'amicus curiae', this could only be done on the condition that the judge merely considered what the software suggested but did not rely exclusively on it in determining the sentence and the size of the penalty to be applied (Supreme Court of Wisconsin, State of Wisconsin v. Eric L. Loomis, Case no. 2015AP157-CR, 5 April–13 July 2016).

In the field of labour law, then, think of algorithmic management of employee performance, the so-called 'algorithmic management'. Managerial decisions are, more and more often, delegated to algorithmic tools that, based on—sometimes opaque—data collection and processing processes, make automatic or semi-automatic decisions concerning personnel. This is a turn of events that, combined with legislation that is still inadequate for this new phenomenon, risks undermining the protection of workers' dignity and fundamental rights, by operating a standardized metric measurement of people's work (e.g., hourly productivity rates) to determine the system of grading levels, benefits and pay parameters.

In some large multinational companies, for example, workers' performance is evaluated using the 'rate' or 'make the beat' metric, i.e. based on an average of the overall, aggregate performance of all employees in the structure, which is constantly monitored, thus determining the standard of performance, the optimal 'rate'. If an employee does not reach the set 'rate', the algorithm triggers an alert to both the employee and the data analysis systems and their managers for consequential evaluations. A repeated series of alerts may result in warnings and, if addressed to precarious workers, even in the non-renewal of contracts (Calderini 2021).

There is, therefore, an obvious risk of new asymmetries in the already unbalanced relationship that binds the parties to an employment relationship, with the real danger of violating the limits that employment law traditionally places on the exercise of employers' powers, especially with regard to that of control. Lastly, the algorithmic decision, in addition to producing potential discriminatory effects, could lead to a breach of the rules protecting the processing of personal data with all the consequences of the case (Bellavista e Santucci 2022).

Coming to deal with the specific profile of the protection of digital religious identity and freedom, both from an individual and collective point of view, the challenge looming on the horizon of present and especially future jurists seems, first of all, to be that of guaranteeing the equal freedom of individuals and confessional groups in the cyber-space, where the risk of the loss of pluralism and discrimination not only on a racial basis but also on a religious basis is feared.

It is necessary, namely, to verify whether and how the cyber technological revolution is destined to affect (or even upset) the current balances that regulate the right to religious freedom in our democratic systems. In other words, one must verify if the current legal system regulating religious pluralism can provide adequate solutions to the development of technological systems, averting the risk of a dematerialization of rights.

Indeed, it does not seem sufficient to invoke the simple recognition of the 'right of access to the Internet' as a fundamental and modern 'human right' through the insertion of a new constitutional provision, given that—as was demonstrated during the Covid-19 epidemic—it is a necessary precondition for the enjoyment of other rights recognized by today's constitutions such as the right to education, the right to work, and the most basic rights of citizenship (Frosini, Pietrangelo 2011; Toscano 2024; Martínez-Torrón 2022; Consorti 2020).

It follows that it also appears necessary to guarantee and protect, both at constitutional and ordinary law level, the correct and safe exercise of traditional rights within the web, as a new 'social space' increasingly governed by algorithms created by private parties outside of public control. Algorithms that decide, for instance, what is politically correct and what is not, and which topics can be published, and which must be 'banned' because they are deemed untrue (so-called 'fake news') or incite hatred (so-called 'hate speech'), sometimes putting in place autocratic censorial conducts because they lack any legal basis and end up infringing the fundamental rights of the digital person. That is, it is necessary to regulate the 'metaverse' objectively, avoiding possible abuses by social network providers, since it is a virtual space in which the differences with reality are reduced to become almost imperceptible, making it difficult to distinguish—especially for weaker subjects such as minors—between what is real and what is fiction, with the consequent need to protect individual rights. In the United Kingdom, for example, an investigation has even been launched to identify the perpetrators of virtual group violence by male avatars against a 16-year-old girl, who—although physically unharmed—suffered an emotional and psychological trauma that, in the opinion of the British investigators, was completely comparable to real violence.

In other words, the guarantees of personal freedom, including that of religion and worship (Bordonali 2005; Ferrante 2017; Ingoglia and Ferrante 2017), must now also be extended to the digital body, to the subjective 'profile' intended as an immaterial projection of the human being (a sort of '*ego*' virtually shifted), whose rights must be equally guaranteed and protected in a public and not merely private key, aiming at a redefinition of the principle of non-discrimination in the now inescapable and constant dialogue between law and technology, operating the insertion of legal values in the algorithmic variables. In other words, a sort of 'value injection' must be made into the algorithms based on constitutional principles, since it must always be remembered that behind the algorithms there are human minds that design them by making a 'choice of criteria' (Romano 2018, p. 28), i.e., operating, upstream, a loading of values (the so-called 'Value Loading Problem') (Hagendorff 2020; Ruffolo et al. 2020; Biancardo 2021; Trezza 2021; Floridi 2022). This implies that where in the dataset (understood as a set of data organized in relational form) there is any prejudice, whether on an ethnic, gender or religious basis, this will end up being transferred with a domino effect to the algorithm which, consequently, will tend to put in place potentially discriminatory algorithmic profiling and evaluations of merit, which will be even more dangerous as they are often invisible and silent.

In other words, it is necessary, as has been effectively pointed out, to follow the "trajectory of the reinterpretation of habeas corpus as habeas data", giving rise to a "legal metaverse", operating upstream an ethical finalization of the algorithms (an ethics-by-design) to protect the digital person (Rodotà 2010).

4.5 Conclusion

In the light of what has been said so far, the need to establish a constructive dialogue between law and technology seems evident to avoid assigning an ancillary role to law with respect to technology and to prevent the latter from dictating content to law.

This dialogical interface between law and technology could also take the form of a renewed 'technology of law' that implies a modification of legal language and the effort to subsume the new in traditional legal categories (think, for instance, of the complex issue of the legal personality of robots) and, where this is not possible, creating new ones. The prospects that arise therefore call for the combined help of ethics and law such as, for example, the drafting of a charter of rights that takes account of this innovative spectrum of coordinates and guidelines/regulations for the development of ethically legitimate artificial intelligence technologies, to avert possible algorithmic discrimination.

In any case, the contrast between the capitalist benefits of the calculation of the legal future—i.e., the 'legal calculability' according to Weber, western capitalism requires legal calculation, i.e., the possibility of predicting the outcome of disputes. (Weber 1980)—and the 'incalculability of law' (understood as the guarantor variable of human rights based on the judge's interpretation of facts), inevitably remains in the background (Irti 2018).

As far as religions are concerned, they are called upon to listen, reflect and engage by proposing an ethical, doctrinal, and spiritual framework within which to metabolize the enormous social impact that algorithm-based technological evolution will have on the universal community in the coming decades.

By reasoning on these issues, one hopes to avert the risk of a role reversal typical of the Hegelian dialectic, i.e. a subversion of the servant-master roles (in our case algorithm-man) based on the awareness acquired by the servant (perhaps through the mechanism of 'machine learning'), with an existential type inversion, in virtue of which the servant, i.e. the algorithm, through an acquired self-awareness, becomes free and the master, i.e. man, becomes a servant (Hegel 1807).

In conclusion, in view of the dreaded risks, there is a need to remove the danger of a technological narcissism with its attendant consequences and to operate an anthropocentric approach that places Artificial Intelligence at the service of people and not vice versa.

References

Alpa G (2020) Diritto e intelligenza artificiale. Profili generali, soggetti, contratti, responsabilità civile, diritto bancario e finanziario, processo civile

Aquinas T (1967) Summa theologiae, I, q. 2, a. 3, resp.: Quarta via sumitur ex gradibus qui in rebus inveniuntur. New York, London

Araldi P, Scifo B (2002) Internet e l'esperienza religiosa in rete, in Vita e Pensiero

Barone G (2021) Machine Learning e Intelligenza Artificiale—Metodologie per lo sviluppo di sistemi automatici. Dario Flaccovio, Palermo

Bassoli E (2022) Algoritmica giuridica. Intelligenza artificiale e diritto. Amon Edizioni, Rome

Bellavista A, Santucci R (2022) Tecnologie digitali, poteri datoriali e diritti dei lavoratori. Giappichelli, Turin

Benanti P (2018a) Le macchine sapienti. Intelligenze artificiali e decisioni umane. Marietti, Bologna

Benanti P (2018b) Oracoli. Tra algoretica e algocrazia. Luca Sossella Editore, Rome

Biancardo A (2021) Problematiche etico giuridiche relative all'utilizzo dell'intelligenza artificiale in ambito sanitario, in Jus online, n. 3, 1–51

Boden M (2019) L'intelligenza artificiale. Il Mulino, Bologna

Bordonali S (2005) Le istanze religiose di fronte ai meccanismi di produzione giuridica, Il Diritto Ecclesiastico, 1–2:82–97

Cabitza F, Floridi L (2021) Intelligenza artificiale: L'uso delle nuove macchine. Bompiani, Milan

Calderini, B (2021) Amazon, il lavoro dettato dall'algoritmo: è peggio del previsto. (Agendadigitale.eu)

Carleo A ed. (2019) Decisione robotica. Il Mulino, Bologna

Ciotola C (2010) Confessione anche on line? Spunti di Riflessione Sul Sacramento della Penitenza, in Diritto e Religioni 2:13–30

Comodo V, Franco Poli G. (2002) Cliccate e vi sarà @perto. Spunti per la missione della Chiesa in internet. Effatà Editrice, Cantalupa (Turin)

Consorti P (2020) Law, religion and covid-19 emergency. DiReSom, Pisa

D'Arienzo M (2019) Zuckerberg e le nuove dimensioni dei rapporti tra diritto e religioni. *A Proposito di Libertà di Coscienza Nell'era Digitale*, in *Diritto e Religioni* 1–2019:384–395

Di Prima F (2013) Giudice amministrativo ed interessi religiosi collettivi. Istanze confessionali, conflitti e soluzioni giurisprudenziali. pp. 29–53. Libellula, Tricase (Lecce).

De La Oliva Santos A (2019) "Giustizia predittiva", interpretazione matematica delle norme, sentenze robotiche e la vecchia storia del "Justizklavier", in Rivista Trimestrale Diritto e Procedura Civile, n. 3, pp 883–895

Decimo L (2021) Templa moderna: i luoghi di Dio. La disciplina giuridica degli edifici di culto. E.S.I., Naples

Domingos P (2016) L'algoritmo definitivo. La macchina che impara da sola e il futuro del nostro mondo. Bollati Boringhieri, Turin

Dostoevsky F (1875) The raw youth. Heinemann, London (1915)

Duffer E (2017) As Artificial Intelligence Advances, What Are its Religious Implications?, in Religion & Politics. (blog)

Dworkin R (2013) Religion without god. Cambridge, Massachusetts, p 17

Epicurus (3rd century B.C.). Letter to meneceus or letter on happiness. (see in Hicks, R.D., 1910, Stoic and Epicurean)

Ferrante M (2017) Diritto, religione, cultura: verso una laicità inclusiva. Stato, Chiese e pluralismo confessionale. Riv. telematica (statoechiese.it)

Ferrari A, Ferrari S (2010) Religion and the secular state, the Italian national reports to 18th world congress of comparative law, in The cardozo electronic law bulletin, Vol. 16

Fioravante R, Vaccaro A (2025) Humanism, dehumanization, integral human development: an overview of boundaries and capabilities of human-centered artificial intelligence in business and organizations. In Fioravante R, Vaccaro A (eds) Humanism and Artificial Intelligence, Springer, Cham, Switzerland

Floridi L (2022) Etica dell'intelligenza artificiale. Sviluppi, opportunità, sfide. Raffaello Cortina Editore, Milan

Francisci S (1901) Doc. Ant. Franc., I, Firenze, 1901, 104

Frosini TE Il diritto costituzionale di accesso ad Internet, RivistaAIC, pp 23–43

Fuccillo A (2023) Il paradiso digitale. Diritto e religioni nell'iperuranio del web. Editoriale Scientifica, Neaples

Garapon A, Lassègue J (2021) La giustizia digitale. Determinismo tecnologico e libertà. Il Mulino, Bologna

Guzzo LM (2020) Il web può essere uno spazio liturgico?, in Il Regno.it

Hagendorff T (2020) The Ethics of AI Ethics. An Evaluation of Guidelines, in Minds & Machines, pp. 1–22

Harari YN (2016) Yuval Noah Harari on big data, Google, and the end of free will, in Financial Times

Hegel (1807) Hegel's 'Phenomenology of Spirit'. (Oxford University Press, 1979)

Helland C (2000) Online-religion/Religiononline and Virtual Communitas. In Jeffrey Hadden, Douglas Cowan (ed) Religion on the Internet. Research, Prospects and Promises, Jai Press, Greenwich, Conn., London, pp 205–224

Huxley J (1975) Religion without revelation. Charles A. Watts & Co. Ltd, London

Ingoglia A, Ferrante M (eds) (2017) Fenomeni migratori, diritti umani e libertà religiosa, LibreriaUniversitaria, Limena

Irti N (2018) Un diritto incalcolabile. Giappichelli,Turin

Karaflogka A (2002) Religious discourse and cyberspace. Religion 32:279–291

Karaflogka A (2006) E-religion. A critical Apparaisal of Religious Discourse on the World Wide Web. Routledge London

Longo A, Scorza G (2020) Intelligenza artificiale. L'impatto sulle nostre vite, diritti e libertà

Marmo R (2020) Algoritmi per l'intelligenza artificiale: Progettazione dell'algoritmo—Dati e Machine Learning—Neural Network—Deep Learning. Hoepli, Milan

Martínez-Torrón J (2022) State religion and COVID-19: can religious freedom be guaranteed in exceptional circumstances? Stato Chiese e pluralismo confessionale. Riv. Telematica (statoechiese.it). https://doi.org/10.54103/1971-8543/18818

Montesquieu (1748) De l'esprit des lois, XI, cap. XVI

Nicolisi S (1987) Il dualismo da Cartesio a Leibniz, reviewed by Priano, G. B., in Rivista di filosofia neoscolastica, n. 4, 628–630

Nicotra IA, Varone V (2019) L'algoritmo, intelligente ma non troppo, in Rivista AIC, n. 4, 1–21

Ostiense, Summa aurea, lib. 5°, tit. De dispensationibus, n. 1

Pascal B (1670) Pensées (Thoughts) Paris

Pierani M, Scialdone M (2021) Vivere con l'Intelligenza Artificiale. Società, consumatori e mercato. Espress, Turin

Pietrangelo M (2011) Il diritto di accesso ad Internet

Quintarelli S (2020) Intelligenza artificiale: Cos'è davvero, come funziona, che effetti avrà. Bollati Boringhieri, Turin
Ricca M (2023) Intercultural spaces of law translating invisibilities. Springer Nature Switzerland Cham. https://doi.org/10.1007/978-3-031-27436-7
Rodotà S (2010) Una Costituzione per Internet? in Politica del diritto, n. 3, 21–34.
Rodríguez Blanco M (2024) Los desafíos de la libertad religiosa conforme a la reciente jurisprudencia española. Quaderni di diritto e politica ecclesiastica, n. 1, 265–304
Romano B (2018) Algoritmi al potere. Calcolo giudizio pensiero, Giappichelli, Turin
Ruffolo U (2020) Intelligenza artificiale Il diritto, i diritti, l'etica. Giuffrè, Milan
Ruffolo U, Riccio G, Uricchio AF (2020) Intelligenza Artificiale tra etica e diritti. Prime riflessioni a seguito del libro bianco dell'Unione europea. Cacucci, Bari
Saint John Paul II (1998). Encyclical 'Fides et ratio'
Santoro R, Palumbo P, Gravino F (2024) Diritto canonico digitale. Editoriale Scientifica, Neaples
Santosuosso A (2020) Intelligenza artificiale e diritto. Perché le tecnologie di IA sono una grande opportunità per il diritto
Spadaro A (2001) Dio nella «rete». Forme del religioso in internet, in La Civiltà cattolica, n. 3625, 15–27
Spadaro A, Twomey T (2020) Intelligenza artificiale e giustizia sociale. Una sfida per la Chiesa, in La Civiltà Cattolica, Quaderno n. 4070, Volume I, 130
Supreme Court of Wisconsin, State of Wisconsin v. Eric L. Loomis, Case no. 2015AP157-CR, 5 April–13 July 2016
Taddei Elmi G, Contaldo A (2020) Intelligenza artificiale. Algoritmi giuridici. Ius condendum o "fantadiritto"? Pacini, Pisa
Tirosh-Samuelson H (2012) Transhumanism as a Secularist Faith, Zygon: J Relig Sci 47:712–719
Toscano M (2024) Emergenza sanitaria e libertà di religione. Giappichelli, Turin
Trezza R (2020) Diritto e intelligenza artificiale. Etica, Privacy, Responsabilità, Decisione. Pacini, Pisa
Trezza R (2021) Legal values" and "algorithmic values": an ethically oriented interpretation of Artificial intelligence, in Iura and legal systems, n. 2, 3–14
Vecoli F (2010) Internet e religioni. Una Introduzione, HumItas 5–6:749–760
Veicoli F (2013) La religione ai tempi del Web. Laterza, Rome—Bari
Ventura M (2021) Nelle mani di dio. La super-religione del mondo che verrà. Il Mulino, Bologna
Weber M (1980) Economia e società, vol. III, Edizioni di Comunità III:17

Chapter 5
Christian Humanism and Technology: New Frontiers for Contemplation

Martin Schlag

Abstract This chapter explores the intersection of Christian humanism and digital technology, particularly Artificial Intelligence (AI). In asserting its centrality in Catholic social teaching, I underscore the need for a Christian humanism that goes beyond secularism and argue for a transcendent worldview. The chapter delves into the role of contemplation, an element of Christian spirituality, in shaping ethical considerations for AI and digital technologies as they might be relevant to business ethics. By emphasizing contemplation, I support a human-centered approach that aligns technology with values such as human dignity, freedom, subsidiarity, solidarity, and the preferential option for the poor. The chapter proposes contemplation to navigate the challenges posed by AI, fostering a mindful and ethical integration of technology in line with Christian humanistic principles. The notion of contemplation was transformed over time. The distinction between active and contemplative life, introduced by Gregory the Great, evolved through figures like Thomas Aquinas, Ignatius of Loyola, and Josemaría Escrivá. I discuss contemplation's role in shaping socio-economic realities according to the three most recent popes. Finally, I explore contemplation in the context of AI in business, following the dual axes of God and human-centeredness.

Keywords Christian humanism · Technology · Contemplation · Artificial Intelligence AI

5.1 Introduction

Digital technology, especially Artificial Intelligence (AI), are ubiquitous topics of socio-ethical concern, also in business ethics. (see Brusoni and Vaccaro 2017; Haenlein et al. 2022) In this chapter, I make Christian humanism fruitful for the debate about the ethical dimensions of digital technology, in particular AI. There are three approaches to Christian humanism. One that considers the concept as an equivocal

M. Schlag (✉)
University of St. Thomas, Saint Paul, MN, USA
e-mail: schl2455@stthomas.edu

R. Fioravante and A. Vaccaro (eds.), *Humanism and Artificial Intelligence*, SpringerBriefs in Philosophy, https://doi.org/10.1007/978-3-031-85478-1_5

contradiction in terms: either a tenet is Christian, or it is humanist (De Lubac 1995, p. 400). A second approach considers Christian humanism to be a watered-down form of cultural Christianity, a sort of "Christianity light" (See Hobson 2018, p. 6). A third group proposes it as a central and indispensable concept of Catholic social teaching (Maritain, Benedict XVI, Francis). I share the conviction of the third group.

Some proponents of Christian humanism have applied this concept to technology. However, they fall short of addressing the growing thirst for spirituality that comes to the fore in cultural movements like creation spirituality or eco-spirituality. A focus on spirituality, of which contemplation is an element, widens the appeal of Christian humanism and can open new vistas on technology.

The purpose of this chapter is to develop some normative implications of an important element of Christian spirituality, and therefore also of Christian humanism: contemplation. Pope Francis has applied the concept of contemplation to socio-ethical issues. I will argue that contemplation has important consequences also for AI and other digital technologies. I structure this chapter as follows. First, I briefly sketch the history of Christian humanism and describe its contemporary formulation and role in Catholic social teaching and thought. Second, I show how contemplation is an important element of Christian humanism and what we mean when we refer to it as a socio-ethical category. As such it has implications for important principles and values of Catholic social teaching, in particular human dignity, freedom, subsidiarity, solidarity, and the preferential option for the poor. Contemplation can even be a way forward out of the impasse between utilitarianism's regulatory zeal, often based on pessimism and fear, on one side, and libertarian optimism, on the other side. Technology requires new virtues. It also requires a new contemplative mindfulness at work. Understanding how contemplation in work is intertwined with new technology helps to grasp some relevant features of humanism that should be enhanced and preserved from dehumanizing processes connected with the use of AI. This has become urgently necessary in the face of antihumanism.

5.2 Christian Humanism

Humanism, in our age, is frequently formulated as a socio-philosophical conception opposed to or at least alternative to religious worldviews. Humanism, in its most general meaning, refers to everything that enhances our potential and well-being as humans, everything that liberates and perfects us, that makes us flourish. *Christian* humanism holds that life according to Christ's teaching and in his grace is the best way to achieve happiness and flourishing on earth and not only in heaven. In contrast to Christian humanism, *secular* humanism strives to achieve human flourishing in an immanent frame that excludes transcendence (Taylor 2007, pp. 15–20). In its historical origins in the Renaissance, however, humanism (in Western civilization) was Christian. Humanism in the Renaissance was an attempt to return to the pure sources of Christianity (the Bible and patristic texts) in opposition to the arid and fruitless disquisitions of decadent scholasticism, stymied by nominalism. In that sense,

Renaissance humanism was not a Pagan revival or anti-Christian movement. It turned against self-referential theological studies that had lost touch with the lived reality of Christian people. The Renaissance Christian humanists (Erasmus of Rotterdam, Thomas More, Luis Vivés, and others) aimed at Church reform, not its excision from social life (Cunningham 1987). In the posterior development, however, humanism turned against Christianity. Kampits (2001) distinguishes five stages of its development, of which the first is Renaissance humanism, as mentioned. The second stage is the new humanism of German classicism that centered on autonomy, reason, freedom, and tolerance as central concepts of enlightened humanism. It contrasted *humanitas* with *animalitas*. The third historical instantiation of humanism is its attempted revival in the so-called "Third humanism" after 1900. Dissatisfied with the positivistic and materialistic environment of the first half of the twentieth century, it stressed the need to revive classical culture and the values of antiquity. At the same time, a fourth form was gathering momentum: the anti-idealistic and materialistic humanism of the nineteenth century that postulated a concrete or "real" humanism to overcome alienation and nature. Marxism and other forms of atheist conceptions of society are examples. The fifth form comprises modern movements that are critical of classical humanism. They severed the link between *humanitas* and metaphysics in its classical expressions and formulated their proposals along the lines of existentialism.

In the face of totalitarianism and the atrocities of the Third Reich and the Second World War, secularist and Christian thinkers alike recognized that they had much in common. Born from suffering, this recognition of a possible reconciliation between the Church and modernity was not only a pragmatic option but the realization, by secular defenders of humanist ideals, that Christianity was the living source of their own humanism. Without an anchor in transcendent faith the ideals of human dignity, the common good, solidarity, justice and mercy, truth and freedom become contingent on the cultural mainstream—as became atrociously evident under the totalitarian regimes of Nazism and Bolshevism. The meaning of concepts is easily reinterpreted and changed to fit into the prevailing political agenda. They are swept away by the currents of cultural change. The incarnational and ecumenical theology of Dietrich von Bonhoeffer is an example among Protestants for Christian humanism (See Zimmermann 2019, pp. 19–20). In the Catholic Church, on which I focus, Jacques Maritain was highly influential. Jacques Maritain's "integral humanism" explicitly endorses both Christian heroism and humanism with the aim of reconstructing the temporal order on Gospel principles. This endeavor requires a new form of sanctity in the world (Maritain 2017, pp. 152–156). Integral humanism integrates faith in Christ into humanism. Christ unifies and grounds all reality. As God, he also embodies humanity and is therefore normative for all human values and ideals. The Second Vatican Council in its Pastoral Constitution Gaudium et Spes endorsed this anthropocentric turn that focused on Christian humanism. In his concluding address to the Council, Paul VI characterized the whole endeavor of the Second Vatican Council as the proclamation of "our own new type of humanism," focused on human needs and joys. Like the Good Samaritan, the Church at the Council bowed down over humanity's suffering and became its servant. Contemplating the countenance of Christ, in whom we recognize the Father, "our humanism becomes Christianity, our Christianity becomes centered on God; in such sort that we may say, to put it differently: a knowledge of man is a prerequisite for a knowledge of God" (Paul VI 1965).

The document that best expressed the Council's humanist intentions is the "Pastoral Constitution on the Church in the modern world Gaudium et Spes." Its title and opening line define its scope:

> The joys and the hopes, the griefs and the anxieties of the men of this age, especially those who are poor or in any way afflicted, these are the joys and hopes, the griefs and anxieties of the followers of Christ. Indeed, nothing genuinely human fails to raise an echo in their hearts. (Second Vatican Council 1965, n. 1)

In prior centuries, the relationship between faith and society had been regulated by concordats between the Church and the State, as two independent institutions endowed with power. Both kept each other in check in an often-strained relationship in which the Church hierarchy (the clergy) taught the moral principles that the lay princes were expected to implement. Evangelization was carried out in a top-down fashion by state coercion that imposed conformity with Church teaching with political means. In Gaudium et Spes, the Catholic Church replaced this approach with a bottom-up strategy. The bottom-up approach counts on the Christian lay faithful who are active in the world as their natural habitat. They are called to permeate the whole fabric of society in which they live and work with the light and warmth of Christ. They are there not because they are sent by the clergy but because it is their natural place to be. For the lay Christians, workers, intellectuals, artists, politicians, and so forth, the world is not a pulpit or stage from which to proclaim Christian values, but a reality Christians are called to shape from the inside. The secular world is theirs originally. Priests and religious are also in the world but they shape it from the outside. They are not immediately active in politics and business, nor are they usually experts in science and technology. The clergy are dedicated to pastoral ministry, caring for individuals and families, and do not usually have the time to engage in secular occupations, at least not on a full-time scale. In accordance with this teaching, the Council recognized the relative autonomy of earthly affairs, thus accepting modernity, understood as the emancipation of secular society from ecclesiastical tutelage (Second Vatican Council 1965, n. 36). With a well-formed conscience, the lay faithful are capable of discerning what the calling to holiness demands of them in the specific worldly circumstances they encounter themselves. This does not render the clergy superfluous. Quite the opposite. Their task is to sanctify, teach, and accompany the lay faithful in the person of Christ, the head of the Church. They do so in humility, knowing that the Church hierarchy can learn from the world while it teaches the world. Indeed, the Church is aware of being the depositary of Christ's grace and revelation of what it means to be fully human. The spirit of dialogue and mutual learning is borne by the certainty that "Christ, the final Adam, by the revelation of the mystery of the Father and His love, fully reveals man to man himself and makes his supreme calling clear" (Second Vatican Council 1965, n. 22).

This quotation underscores that the humanism of the Second Vatican Council is Christocentric and theocentric. The text insists that without the creator the creature would become nothing (Second Vatican Council 1965, n. 36). God is not seen in competition with the human person or her freedom but as the foundation that enables true human flourishing.

This was the conviction that Paul VI expressed in his encyclical *Populorum Progressio*, in which—quoting Jacques Maritain and Henri de Lubac—he calls for a new humanism. Development, the new name for peace, is possible only with a "full-bodied humanism" that includes the transcendent dimension of faith in the God:

> True humanism points the way toward God and acknowledges the task to which we are called, the task which offers us the real meaning of human life. Man is not the ultimate measure of man. (Paul VI 1967, n. 42)

John Paul II too was convinced of Christian humanism. As an episcopal member of the Second Vatican Council, he made an important contribution to its anthropocentric turn. As pope, from his first encyclical, he underscored the human dimension of the mystery of Redemption (John Paul II 1979, n. 10). In his long pontificate, he set humanism against economism and all forms of alienation by social, economic, and political powers. His defense of innocent human life from the moment of conception until natural death is part of his Christian humanism. As is the way he interpreted the preferential option for the poor as a particular form of justice and charity. On his many trips to the ends of the world, he was able to put his conviction into practice that the Word of God was made incarnate not only in human nature but in a specific human culture and history.

Benedict XVI was an outspoken advocate for Christian humanism as is Pope Francis. The central theme of Pope Benedict XVI, which is expressed in the seashell in his coat of arms,[1] is the mystery of God. Benedict's insistence on "a true humanism," therefore, is theocentric: it "acknowledges that man is made in the image of God and wants to help him to live in a way consonant with that dignity" (Benedict XVI 2005, n. 30). After the financial crisis in 2007 and 2008, his appeals become stronger. The socio-economic situation required "efforts of holistic understanding and a new humanistic synthesis" (Benedict XVI 2009, n. 21). Not surprisingly in an encyclical written to commemorate an anniversary of Paul VI's encyclical *Populorum Progressio*, Benedict XVI pits humanistic principles against a technical mindset that threatens to reduce the human person to an object open to manipulation. In his endeavors to defend the centrality of the human person, Benedict XVI repeated notions dear to Maritain and Paul VI: authentic humanism is integral humanism, in other words Christian humanism:

[1] The seashell is a symbol for the story of St. Augustine who one day was walking on the seashore pondering the mystery of the Holy Trinity. He came across a boy who was ladling seawater with a shell into a hole in the sand. In answer to Augustine's question what he was doing, the boy answered that he was filling the ocean into the hole. Augustine understood that he was attempting to do just what the boy was doing, in as futile a manner as the boy's game: trying to fit God into his own mind.

> The greatest service to development, then, is a Christian humanism that enkindles charity and takes its lead from truth, accepting both as a lasting gift from God. Openness to God makes us open towards our brothers and sisters and towards an understanding of life as a joyful task to be accomplished in a spirit of solidarity. On the other hand, ideological rejection of God and an atheism of indifference, oblivious to the Creator and at risk of becoming equally oblivious to human values, constitute some of the chief obstacles to development today. A humanism which excludes God is an inhuman humanism. Only a humanism open to the Absolute can guide us in the promotion and building of forms of social and civic life — structures, institutions, culture and ethos — without exposing us to the risk of becoming ensnared by the fashions of the moment. (Benedict XVI 2009, n. 78)

In continuity with his predecessor, Francis has called for "a genuine and profound humanism to serve as the basis of a noble and generous society" (Francis 2015a, n. 181). His hope is that faith can inspire a humanism "capable of bringing together the different fields of knowledge, including economics, in the service of a more integral and integrating vision" (Francis 2015a, n. 141). We urgently need such a humanism. Francis uses the expression Christian humanism sparingly, even though he makes no secret of his faith that is operative in works of charity (Francis 2020a, n. 86). In an occasion where he did use the expression Christian humanism, he referred to it as the "humanism of the mind of Jesus," characterized by three traits: humility, disinterest, and beatitude (Francis 2015b).

The texts of recent official Catholic teaching that I have referenced above point to Christ as the one who inspires humanity with justice, warmheartedness, and social concern by adding a transcendent motivational horizon. God identifies with the "least of the brethren" and promises eternal reward to those who care for them (See Mt 25:31–46). Christian humanism, however, is not completely congruent with or identical to social concern, as important as it is. The Church is the Bride of Christ, not an NGO (Francis 2013a). Reducing the Church to an NGO or some other institution of social beneficence and humanitarian aid would be social horizontalism that tends to neglect the supernatural belief in the full revelation of God in Christ. God reveals himself as love but also as truth. Truth can be unpleasant and divisive. Social horizontalism easily succumbs to the danger of eschewing the contradiction of preaching Jesus crucified and might fail to place transcendent claims over and above inner-worldly ones. In Christian teaching, there are moral demands that mainstream culture accepts and others that it violently and passionately rejects. In the present cultural situation, it is difficult not to see that the postwar reconciliation between modernity and Church has been unilaterally revoked by secularism. In this chapter, we cannot pursue this question in the depth it deserves as it is an aspect of the complex relationship between nature and grace. We can only state that mainstream culture blends out the bothersome elements of Christianity that antagonize the zeitgeist and strives to keep the values of humanity that it cherishes. Christian humanism resists such appropriation. It cannot become a form of secularism that limits life to an immanent frame and conceives of human flourishing without transcendence. In other words, there are no Christian values without Christian faith, without Christ crucified and alive in humans through the Holy Spirit. Christ is the big disturber who shakes us out of the systems and structures we have fabricated and in which we feel comfortable and cozy. That is why Christian humanism presupposes an attitude of humble receptivity and openness to conversion. If we resist the promptings of the Holy Spirit, our hearts harden, our love cools off. Christian humanism points us beyond ourselves and our personal interests, helps us to focus on the needs of others.

Such an attitude is a valuable orientation also for technology. It can undergird the human-centered purpose of digital (and all other) technology. Recent business ethics literature calls for precisely such a fundamental orientation of digital technology, in particular of AI, toward the human person. Business ethics contributes to a human-centered use of AI and other digital technologies (Martin and Freeman 2004; Martin et al. 2019; Figueroa-Armijos et al. 2023; Levine 2019; Leclercq-Vandelannoitte 2019; Kim and Scheller-Wolf 2019; Leicht-Deobald et al. 2019).

As I will show below, the attitude of humble receptivity, in the Christian tradition, is expressed with the word contemplation.

5.3 Christian Humanism and Contemplation

5.3.1 Origins and Development

Contemplation as spiritual practice is by no means limited to Christianity. Buddhism and other oriental religions consider it central to their own traditions. However, Christianity like no other religion teaches to behold the face of God in Jesus Christ, and thus, thought veiled, in all humans. Christians believe that God has become visible in the world in Jesus and that he, the Logos, has recapitulated all the world.

Hellenist philosophy in whose terms the Christian faith was expressed by the early Christian theologians cherished contemplation ("the theoretical life") as the highest realization of human flourishing. This, however, is not the thrust of the Bible that is focused on conversion and faith, not on theory. It is interesting to note that the noun contemplation (*theoria*, in Greek) only occurs once in the New Testament, in connection with Christ's passion on the cross: "When all the people who had gathered for this spectacle (*theorian tauten*) saw (*theoresantes*) what had happened, they returned home beating their breasts" (Lk 23:48). This sentence points us to the dynamism of contemplation as a call to conversion that also underlies the use of the word as a verb in the New Testament: those who behold the Passion are drawn into the self-giving sacrifice of Christ. The verb *theoreo* (to look, to contemplate) occurs 39 times in the gospels. As has just been said, it is most frequently used in connection with the Passion and Resurrection of Jesus Christ (See Mt 27:55; 28:1; Mc 15:47; 16:4; Lk 23:35; 23:48; 24:37.39). In the gospel according to John, however, there is an additional dimension of the word that comes closer to our contemporary understanding of contemplation in the context of spirituality. In Jn, the verb *theorein* is used to express the perception of the divine nature of Jesus when seeing his miracles or hearing his words. Contemplating Jesus means beholding and believing in the Son whom the Father sent (Jn 2:23; 4:19; 6:2; 6:19; 6:40; 6:62; 7:3). Jesus uses *theorein* to refer to the deeper way of seeing and beholding God's glory in himself:

"whoever sees (*theoron*) me sees (*theorei*) the one who sent me" (Jn 12:45). And a few paragraphs later Jesus prays to his Father God for his disciples: "Father, they are your gift to me. I wish that where I am they also may be with me, that they may see (*theorosin*) my glory that you gave me, because you loved me before the foundation of the world" (Jn 17:24).

Paul was the first theologian, deeply steeped in Hellenistic culture, literature, and philosophy. He must have been aware of the importance of the contemplative life in antique society. Nevertheless, the words *theorein* and *theoria* do not appear once in his letters. He was more concerned about the power of the Holy Spirit that is alive in those who believe. Following suit, the earliest theologians of the apostolic age (up to the end of the second century AD) pay little attention to theoretical life. This changes with Clement of Alexandria and Origen who strive to explain the Christian revelation with the philosophical concepts of Hellenism. Contemplation is here to stay as the highest form also of Christian life. However, the Christian theologians of the early Church transformed the concept by linking it to the adoration of the triune God. Like the pagan Greek philosophers, the Church fathers aspired to seek and behold the truth. However, this truth had made itself visible as love in the person of Jesus Christ. Contemplation of Christ is authentic only if it leads to charity for our neighbor especially the least of our brethren. Christian contemplation is thus not merely theoretical speculation or philosophizing. It implies a spirit-filled penetration of the revelation of God in Christ who discloses the depths of God in a way that is inaccessible to mere human intellect, strength, and means. At the same time, faith is alive in works of charity. Christian contemplation means an active attitude of beholding God in the outcast and oppressed who do not usually interact with the leisure class who can dedicate themselves to the pursuit of intellectual activities. From the outset, therefore, contemplation is integral to Christian humanism. Contemplation means gazing at the face of God and looking at the world with the compassionate eyes of Christ. Contemplation opposes a manipulative mindset that wishes to grasp the world for oneself. It receives creation as a gift that surprises us, makes us wonder and admire the world and the people around us. Authentic Christian contemplation is a spirit of contemplation true to Jesus himself. It is humanistic because it is sustained by a vertical axis toward God and a horizontal axis that unites us with our neighbor. Unfortunately, these two axes get dissociated easily, on a practical level because of our weaknesses, but also theoretically by a distinction that was misunderstood.

Gregory the Great (died 604) introduced the distinction I have in mind. It is a distinction that has deeply influenced Christianity throughout the centuries. He applied the old Hellenistic concepts of *vita activa* (active life) and *vita contemplativa* (contemplative life) to the different states of life a Christian can choose: to live in the world of work and active configuration of society (active life), or to withdraw into a religious order in the quiet refuge of a monastery (contemplative life). Gregory, and most other spiritual masters after him, granted contemplative life the higher dignity and closeness to God. Those in the world could save their souls by obeying the Ten Commandments but holiness and contemplation were practically unattainable for them. The contemplatives were the religious who were called to a higher form of life, dedicated to God exclusively. This is not what the Catholic Church teaches in our day and age. However, it took centuries for a change to take place. We can associate three saints with a progressive widening of the circle of those called to contemplation. Thomas Aquinas coined the phrase "*contemplata tradere*" (hand on what you contemplate). With this, Aquinas encouraged preachers to meditate on the teachings of the gospel before they preach to others. Thomas is trying to make the point that priests who are active in preaching are better than those who merely contemplate. Aquinas thus opens the concept of contemplation to an appreciation of an active life of pastoral service. Ignatius of Loyola expanded on this notion. He taught his followers to be "*contemplativus in actione*" (contemplative in action), addressing the priests and religious in pastoral ministry (action) to live out of a spirit of prayer and to be aware of God's loving presence in dealing with others. Josemaría Escrivá finally demanded of his spiritual children to be contemplatives in the middle of the world. He had in mind the manifold walks of life and the countless modes in which human work unfolds in society. His challenge was to open secular work to sanctity. The world emerged holy from the hands of God; our sins have defiled it. However, nothing humanly good is barred from being assumed by the incarnate word of God, only sin is. Escrivá's teachings were corroborated by the Second Vatican Council. It reminded all Christians of the universal call to holiness, of which the laypeople are main addressees. They have a secular nature and exercise secular work amid society and at the same time are called to mystical union with God. Mystical union is another name for contemplation.

In the Christian tradition, we find different descriptions and definitions of contemplation. Contemplation is generally considered to be "the summit of prayer life." (Belda 1998) Various definitions of contemplation from the tradition of Catholic spirituality confirm this affirmation: "Contemplation is when the mind is in some sort lifted up to God and held above itself, so that it tastes the joys of everlasting sweetness" (Guigo II 1981, p. 68); "an infused loving knowledge that both illumines and enamors the soul, elevating it step by step to God, its Creator. For it is only love that unites and joins the soul to God" (John of the Cross 1991, p. 440); "…a single concentrated look at what we love—concentrated reflection that has greater energy, greater power to move the will" (Francis de Sales 1997, p. 146). The common denominator of these medieval and early modern quotations is that contemplation is "an attentive gaze, marked by simplicity and constancy" (Belda 1998, p. 330). Contemplation is often experienced as an Exodus from sin, addictions, and futile pursuits to a life of fullness that leads back to a different perception of the challenges of this world. Thomas Merton expressed this beautifully: "Contemplation, at its highest intensity, becomes a reservoir of spiritual vitality that pours itself out in the most telling social action" (Merton 2012, p. 56). The path to contemplation begins with a period of purification that leads to an illumination and elevation of the human mind, that finally—as if a stream—empties out into the great ocean of union with God.

5.4 Contemplation that Shapes the World

It is interesting to note that in recent years, the popes have linked contemplation with shaping the socio-economic realities of the societies we live in. John Paul II's concept of contemplation, for instance, was two-directional. One direction leads the Christian to raise his or her mind to God; the other makes the believer engage in the world. This latter understanding was the meaning that John Paul II usually read into the term "contemplation" or "contemplative outlook," which he used repeatedly in his documents. Contemplation as a contemplative outlook at the world comprises the prophetic dimension of denouncing sin and injustices. In the name of God, a prophet—or a contemplative—gives his or her voice to those who have none or are too weak to raise theirs.

Benedict XVI's emphasis was on the importance of contemplation as the source of Western culture. Important achievements of our political and economic system (democracy, accountancy, social banking systems, besides the education of barbarian tribes through the transmission of Roman learning) stem from the wish to give glory to God. In a certain way, these achievements are a byproduct of the human desire to transcend mere material needs and stretch out to our highest calling. The thirst for God leads us to shun the murky puddles of sensual satisfaction and raise our mind to the deepest source of happiness, which is God, mediated by compassionate service to those surrounding us.

In Pope Francis's writings, finally, contemplation has become a category of Catholic Social Thought. For him, contemplation means overcoming reductionism by perceiving the beauty of creation and of the other person who "is beautiful above and beyond mere appearances" (Francis 2013b, n. 199). The contemplative gaze discovers God's presence in our cities (Francis 2013b, n. 71) and discloses the mystical meaning of creatures (Francis 2015a, n. 233). Fraternity in solidarity is based on grateful contemplation (Francis 2015a, n. 214) that receives creation and the other human beings with reverence (Francis 2015a, n. 127): "Authentic contemplation always has a place for others" (Francis 2013b, n. 281). In his Wednesday catechesis on the Catholic social principles, Francis links contemplation to solidarity by attributing solidarity to the outpouring of the Holy Spirit at Pentecost, the great Christian "anti-Babel:" "With Pentecost, God makes himself present and inspires the faith of the community united in diversity and in solidarity" (Francis 2020b). God creates community by inspiring faith in a common Father who makes us discover each other and all creatures as brothers and sisters. The way to healing when community is ruptured, is "a mystical fraternity, a contemplative fraternity" (Francis 2013b, n. 92 [emphasis in the original]). Francis rejects egotistic anthropocentrism, exploitation, and reduction of creatures to their usefulness. He grounds our capacity to discover the intrinsic value of non-human beings in contemplative spirituality and singles out our "mystical capacity" as a protective antidote to the evil tendency to treat others as slaves. He stays in a theocentric framework that regards the world as a gift of the Creator (Francis 2020c). The notion of contemplation, as formulated by the recent popes, has implications for the world of business, as part of the socio-economic reality and human relations that we view with the eyes of God, his creative and redemptive gaze. Contemplation is not an opium for the people that sublimates unjust structures and situations but a penetrating critical glance that births social change. Contemplation, as part of an effective and healthy spirituality, must also affect the way we conduct business and the manner of our relationships with others and technology. It is not surprising, therefore, that contemplation has had some, though too little, impact on business literature.

5.5 Contemplation in Business

The spirituality of work, as an academic topic, has been the focus of substantial research in business literature, especially in recent years (Schlag and Melé 2019, pp. 1–7). Specifically, publications have dealt with the general importance of spirituality and religion for business and society (See Chan-Serafin, Brief, and George 2013; Van Buren III, Syed, and Mir 2020), but also with specific topics like mindfulness and meditation, (See Donaldson et al. 2019; Valcour 2015) and in a lesser degree with the notion of contemplation in work. Schwanda and Sisemore (2020) have rediscovered the spiritual, mental, and emotional benefits derived from the Christian Puritan tradition of prayer, meditation, and contemplation. These authors point out that the prevailing literature on meditation and mindfulness generally uses concepts that are of Buddhist origin but has extracted the concept of mindfulness from any religious context. What remains is mindfulness understood as "a peace and acceptance that is without content," with the good intention to "calm and center modern minds." Grandy and Sliwa (2017) offer both a conceptual and an empirical study on "contemplative leadership" in the context of various Christian churches. They propose contemplative leadership as a virtuous activity that is a "reflexive, engaged, relational, and embodied practice." The authors combine the eight C's of contemplative leadership according to Kim Nolan[2] with the ethical approaches of Alasdair MacIntyre and Emmanuel Levinas. Catholic authors too have dedicated pages to contemplation, specifically in business. (Naughton 2019; Wishloff 2020). Naughton's book is centered on work as a vocation to holiness. Following the German Thomist philosopher Joseph Pieper, Naughton focuses on leisure, another word for contemplation. Naughton identifies it as the wellspring of our striving for holiness in work. "We are looking, then, for an integrated dynamic of receiving and giving, of rest and work, of contemplation and action.... We can therefore say, 'Action occurs not... to the detriment of contemplation, but as its fulfillment'" (Naughton 2019, p. 38, quoting von Balthasar). Holiness, sourced by contemplation as its wellspring, flows over into our endeavor to produce good goods, to offer services that serve others, to create good work as employers

[2] These are Calling (clear purpose/meaning); compassion (altruism, love); care for others (sense of belonging, interconnectedness); centered communication (balance between emotion and reason in articulation); cultivate stillness (engagement in contemplative practices); clarity (wisdom, self, and other awareness); currency of time (mindfulness); and contagious joy (positive energy). Taken from Grandy and Sliwa (2017, p. 426).

and employees, and to aspire to good wealth that is truly valuable. Contemplation in business places a vertical axis into our business activities that unites us with God. Amid the hustle and bustle of industry and interaction we stay anchored or rather stretched out to what is above, to the last transcendent reason why we strive and toil. Without such a transcendent purpose, work can still have a human meaning and be good, but it is more difficult to persevere when things get rough. It is also easier to lose one's bearings and to pursue selfish aims that harm others or the environment without the transcendent horizon. If we are aware of the eternal echo of all we do, our aspirational narratives are enriched beyond the mere materiality of the here and now of economic exchange and increase of wealth. The horizontal axis that links us with our fellow creatures needs the vertical beam to stay high up at the right level of human dignity and not get stuck in the mud of our base instincts. Contemplation in the tradition of Christian humanism thus structures our lives in the two directions of God and neighbor.

5.6 Contemplation and AI

What could contemplation in the tradition of Christian humanism contribute to solving the ethical challenges posed by digital technologies and AI in particular? As has just been stated, contemplation centers us on God and on our fellow creatures. I turn first to the vertical axis of our relationship with God. How could AI possibly center us on God? One possible way AI could help us stay centered on God is by providing us with daily reminders of God's presence and love. For example, an AI assistant can send short inspirational quotes or messages at a specific time every day, reminding us of God's grace and love. Additionally, an AI assistant could help us manage our schedule and prioritize important spiritual practices, such as daily prayer, meditation, or scripture reading. Humans can work with AI to create a personalized schedule that incorporates spiritual practices and includes daily reminders from AI.

On a deeper technical level, transformer architecture could help us discover regularities and sequences in reality that escape our attention. Maximus the Confessor referred to such regularities and sequences as the *logoi*, dispersed by God throughout nature as its architectonical principles. What I mean by this is the following. The transformer architecture in neural networks revolutionized natural language processing and other sequential tasks. Similarly to a translator who reads a sentence word by word, focusing on each word's context to understand and translate, transformers break down input sequences into manageable chunks called tokens and process them simultaneously, allowing for parallelization. Key to transformers is the attention mechanism, like a spotlight directing focus on relevant words. Each word attends to others with varying weights, capturing intricate relationships with surprising speed and precision. This attention mechanism, coupled with self-attention, enables the model to consider global context efficiently. Transformers consist of encoder and decoder blocks, resembling the translator's comprehension and generation phases. The encoder grasps input features, while the decoder generates output. Importantly, transformers excel at capturing dependencies regardless of distance, overcoming limitations in traditional sequential models. Transformers, with their attention mechanism and parallel processing, have greatly enhanced our ability to understand and generate sequences, structures, and principles of being, impacting fields beyond language processing, from image recognition to drug discovery. This capability to discover hidden laws in nature is reminiscent of the idea of the search for the *logoi* embedded in creation that Maximus the Confessor wrote about (See Maximus 2003, pp. 20–25). For Maximus, the Incarnation of the *Logos* in Jesus Christ is the supreme mediation between the *logoi*, the architectonical principles of this world, and the Trinity. The *Logos* discloses the magnificent intricacy and beauty of the transfigured cosmos through the *logoi*, the providential principles of creation and Scripture. The *Logos* recapitulates all the *logoi* in himself in creation. In the history of salvation, the *Logos* in his life on earth, and through the liturgy of the Church over the centuries, guides humanity to the fullness of salvation at the end of time. Through grace we humans take part in the mediation of the *Logos*. The transformation is only possible because God united Himself to us in Jesus Christ, true God, and true man. However, the more we know of the *logoi*, the more we are aware of the broad and complex theater in which God's incarnational mission is playing itself out to full completion. In a deeply theological manner, AI enables us to be more united to God on a natural level.

I now turn to the implications of AI in business for the horizontal plane on which Christian humanism directs us toward our neighbor. Basically, contemplation in AI commits us to a human-centered approach, true to the fundamental convictions of Christian humanism. The human-centeredness of AI in the business realm is a delicate balance between avoiding harm and unlocking unprecedented positive potentials. On the cautious side, there is a growing concern about the ethical implications of AI, including issues related to bias, privacy, and job displacement. Ensuring that AI systems are developed with a strong emphasis on fairness and accountability is crucial to prevent exacerbating existing societal disparities (See Martin 2023).

However, the symbiotic relationship between AI and humans holds immense promise, particularly in enhancing productivity and innovation. AI technologies can automate routine tasks, freeing up human workers to focus on more creative and strategic endeavors. This shift can lead to a workforce that is more engaged, empowered, and capable of tackling complex challenges that require uniquely human skills such as critical thinking, emotional intelligence, and creativity (The Economist 2023). Moreover, as was stated above, AI-driven insights and analytics enable businesses to make data-driven decisions, uncover patterns, and forecast trends with unprecedented accuracy. This not only enhances operational efficiency but also fosters a culture of continuous improvement. Companies can leverage AI to personalize customer experiences, streamline supply chain management, and optimize resource allocation, resulting in a more responsive and customer-centric approach. The collaborative potential of humans and AI is exemplified in human-AI partnerships, where machines augment human capabilities rather than replace them. In fields like healthcare, AI assists medical professionals in diagnostics and treatment planning, leading to more accurate and efficient healthcare delivery. In creative industries, AI tools aid artists and designers in ideation and content creation, with all the problems this causes for copyright and intellectual property.

Human-centeredness of technology, in general, and of AI specifically is defined by its capacity to convey truth and goodness to humans as individuals and as societies. Arguably, AI increases our capacity to receive truth and goodness when it is used well. Of course, I am not blind to potential abuse of AI and its destructive consequences. Nevertheless, considering that contemplation is the participation of the rational creature in the truth and goodness of God, would it not be correct to say that the use of AI and technology in general increases contemplation rather than decrease it? Contemplation is too frequently seen as a quietistic practice that is incompatible with work in the world. However, work can be contemplative if it shares in goodness and truth (Schindler 2015).

5.7 Conclusion

In this chapter I have approached technology and AI with optimism. Christian humanism teaches us to view the world, human work, and ingenuity in a positive light, as things God gives us and as he sees them. Such an attitude is a necessary step to overcome the dangers inherent in every human invention. To cleanse people, cultures, and activities from evil, we must first love and affirm them. Following the double axis of God and human-centeredness that contemplation, as a central element of Christian humanism, implants in us we discover that good technology and AI enhance contemplation. They do not diminish it. This might seem counterintuitive because technology is usually experienced as a noisy distraction from a withdrawn life of contemplative prayer. However, religious monastic models are inadequate molds for an active life in the world. Christian humanism requires new forms of sanctity that embrace the world and work in it as the very matter out of which holiness is made. The challenge lies in truly conveying human good by technological means and exercising one's profession at least in such a manner that it could be ordered toward God as last end. The ultimate battlefield both for monks and people in the world is the human heart.

References

Belda (1998) Contemplatives in the Midst of the World. Romana [Bulletin of the Prelature of the Holy Cross and Opus Dei], 27 (1998), 326–340, 329. Unfortunately this study is not available on the website in English https://en.romana.org/archive/; it is available in Spanish: https://es.romana.org/27/estudio/contemplativos-en-medio-del-mundo-de-manuel-belda/; and in Italian: https://romana.org/27/studio/contemplativi-in-mezzo-al-mondo/

Benedict XVI (2005) Encyclical Deus Caritas Est [God is love], from https://www.vatican.va/content/benedict-xvi/en/encyclicals/documents/hf_ben-xvi_enc_20051225_deus-caritas-est.html

Benedict XVI (2009) Encyclical Caritas in Veritate [Charity in Truth], from https://www.vatican.va/content/benedict-xvi/en/encyclicals/documents/hf_ben-xvi_enc_20090629_caritas-in-veritate.html
Brusoni S, Vaccaro A (2017) Ethics, technology and organizational innovation. J Bus Ethics 143:223–226. https://doi.org/10.1007/s10551-016-3061-6
Chan-Serafin S, Brief AP, George JM (2013) How does religion matter and why? religion and the organizational sciences. Organ Sci 24(5):1585–1600. https://doi.org/10.1287/orsc.1120.0797
Cunningham LS (1987) Humanism. In: Komonchak JA, Collins M, Lane DA (eds) The new dictionary of theology. The Liturgical Press, pp 498–500
De Lubac, Henri (1995) The Drama of Atheist Humanism. Ignatius Press
Donaldson E, Lewis R, Yarker J (2019) What outcomes have mindfulness and meditation interventions for managers and leaders achieved? A systematic review. Eur J Work Organ Psy 28(1):11–29. https://doi.org/10.1080/1359432X.2018.1542379
Figueroa-Armijos M, Clark BB, da Motta Veiga SP (2023) Ethical perceptions of AI in hiring and organizational trust: the role of performance expectancy and social influence. J Bus Ethics 186:179–197. https://doi.org/10.1007/s10551-022-05166-2
Fiorvante R, Vaccaro A (2025) Humanism, dehumanization, integral human development: an overview of boundaries and capabilities of human-centered artificial intelligence in business and organizations. In R. Fiorvante and A. Vaccaro (eds) Humanism and artificial intelligence. Springer
Francis de Sales (1997) Treatise on the love of god. In W.M. Wrights (eds) Francis de Sales, Introduction to the devout life and treatise on the love of god. Crossroad
Francis (2013a) "Missa Pro Ecclesia" with the Cardinal Electors: Homily of the Holy Father Pope Francis, from https://www.vatican.va/content/francesco/en/homilies/2013/documents/papa-francesco_20130314_omelia-cardinali.html
Francis (2013b) Evangelii Gaudium. Libreria Editrice Vaticana
Francis (2015a) Laudato Si', from https://www.vatican.va/content/francesco/en/encyclicals/documents/papa-francesco_20150524_enciclica-laudato-si.html
Francis (2015b) Address at meeting with the participants in the fifth convention of the Italian Church, from https://www.vatican.va/content/francesco/en/speeches/2015/november/documents/papa-francesco_20151110_firenze-convegno-chiesa-italiana.html
Francis (2020a) Fratelli Tutti, from https://www.vatican.va/content/francesco/en/encyclicals/documents/papa-francesco_20201003_enciclica-fratelli-tutti.html
Francis (2020b) Healing the world—5. Solidarity and the virtue of faith, from https://www.vatican.va/content/francesco/en/audiences/2020/documents/papa-francesco_20200902_udienza-generale.html
Francis (2020c) Healing the world"—7. Care of the common home and contemplative dimension, from https://www.vatican.va/content/francesco/en/audiences/2020/documents/papa-francesco_20200916_udienza-generale.html
Grandy G, Sliwa M (2017) Contemplative leadership: the possibilities for the ethics of leadership theory and practice. J Bus Ethics 143:423–440. https://doi.org/10.1007/s10551-015-2802-2
Guigo II (1981) The ladder of monks: a letter on the contemplative life. In E. College and J. Walsh (Trans.). The ladder of monks: a letter on the contemplative life and twelve meditations. Cistercian Publications
Haenlein M, Huang M, Kaplan A (2022) Guest editorial: Business ethics in the era of artificial intelligence. J Bus Ethics 178(4):867–869
Hobson T (2018) God created humanism: the christian basis of secular values. Society for Promoting Christian Knowledge
John of the Cross (1991) The dark night of the soul. In K. Kavanaugh, O. Rodriguez (Trans.), The collected works of St. John of the Cross. ICS Publications
John Paul II (1979) Redemptor Hominis [Redeemer of Man], from https://www.vatican.va/content/john-paul-ii/en/encyclicals/documents/hf_jp-ii_enc_04031979_redemptor-hominis.html

Kampits P (2001) Humanism. In: Fahlbusch E, Lochman JM, Mbiti J, Pelikan J, Vischer L (eds) G.W. Bromiley (Trans.) The Encyclopedia of Christianity (pp 605–608). Eerdmans

Kim TW, Scheller-Wolf A (2019) Technological unemployment, meaning in life, purpose of business, and the future of stakeholders. J Bus Ethics 160:319–337. https://doi.org/10.1007/s10551-019-04205-9

Leclercq-Vandelannoitte A (2019) Is employee technological "Ill-Being" missing from corporate responsibility? The Foucauldian ethics of ubiquitous IT uses in organizations. J Bus Ethics 160:339–361. https://doi.org/10.1007/s10551-019-04202-y

Leicht-Deobald U, Busch T, Schank C, Weibel A, Schafheitle S, Wildhaber I, Kasper G (2019) The Challenges of algorithm-based HR decision-making for personal integrity. J Bus Ethics 160:377–392. https://doi.org/10.1007/s10551-019-04204-w

Levine L (2019) Digital trust and cooperation with an integrative digital social contract. J Bus Ethics 160:393–407. https://doi.org/10.1007/s10551-019-04201-z

Maritain J (2017) Integral humanism. In O. Bird (Ed. and Trans.), J. Evans and Richard O'Sullivan (eds) The collected works of Jacques Maritain (pp. 141–345. University of Notre Dame Press

Martin KE, Freeman RE (2004) The separation of technology and ethics in business ethics. J Bus Ethics 53:353–364. https://doi.org/10.1023/B:BUSI.0000043492.42150.b6

Martin K, Shilton K, Smith J (2019) Business and the ethical implications of technology: introduction to the symposium. J Bus Ethics 160:307–317. https://doi.org/10.1007/s10551-019-04213-9

Martin K (2022) Ethics of data and analytics: Concepts and cases. CRC Press

Maximus the Confessor (2003) On the cosmic mystery of Jesus Christ: selected writings from St. Maximus the Confessor. P.M. Blowers and R.L. Wilken (Trans.). St Vladimir's Seminary Press

Merton T (2012) On Christian contemplation. P.M. Pearson (Ed.). New Directions Publishing Corporation

Naughton MJ (2019) Getting work right: Labor and leisure in a fragmented world. Emmaus

Paul VI (1965) Address during the last general meeting of the Second Vatican Council, from https://www.vatican.va/content/paul-vi/en/speeches/1965/documents/hf_p-vi_spe_19651207_epilogo-concilio.html

Paul VI (1967) Populorum Progressio [The Progress of Peoples], from https://www.vatican.va/content/paul-vi/en/encyclicals/documents/hf_p-vi_enc_26031967_populorum.html

Schindler DC (2015) Work as contemplation: on the platonic notion of techne. Communio 42:594–617

Schlag M, Mele D (2019) A catholic spirituality for business: the logic of gift. The Catholic University of America Press

Schwanda T, Sisemore TA (2020) Experiencing god through head and heart: the puritan practices of meditation and contemplation and their relevance to modern psychology. J Psychol Christ 39(1):40–48. https://doi.org/10.1177/1939790921105599l

Second Vatican Council (1965) Pastoral Constitution on the Church in the Modern World Gaudium et Spes, from https://www.vatican.va/archive/hist_councils/ii_vatican_council/documents/vat-ii_const_19651207_gaudium-et-spes_en.html

Taylor C (2007) A secular age. The Belknap Press of Harvard University Press

The Economist (2023) A technology need not be world ending to be world changing. Online edition, April 20, 2023

Valcour M (2015) A 10-Minute Meditation to help You Solve Conflicts at Work. Harvard Business Review, April 27, 2015, 2–5

Van Buren III HJ, Syed J, Mir R (2020) Religion as a macro social force affecting business: concepts, questions, and future research. Bus Soc 59(5):799–822. https://doi.org/10.1177/0007650319845097

Wishloff J (2020) Work is love made visible: A meditation on grace. The American Journal of Economics and Sociology 79(4):1181–1208. https://doi.org/10.1111/ajes.12351

Zimmermann J (2019) Dietrich Bonhoeffer's Christian humanism. Oxford University Press

Chapter 6
AI and the Future of Virtues in the Workplace

Francesco Vincenzo Giarmoleo, Marta Rocchi, and Ignacio Ferrero

Abstract This chapter explores the ethical implications of Artificial Intelligence (AI) on the evolving landscape of the workplace. Employing the framework of virtue ethics as its analytical lens, the chapter explores the cultivation of a virtuous character in individuals involved in the design, deployment, and use of AI-based technologies in organizations. Acknowledging the limited attention virtue ethics has received in AI ethics research, this work aims to fill the gap by considering whether an AI-enhanced workplace helps or prevents develop the cardinal virtues: practical wisdom, justice, courage, and temperance.

Keywords Ethics · Artificial intelligence · Virtues

6.1 Introduction

The profound transformation brought by AI in the workplace and its applications for reshaping work dynamics is a topic of keen interest (Ashri 2019; Davenport and Miller 2022; Pereira et al. 2023). The emergence of new technologies introduces a spectrum of ethical challenges including potential job displacement, manipulative marketing strategies, and enhanced surveillance of employees (Haenlein et al. 2022). Notably, AI has prompted ethical analyses from various perspectives. Deontological ethics, linked to Immanuel Kant, focuses on evaluating actions according to defined rules or principles. In the realm of AI, this perspective predominantly

F. V. Giarmoleo (✉)
ISSA School of Applied Management, University of Navarra, Pamplona, Spain
e-mail: fgiarmoleo@unav.es

M. Rocchi
DCU Business School, Dublin City University, Dublin, Ireland

I. Ferrero
School of Economics and Business, University of Navarra, Pamplona, Spain

R. Fioravante and A. Vaccaro (eds.), *Humanism and Artificial Intelligence*, SpringerBriefs in Philosophy, https://doi.org/10.1007/978-3-031-85478-1_6

involves establishing ethical guidelines and principles for AI development and use, raising questions about respecting human rights, autonomy, and dignity. Another ethical approach is consequentialism, which assesses the morality of actions based on their outcomes. In AI ethics, consequentialism delves into the potential consequences of AI applications, evaluating their impact, including concerns about job displacement and economic inequalities. Virtue ethics, whose one of the fathers is considered to be Aristotle, concentrates on nurturing virtuous character traits in individuals. Applied to AI, virtue ethics contributes by promoting virtuous behavior in the design, deployment, and use of AI technology challenging developers to create a technology that enhances excellent character traits in individuals and contributes to the good of society. Within AI ethics, this perspective underscores the importance of considering the flourishing of individuals impacted by AI systems and urges developers to incorporate empathy and human-centered values into AI design. Virtue ethics provides a complementary perspective to rule-based and consequence-based ethical frameworks. Although virtue ethics is focused on the importance of cultivating virtues, it integrates norms and consequences (Sison et al. 2017). It recognizes that ethical norms and principles are essential guides to action, but it places them in the broader context of character development. Nor does it ignore consequences. Because its ultimate goal is human flourishing, it encourages agents to contemplate the implications of their actions for their character, the character of others, and the good of society, highlighting the importance of personal and professional character in shaping the design and use of AI-based technologies.

However, in the vast realm of research in AI ethics, virtue ethics has received limited attention (Giarmoleo et al. 2024; Gorichanaz 2022). This chapter advances virtue ethics research within the context of the future workplace, seeking to define virtuous AI-enabled workplaces and the necessary virtues in this evolving setting. By delving into this issue, we gain insights into the moral consequences of widespread AI adoption and its impact on human character, promoting virtuous behavior and ethical decision-making. Specifically, we study the impact of AI utilization in workplaces on the development of cardinal virtues, namely practical wisdom, justice, courage, and temperance.

Examining the impact of AI through the framework of cardinal virtues yields two noteworthy advantages. Firstly, the cardinal virtues provide a well-established and systematic approach to ethical evaluation, thereby offering clear guidance for virtuous behavior. This framework serves to enhance the understanding of AI's ethical implications, contributing to the promotion of responsible AI development. Secondly, the incorporation of cardinal virtues into AI analysis encourages personal development and moral growth among professionals who design and/or use AI-based technologies, fostering ethical responsibility and awareness in the utilization of AI systems. The chapter builds on contributions that recognize that technologies can also be used to promote virtuous behaviors (Brusoni and Vaccaro 2017). Specifically, AI can be leveraged to promote human flourishing at the individual, organizational, and stakeholder levels (Fioravante and Vaccaro 2025).

The purpose of this chapter is to study how we can cultivate human excellence in the workplaces of the future, particularly in light of the intricate implications related to the use of AI-based technologies. In this context, professionals are encouraged to embark on a journey of self-improvement aimed at nurturing ethical responsibility and heightened awareness in the deployment of AI systems. This transformative paradigm seeks not only to address immediate ethical concerns but also to cultivate a community of AI practitioners deeply attuned to the moral dimensions of their professional endeavors.

6.2 Virtues: Developing Personal Excellence in the AI-Enhanced Workplace

Virtue ethics encompasses the evaluation of ends and outcomes (goods), the establishment of necessary norms to prevent harm and promote societal well-being (norms), and the cultivation of habits (virtues) (Rocchi and Bernacchio 2022a), through the repetition of good actions. We now focus in particular on the virtues, which are habitual dispositions to do the good (Aristotle 1999), and how an AI-enhanced workplace can help develop or hinder their development. As there are many and different virtues, we focus in particular on four of them, which are called "cardinal virtues": practical wisdom, justice, courage, and temperance.

Already present in the ancient Greek philosophy tradition, moral philosophers across various cultural and religious traditions have worked on these virtues, characterizing their conceptual meaning and practical relevance. They represent the excellence of human behavior, and are essential to living the good life, which leads to *eudaimonia* (i.e. flourishing, or happiness). For instance, in *The Republic*, Plato (2008) extensively discusses these virtues; and so does Aristotle (1999) in the *Nicomachean Ethics*, where he provides detailed insights into these virtues and explores methods for their cultivation. Christian philosophers and tradition also place significant importance on these virtues. The Christian theologian and philosopher Thomas Aquinas (1964) further developed a moral theology rooted in the virtues, leaving a lasting impact on Catholic tradition.

According to Aristotle, virtue represents a balance between extremes. For example, regarding the virtue of courage, recklessness or the disregard of fear can result in perilous actions that jeopardize lives, while a deficiency of courage can lead to inertia and an unwillingness to confront challenges. Virtue aims to circumvent these detrimental extremes. Moreover, personal excellence is attained through the intentional cultivation and reinforcement of virtuous habits, achieved through repeated virtuous actions, leading to a virtuous character (Sison and Ferrero 2015). This process involves consistently making choices that embody virtuous qualities. As individuals engage in these virtuous actions over time, they shape and refine their character, aligning it with the ultimate human purpose or end, *eudaimonia*, often described as a state of flourishing and fulfilment.

In the context of future augmented workplaces, characterized by the presence of AI-based technologies, some questions emerge: how can these workplaces contribute to the enhancement of these virtues? Do AI-based technologies encourage or prevent the development of virtuous workers? The next section looks at how AI-powered workplaces can help or prevent cultivating cardinal virtues. For each one, we will consider one specific AI-based technology related specifically to the augmented workplace, and will highlight three key aspects to orient this technology towards human flourishing.

6.2.1 Practical Wisdom and Algorithmic Decision-Making

Practical wisdom (or prudence) "is not only itself a virtue, it is the keystone of all virtue, for without it one cannot be virtuous" (MacIntyre 1973 [1966], p. 74); it is the measure and guide for the other virtues (Pieper 2017). Practical wisdom is the virtue that represents the ability to identify the good end to pursue, make informed decisions to achieve it, apply discernment, and use knowledge wisely. It analyzes complex situations, detects antecedents and implications, aims at doing the right thing given a set of particular circumstances, and effectively safeguards the inherent moral good relevant to the situation (Ferrero et al. 2020).

The extensive literature on the relevance of practical wisdom in business decision-making settings (Bachmann et al. 2018; Ferrero et al. 2020; Schwartz et al. 2020) underscores its critical role in facing the challenges raised by the increasing integration of AI-based technologies in decision-making across diverse organizational contexts (Lindebaum et al. 2020). While these technologies present novel strategic prospects, they simultaneously introduce concerns (Newell and Marabelli 2020). The literature warns that the growing reliance on AI for accessing information could lead to a decline in individuals' ability to think critically and discern, potentially resulting in a moral deskilling (Green 2019) specifically related to practical wisdom. This tendency highlights the importance of maintaining and nurturing practical wisdom in decision-making processes to counteract the potential erosion of this vital virtue in advancing AI applications in decision-making settings highly augmented by algorithmic decision systems. Regarding the workplace, it is concerning for workers to potentially lose skills associated with complex tasks, including judgment, intuition, and awareness of context (Bankins and Formosa 2023).

Furthermore, considering the ability of AI to analyze data, learn from it, and make decisions, we could ask ourselves if it was better to delegate entirely the decision-making process to AI, rendering practical wisdom almost obsolete. Some scholars acknowledge the necessity of practical wisdom, although proposing a reinterpretation. For example, Polizzi and Harrison emphasize the need for a new understanding of practical wisdom in the digital age, called "cyber-wisdom" (2022). While future predictions are challenging amidst rapid technological advancements, it is unlikely that practical wisdom will become irrelevant. AI decisions heavily rely on data; consequently, AI-generated outcomes, although technically accurate, might raise ethical concerns. The present work argues that AI will prove to be a valuable instrument in enhancing human decision-making, provided that practical wisdom remains pertinent in safeguarding three essential elements.

Firstly, practical wisdom will be indispensable in integrating ethical frameworks into algorithmic decision-making processes. AI-powered machines' inherent limitations in comprehending the ethical nuances of specific situations underscore the crucial role of human oversight, since practical wisdom involves the ability to make thoughtful and balanced decisions, carefully considering the circumstances and consequences of actions. For example, in the field of Human–Computer Interactions (HCI), prudential judgment guides the design of systems that provide better moral choices and ethical considerations while fostering virtuous practices (Gorichanaz 2022).

Secondly, relying solely on AI-driven decision-making, without the critical oversight of humans, can lead to shallow analysis and poor decisions. Practical wisdom provides wise individuals with a broader and deeper view of situations (Baehr 2012), cultivated through long and profound learning process, often of years of experience, reflection, and learning (Ferrero et al. 2020); it is not something acquired overnight, it requires time and commitment. AI systems are proficient at swiftly processing extensive volumes of data, but they might encounter difficulties in grasping the full context, nuanced details, and complexities of intricate situations. Unlike human decision-makers, AI lacks the capacity to consider other aspects of a specific situation, like unforeseen circumstances or emotional factors, which might be overlooked by data-driven algorithms. Indeed, understanding and appropriately responding to human emotions, such as empathy, are pivotal aspects of ethical and effective decision-making (Mencl and May 2009; Pohling et al. 2016). Wise individuals, who can demonstrate compassion and empathy by understanding others' perspectives (Csikszentmihalyi et al. 2014), could bridge the gap between human understanding and AI decision-making, which currently lacks this ability.

Finally, explainability is fundamental for the ethical and responsible deployment of AI, serving as a cornerstone in ensuring accountability and making the decision-making processes of algorithms interpretable. This is necessary because AI systems function within predetermined parameters, making them vulnerable to difficulties when encountering unforeseen scenarios. Precisely, the development of these emerging technologies "presents challenges far too complex, dynamic, and context-sensitive to be resolved simply by applying standing moral rules or principles intended to govern all possible cases" (Vallor 2016, p. 110). Achieving explainability requires employing interpretable models and fostering transparency by providing employees with information about algorithmic processes. This will raise awareness about the inherent opacity that algorithms may possess. Practical wisdom finds the right balance between transparency and the complexity of the models, allowing informed decisions without overwhelming users. Moreover, it involves the perspectives and needs of end-users, ensuring that explanations are meaningful and empower users to make informed decisions.

6.2.2 Justice and AI-Powered Predictive Analytics

Justice is the virtue of giving each person what is due to her (Pieper 2017). Its significance lies in fostering a society based on equality (Ake 2017), human dignity (Pritchard 1972), and social justice (Garlington and Collins 2021). It pertains to the interactions between individuals, and the bidirectional relationship between the community and the individuals (Pieper 2017). In the workplace augmented by AI, the prevalence of algorithms for scrutinizing data, recognizing patterns, and forecasting future scenarios will be paramount. This synergistic blend of machine learning and data analytics empowers individuals to make informed decisions by providing invaluable insights.

For this reason, justice is a necessary virtue to assess the impact of this technology on the basic rights, dignity, and welfare of individuals and groups (Vallor 2016). For instance, if AI is not carefully designed and trained, it could perpetuate and exacerbate bias, leading to increased injustice and discrimination. AI systems often rely on large datasets for training, and if these datasets contain historical biases or reflect existing societal inequalities, the algorithms can learn and perpetuate those biases (Agarwal et al. 2023; Johnson 2021). Moreover, if the developers do not contemplate diversity and inclusivity, they may not adequately consider the needs and perspectives of underrepresented groups, leading to unjust and biased decisions, especially regarding gender (Nadeem et al. 2022) and racial bias (Ntoutsi et al. 2020). This issue is particularly urgent in the AI field, characterized by the dominance of Western viewpoints (Aggarwal 2020). Consequently, AI systems could produce discriminatory outcomes across various domains, especially during recruitment processes (Soleimani et al. 2021). For instance, in 2014, Amazon developed an AI-based system for personnel selection that learned to consider men "preferable" and began discriminating against women. A year later, Amazon implemented a tool, based on AI, for personnel selection that, due to certain erroneous biases in its algorithm, preferred and chose female candidates over male candidates. The virtue of justice will play a pivotal role in guiding these technologies to avoid biases and discrimination toward fostering human flourishing. To achieve that, justice should address three key points.

First, AI algorithms can be employed to analyze historical data from successful employees, identifying patterns related to skills, qualifications, and performance, reducing discriminatory decisions, and making it easier to reward merit. For instance, Houser (2019) argues that AI can be used as a means to mitigate unconscious bias and variability in human decision-making, particularly in the context of promoting gender diversity in the tech industry. Newstead et al. (2023) provide actionable strategies for managers to leverage AI to promote greater gender equity in leadership. The same AI can be used to promote a more inclusive work environment. For instance, Mateos-Sanchez et al. (2022) propose an educational tool aimed at enhancing social skill development and inclusion for people with intellectual disabilities, both preparing users for real-life situations and supporting active learning methodologies.

Second, only human beings are able to ensure that AI implementation empowers everyone, not just a selected few. On one hand, AI applications such as chatbots and virtual assistants can enhance people's access to information and resources. On the other hand, it is essential for employees to understand how AI contributes to decision-making and use it to express their opinions. AI can monitor and analyze employee feedback and comments, providing insights into the overall sentiment within the workplace and identifying potential issues related to diversity and inclusion. This proactive approach allows for timely interventions and adjustments to policies or practices, promoting a just and harmonious work environment. Encouraging human feedback in the process is crucial, considering Palladino's observation (2023) that AI technologies may seem neutral on the surface, but their design is shaped by numerous human decisions.

Third, AI-powered analytics can be used to identify skill gaps and training needs within the workforce. This ensures the equitable distribution of professional development opportunities, providing all employees with the chance to upgrade their skills and advance in their careers. In addition, considering factors such as retirement trends, skill gaps, and demographic shifts, the organization can make strategic decisions to maintain a balanced workforce. This would allow an environment with fair distribution of opportunities, balanced representation of diversity, equitable succession planning, and inclusive talent development.

6.2.3 Courage and AI-Powered Virtual Reality Training

Courage is a virtue that signifies the capacity to act resolutely and honorably in challenging or dangerous circumstances (Rorty 1986). It is highly significant because it empowers individuals to surmount obstacles, champion what is just, and uphold their moral principles (Lachman 2007). The essence of courage does not lie in exposing oneself to any form of risk, but only to that which is in accordance with reason (Pieper 2017). Courage is fundamental for both personal and societal advancement, as it compels people to take brave actions for the greater good (Misztal 2007).

This virtue encompasses several essential characteristics. It represents the middle ground between cowardice and recklessness (Aristotle 1999), it is not the absence of fear but rather the ability to confront it (Goud 2005); it can be described as "a reliable tendency to intelligently balance measured and justified fears with measured and justified confidence and hope" (Vallor 2016, p. 129). Therefore, this virtue helps the agent to overcome cowardice and avoid recklessness or acting blindly by passion or ignorance of the danger. It can manifest in diverse forms, including both physical courage (facing physical dangers) and moral courage (defending ethical principles) (Olsthoorn 2007). Courage is often closely associated with integrity and honesty since it involves the readiness to speak the truth (Matt 2015), even when doing so may be inconvenient or unpopular, and to uphold what is right and morally sound. Individuals who stand up against discriminatory systems often exhibit moral courage in their actions.

AI could have the potential to hinder the development of courage, boosting cowardice, since AI systems are often designed to minimize risks and optimize outcomes. Consider, for instance, sectors such as finance and healthcare. The use of AI can inadvertently foster excessive risk aversion among individuals, causing them to shy away from any situation or decision involving even a slight level of risk. On the other side, when AI systems take over various tasks and decision-making processes, employees may perceive a diminished sense of initiative in their work. This reduced autonomy can result in decreased motivation to actively contribute to their organizations. Excessive reliance on machines for courageous or risky actions can diminish individuals' opportunities to develop courage through direct action (Kirkpatrick 2015). Conversely, AI-generated confidence in automated decision-making can discourage individuals from critically assessing risks, thus encouraging reckless actions. For example, healthcare providers or emergency responders may become overly reliant on AI recommendations, potentially overlooking critical information. On the contrary, AI can encourage the agent to act courageously. In particular, AI-powered virtual reality (VR) training can create simulated environments that replicate real-world workplace scenarios where employees need to make courageous decisions. This technology holds various workplace implications (Sagnier et al. 2021) and has been applied to optimize workplace layouts, leading to enhanced productivity (Muttaqin et al. 2020). Moreover, this approach is already relevant for roles involving high-risk situations, like the military field (Wang et al. 2020).

In the augmented workplace, virtual reality simulations would be beneficial for courage development at least in three ways. Firstly, by exposing individuals to daily challenges they can face in the workplace, such as handling difficult conversations, employees can practice and build their courage in a safe and controlled setting. For instance, a variant of VR training was employed to instruct teachers in handling challenging behaviors exhibited by students (Chen 2022), resulting in an increase in confidence through proactive student engagement, and issuing effective oral commands. Another tailored VR simulation aims to empower young job seekers with positive results (Prasolova-Førland et al. 2019). Moreover, recreating daily situations or engaging in challenging professional activities can enhance the workplace environment, fostering improved mutual understanding and the refinement of individual skills. VR is progressively employed for training non-technical skills, holding significant relevance for management practice as well (Philip et al. 2023). The VR simulator reveals the potential to enhance teamwork skills with a positive impact (Amat et al. 2023), as already happens in healthcare to improve empathic communication (Guetterman et al. 2019).

Secondly, it is essential to provide individuals with appropriate coaching following the VR simulation, allowing users to receive feedback and improve their performance. There are several assessment tests and evaluation methods employed to validate the effectiveness of VR training (Xie et al. 2021). While AI algorithms can suggest strategies in specific situations, the role of human coaching is irreplaceable in this task. Human coaches possess emotional intelligence, which allows them to understand the nuances of emotions, and provide empathy and motivation, while AI algorithms might encounter difficulties in this aspect. In particular, human coaches can adapt their verbal and non-verbal cues to effectively convey messages. Moreover, trustworthiness is a crucial component of coaching, perceived in terms of ability, integrity, and benevolence (Schiemann et al. 2019), especially in personal development areas. At the same time, in sensitive domains such as healthcare, trustworthiness is imperative for a dependable AI. As highlighted by Paladino (2023), the principal challenge lies in establishing trustworthiness. Paladino advocates for striking a delicate equilibrium between the algorithm's efficacy and its explicability, ensuring that results are comprehensible and can be explained to patients, physicians, and competent authorities. Simultaneously, he acknowledges the call to enhance transparency, a crucial measure for detecting and critically analyzing biases within the system. This is a potential area of improvement in the virtue of courage, as it helps individuals to understand the setting and think of concrete ways to overcome difficult situations, avoiding cowardice or recklessness.

Thirdly, the organization should adapt its policies to systematically integrate VR simulations in its procedures. Organizations aiming to achieve this goal should dedicate resources, possibly establishing a specialized team tailored to address unique requirements during the implementation of VR simulations. These professionals may consist of existing employees or new hires, and their role would involve supporting the organization's activities. In such instances, individuals responsible for these policies could undergo training to proficiently integrate VR for policy improvement. These professional figures would also tailor training programs to suit the unique needs of each individual, ensuring personalized learning experiences. Utilizing VR for personalized learning enhances cognitive processes such as information discovery, processing, memorization, and recall (Horváth 2021), enhancing workplace safety (Rebelo et al. 2019). In augmented workplaces, rather than implementing a standardized VR simulation for all employees, it could be advantageous to expose individuals to tailored and challenging scenarios, closely monitoring their progression. This ensures that the training remains stimulating and relevant, progressively pushing individuals to expand their comfort zones and develop a heightened sense of courage in various workplace contexts.

6.2.4 Temperance and AI Workforce Management Tools

Temperance is characterized by self-control, moderation, and self-discipline (Sanz and Fontrodona 2019). While the other cardinal virtues relate to one's interaction with the external world, the purpose of temperance is to bring order to the inner self of a person (Pieper 2017). Since temperance involves skillfully managing desires and passions (Young 1988), it plays a crucial role in helping individuals manage their desires and impulses in a balanced way. AI-based technologies expand the abundance and diversity of personalized products, accelerate the acquisition, consumption, and replacement of these items, and amplify addictive consumption patterns through sophisticated software design (Vallor 2016). In this context, self-control is more necessary than ever before. Emerging situations, influenced by modern technologies like remote work, emphasize the importance of this virtue in reestablishing a harmonious balance in many activities performed by individuals (Rocchi and Bernacchio 2022b).

Temperance in the workplace entails avoiding the extremes of laziness and excessive work. Some uses of AI-based technologies can facilitate laziness. AI systems play a significant role in decision-making by offering data analysis and recommendations. While this support can be invaluable, there is a concern that heavy reliance on AI might reduce employees' cognitive efforts, hindering the development of temperance by promoting laziness. Literature alerts on potential malicious effects related to AI-based tools like ChatGPT, that could cause a decline in critical thinking (Malinka et al. 2023). On the flip side, if AI is used for surveillance in the workplace (Bales and Stone 2020), it might encourage a culture of constant work. This could lead to overwork and a lack of balance in employees' lives. Excessive self-control may result from AI-driven performance metrics and continuous monitoring, as employees fear not meeting productivity targets. In particular, the use of wearable devices constantly conveys picking targets and evaluates employees' performance: this can lead to increased emotional and physical exhaustion (del Pero et al. 2022).

In the modern era influenced by technology, temperance can be characterized as "an exemplary ability to choose, and ideally to desire for their own sakes, those goods and experiences that most contribute to contemporary and future human flourishing" (Vallor 2016, p. 124). When used as workforce management tools, AI-based technologies can serve the cause of temperance by encouraging the right experiences for human flourishing, channeling them into three main areas.

Firstly, AI-powered emotion recognition software can help handle specific moments of stress. AI-based applications can monitor physical and mental wellbeing (Mody and Mody 2019). For example, AI can analyze facial expressions, voice tone, and other physiological indicators to assess employees' stress levels, and can prompt interventions. For instance, if an employee shows signs of frustration, the system could suggest taking a break or mindfulness exercises. In particular, AI can be leveraged to offer a form of mental health support through chatbots or virtual assistants (Graham et al. 2019). These AI-driven resources can provide valuable guidance and resources for managing mental health and coping with workplace stress, encouraging employees to seek assistance when needed.

Secondly, AI can analyze work patterns to provide insights into workload balancing. AI-driven tools can be employed to assist employees in managing their workloads and maintaining a healthy work-life balance (Pawlicka et al. 2020). For instance, by considering factors such as meeting durations, task complexity, and designated break times, AI can help employees structure their workdays more efficiently, fostering a balanced and sustainable approach to task management. AI can also aid in time management, preventing procrastination (Costa 2021), so helping develop the virtue of temperance. This proactive scheduling approach aims to prevent burnout and improve time management.

Thirdly, AI can contribute to establishing or reinforcing organizational policies that promote temperance by aligning work expectations with sustainable work practices. This goal can be achieved in two ways. On the one hand, organizations could implement and encourage the use of AI tools in workers' daily activities, to serve as reminders for taking breaks, and monitor overtime hours. For instance, the combination of sensor wristbands, a smartphone app, and AI can be used to predict and recommend individual breaks for warehouse workers, aiming to mitigate health and productivity risks associated with frequent mental and physical workloads (Kretschmer et al. 2021). AI can also be used to improve the physical workplace. In particular, AI use can be extended to wearable sensors for testing and validating cooperative workplaces from an ergonomic perspective (Caporaso et al. 2022).

On the other hand, while many AI devices focus on monitoring human performance, such as biomechanical functions and physical activity, emerging intelligent systems actively monitor mental health (Patel et al. 2022). By analyzing data on working hours, AI can provide alerts or suggestions when employees are consistently exceeding healthy limits, promoting awareness and encouraging individuals to take necessary steps to preserve their well-being. Moreover, the organization could provide employees with AI-assisted health programs, such as brief exercises that can effectively alleviate common physical symptoms due to work activities, like neck/shoulder pain/stiffness and low back pain within a 12-week period (Anan et al. 2021).

The following table 6.1 can serve as an eventual summary of the analysis:

6.3 Conclusions

This study suggests that the advancement of AI technology in the workplace underscores the imperative of incorporating the virtue ethics framework to address emergent challenges and unforeseen consequences in both AI development and deployment. In the augmented workplace of the future, challenges arise from the risk of replacing human judgment with AI-driven decisions, potentially perpetuating biases, undermining justice, and leading to deskilling. On the positive side, virtuous individuals can leverage AI to enhance decision-making, reduce bias, address fears, and promote a healthy work-life balance for all.

The inherent human-centered nature of virtue ethics constitutes a fertile ground for prospective research. Firstly, we have considered whether an AI-enhanced workplace helps or prevents develop the cardinal virtues: practical wisdom, justice, courage, and temperance. Secondly, we propose creativity and empathy as additional virtues to enhance the capabilities of future workplace practitioners. In the evolving landscape where AI excels in data processing, the human ability to think creatively, adapt to changing circumstances, and generate original ideas becomes increasingly crucial. Another vital virtue is empathy. While AI can recognize human emotions, empathy remains a distinctly human trait. It involves the capacity to adopt alternative perspectives, and understand others' emotions. Both creativity and empathy are likely to be pivotal virtues in the workplaces of the future.

Thirdly, it would be advantageous to incorporate not only conceptual research but also qualitative and quantitative methodologies. There is a necessity to quantify the impact of virtues in AI-shaped workplaces. This can be achieved through various

Table 6.1 The cardinal virtues in the AI-enhanced workplace

Virtue	Definition of the virtue	AI-powered context of virtue analysis in the future workplace scenario	How the AI-powered context can prevent the virtue development in the future workplace	How the AI-powered context can help in developing the virtue in the future workplace
Practical wisdom	Practical wisdom is the virtue of identifying the good end to pursue and choose the best means to achieve it	Algorithmic decision-making	- Risk of replacing human judgment with AI-driven decision-making - Over-reliance on AI and moral deskilling	- Integrate human judgment into algorithmic decision-making processes - Continuous monitoring of algorithms - Ensure explainability of the algorithmic decision
Justice	Justice is the virtue of giving each person what is due to her; it encompasses the equitable treatment of individuals and groups	AI-powered predictive analytics	- It may perpetuate and amplify bias if datasets carry historical biases or if AI development teams lack diversity and inclusivity	- Analyze employees' historical data, reduce bias in decision-making and promote merit-based rewards - Broaden access to information and fostering inclusivity - Identify skill gaps and ensure fair distribution of professional development opportunities for career advancement

(continued)

Table 6.1 (continued)

Virtue	Definition of the virtue	AI-powered context of virtue analysis in the future workplace scenario	How the AI-powered context can prevent the virtue development in the future workplace	How the AI-powered context can help in developing the virtue in the future workplace
Courage	Courage is the virtue of keep pursuing the good even in the middle of adverse circumstances	AI-powered virtual reality training	- AI may promote excessive risk aversion - When AI handles tasks and decisions, employees might feel less initiative and limit their active contributions - AI-generated confidence in automated decisions may discourage critical risk assessment, potentially leading to reckless actions	- Tailor simulations to specific personal and organizational needs is crucial for meaningful training - Ensure human feedback. Integrating human coaches is necessary due to emotional intelligence and trust - Adapt organizational policies to systematically integrate VR simulations in its procedures. Specialized teams should adjust scenarios for personalized and challenging experiences
Temperance	Temperance is the virtue of self-control, moderation, and restraint in one's actions and desires	AI-based workforce management tools	- Heavily relying on AI may cause deskilling and laziness - It may contribute to a decline in critical thinking - AI-driven surveillance may promote a culture of continuous work, risking employee well-being	- Ensure personalized well-being recommendations in specific moments of stress - Encourage balanced task distribution and efficient time management - Adapt organizational policies and procedures to foster a healthy work-life balance for all

means. For instance, designing surveys and questionnaires could prove valuable for collecting data on individuals' perceptions of virtues and their development in the workplace. Analyzing individual performances may further help identify correlations between the development of virtues and job success in the AI-enhanced workplace. By employing qualitative and quantitative methods, researchers can gain a more comprehensive understanding of how virtues influence the dynamics of AI-influenced work environments.

Finally, future research can consider the development of learning strategies, specifically within business curricula, to place a greater emphasis on the teaching of virtues in the context of AI-enhanced organizations (Moosmayer et al., 2024). This can be approached in diverse ways. One approach is to incorporate modules or lessons that highlight the practical application of business virtues in daily scenarios. Another strategy is to implement mentoring programs focused on assisting students in cultivating virtues and fostering character development, to better prepare them for their work in AI-enhanced organizations, where they can develop their potential as individuals and workers.

References

Agarwal R, Bjarnadottir M, Rhue L, Dugas M, Crowley K, Clark J, Gao G (2023) Addressing algorithmic bias and the perpetuation of health inequities: An AI bias aware framework. Health Policy Technol 12(1):100702

Aggarwal N (2020) Introduction to the special issue on intercultural digital ethics. Philos Technol 33(4): 547–550. https://doi.org/10.1007/s13347-020-00428-1

Ake C (2017) Justice as equality. Justice (pp. 121–141). Routledge.

Amat AZ, Adiani D, Tauseef M, Breen M, Hunt S, Swanson AR, ... Sarkar N (2023) Design of a desktop virtual reality-based collaborative activities simulator (ViRCAS) to support teamwork in workplace settings for autistic adults. IEEE Trans Neural Systems Rehabil Eng 31: 2184–2194.

Anan T, Kajiki S, Oka H, Fujii T, Kawamata K, Mori K, Matsudaira K (2021) Effects of an artificial intelligence–assisted health program on workers with neck/shoulder pain/stiffness and low back pain: Randomized controlled trial. JMIR Mhealth Uhealth 9(9):e27535

Aquinas T (1964) Summa theologiae: Latin text and English translation, introductions, notes, appendices, and glossaries (T. Gilby, Ed.). Blackfriars

Aristotle. (1999) Nicomachean ethics. Hackett Publishing Co, Indianapolis

Ashri R (2019) The AI-powered workplace: How artificial intelligence, data, and messaging platforms are defining the future of work. Apress

Bachmann C, Habisch A, Dierksmeier C (2018) Practical wisdom: Management's no longer forgotten virtue. J Bus Ethics 153:147–165

Baehr J (2012) Two types of wisdom. Acta Analytica 27:81–97. https://doi.org/10.1007/s12136-012-0155-3

Bales RA, Stone KVW (2020) The Invisible web at work- artificial intelligence and electronic surveillance in the workplace. Berkeley J Employ Labor Law 41(1):1–62. https://doi.org/10.1007/s10551-023-05339-7

Bankins S, Formosa P (2023) The ethical implications of artificial intelligence (AI) for meaningful work. J Bus Ethics 1–16. https://doi.org/10.1007/s10551-023-05339-7

Brusoni S, Vaccaro A (2017) Ethics, technology and organizational innovation. J Bus Ethics 143:223–226. https://doi.org/10.1007/s10551-016-3061-6

Caporaso T, Grazioso S, Di Gironimo G (2022) Development of an integrated virtual reality system with wearable sensors for ergonomic evaluation of human–robot cooperative workplaces. Sensors 22(6):2413. https://doi.org/10.3390/s22062413

Chen C (2022) Immersive virtual reality to train preservice teachers in managing students' challenging behaviours: A pilot study. Br J Edu Technol 53(4):998–1024. https://doi.org/10.1111/bjet.13181

Costa C (2021) Procrastinate no more. How to overcome procrastination with machine learning. An exploration of design as a bridge between data science and human beings. https://www.politesi.polimi.it/bitstream/10589/175396/3/D%26E%20-%20Camilla%20Costa%20-%20Procrastinate%20no%20more.pdf

Csikszentmihalyi MN, Jeanne. (2014) The role of emotions in the development of wisdom. A handbook of wisdom: psychological perspectives, pp 220–242. https://doi.org/10.1007/978-94-017-9094-9_4

Davenport TH, Miller SM (2022) Working with AI: real stories of human-machine collaboration. The MIT Press. https://doi.org/10.55613/jeet.v32i1.108

del Pero AS, Wyckoff P, Vourc'h A (2022) Using artificial intelligence in the workplace: What are the main ethical risks? OECD Social, Employment and Migration Working Papers, No. 273, OECD Publishing, Paris, https://doi.org/10.1787/840a2d9f-en

Ferrero I, Rocchi M, Pellegrini MM, Reichert E (2020) Practical wisdom: A virtue for leaders. Bringing together Aquinas and Authentic Leadership. Business Ethics: A European Review. 29. https://doi.org/10.1111/beer.12298

Fioravante R, Vaccaro A, (2025) Humanism, dehumanization, integral human development: An overview of boundaries and capabilities of human-centered artificial intelligence in business and organizations. In: Fioravante R. Vaccaro A. (2025) (eds.) Humanism and artificial intelligence, Springer

Garlington SB, Collins ME (2021) Addressing environmental justice: Virtue ethics, social work, and social welfare. Int J Soc Welf 30(3):353–363. https://doi.org/10.1111/ijsw.12466

Giarmoleo FV, Ferrero I, Rocchi M, Pellegrini M (2024) What ethics can say on artificial intelligence: Insights from a systematic literature review. Bus Soc Rev. https://doi.org/10.1111/basr.12336

Gorichanaz T (2022) Designing a future worth wanting: applying virtue ethics to HCI. ArXiv Preprint. https://doi.org/10.48550/arXiv.2204.02237

Goud NH (2005) Courage: Its nature and development. J HumIstic Couns, Educ Dev 44(1):102–116. https://doi.org/10.1002/j.2164-490X.2005.tb00060.x

Graham S, Depp C, Lee EE, Nebeker C, Tu X, Kim H-C, Jeste DV (2019) Artificial intelligence for mental health and mental illnesses: An overview. Curr Psychiatry Rep 21:1–18. https://doi.org/10.1007/s11920-019-1094-0

Green BP (2019) Artificial intelligence, decision-making, and moral deskilling. Markkula Center for Applied Ethics

Guetterman TC, Sakakibara R, Baireddy S, Kron FW, Scerbo MW, Cleary JF, Fetters MD (2019) Medical students' experiences and outcomes using a virtual human simulation to improve communication skills: Mixed methods study. J Med Internet Res 21(11):e15459

Haenlein M, Huang MH, Kaplan A (2022) Guest editorial: Business ethics in the era of artificial intelligence. J Bus Ethics 178(4):867–869. https://doi.org/10.1007/s10551-022-05060-x

Horváth I (2021) An analysis of personalized learning opportunities in 3D VR. Frontiers in Computer Science 3:673826. https://doi.org/10.3389/fcomp.2021.673826

Houser KA (2019) Can AI solve the diversity problem in the tech industry: Mitigating noise and bias in employment decision-making. Stan. Tech. L. Rev. 22:290. Available at SSRN: https://ssrn.com/abstract=3344751

Johnson GM (2021) Algorithmic bias: On the implicit biases of social technology. Synthese 198(10):9941–9961. https://doi.org/10.1007/s11229-020-02696-y

Kirkpatrick J (2015) Drones and the martial virtue courage. J MilY Ethics 14(3–4):202–219. https://doi.org/10.1080/15027570.2015.1106744

Kretschmer V, Mättig B, Fiolka M (2021) Dynamic break management in logistics on the basis of individual vital data: designing the user interface of an ai-based mobile app for employees in order picking. 483–490. https://doi.org/10.1007/978-3-030-74608-7_60

Lachman VD (2007) Moral courage: A virtue in need of development? Medsurg Nurs 16(2):131

Lindebaum D, Vesa M, Den Hond F (2020) Insights from "the machine stops" to better understand rational assumptions in algorithmic decision making and its implications for organizations. Acad Manag Rev 45(1):247–263. https://doi.org/10.5465/amr.2018.0181

MacIntyre AC (1973) A short history of ethics. A history of moral philosophy from the homeric age to the twentieth century, 5th edn. The MacMillan Company, New York, NY

Malinka K, Peresíni M, Firc A, Hujnak O, Janus F (2023) On the educational impact of ChatGPT: Is Artificial Intelligence ready to obtain a university degree? In Proceedings of the 2023 Conference on Innovation and Technology in Computer Science Education V. 1 (pp. 47–53). https://doi.org/10.1145/3587102.3588827

Mateos-Sanchez M, Melo AC, Blanco LS, García AMF (2022) Chatbot, as educational and inclusive tool for people with intellectual disabilities. Sustainability 14(3):1520. https://doi.org/10.3390/su14031520

Matt BF (2015) Speaking truth to power: The courageous organizational dissenter. In Moral Courage in Organizations (pp. 157–170). Routledge

Mencl J, May DR (2009) The effects of proximity and empathy on ethical decision-making: An exploratory investigation. J Bus Ethics 85:201–226. https://psycnet.apa.org/doi/10.1007/s10551-008-9765-5

Misztal, Barbara (2007) Intellectuals and the public good: creativity and civil courage. https://doi.org/10.1017/CBO9780511488825

Mody V, Mody V (2019) Mental health monitoring system using artificial intelligence: A Review. 1–6:1–6. https://doi.org/10.1109/I2CT45611.2019.9033652

Moosmayer DC, Rocchi M, Ferrero I (2024) Virtue as competence: a conceptual integration of competence thinking with MacIntyrean. Virtue Ethics British J Manag. https://doi.org/10.1111/1467-8551.12897

Muttaqin BI, Prastyabudi A, Zunaidi W, Rizqa. (2020) Workplace design selection framework to increase productivity by using virtual reality. AIP Conf Proc 2217:030118. https://doi.org/10.1063/5.0000641

Nadeem A, Marjanovic O, Abedin B (2022) Gender bias in AI-based decision-making systems: A systematic literature review. Australas J Inf Syst, 26. https://doi.org/10.3127/ajis.v26i0.3835

Newell S, Marabelli M (2020) Strategic opportunities (and challenges) of algorithmic decision-making: A call for action on the long-term societal effects of 'datification'. In Strategic information management (pp. 430–449). Routledge

Newstead T, Eager B, Wilson S (2023) How AI can perpetuate–Or help mitigate–Gender bias in leadership. Organizational Dynamics, 100998. https://doi.org/10.1016/j.orgdyn.2023.100998

Ntoutsi E, Fafalios P, Gadiraju U, Iosifidis V, Nejdl W, Vidal M, Ruggieri S, Turini F, Papadopoulos S, Krasanakis E (2020) Bias in data-driven artificial intelligence systems—An introductory survey. Wiley Interdiscip Rev: Data Min Knowl Discov 10(3):e1356. https://doi.org/10.1002/widm.1356

Olsthoorn P (2007) Courage in the military: Physical and moral. J MilY Ethics 6(4):270–279.

Paladino MS (2023) Inteligencia Artificial en Medicina. Reflexiones éticas desde el pensamiento de Edmund Pellegrino. Cuad. Bioét, 25–35

Patel V, Chesmore A, Legner CM, Pandey S (2022) Trends in workplace wearable technologies and connected-worker solutions for next-generation occupational safety, health, and productivity. Adv Intell Syst 4(1):2100099

Pawlicka A, Pawlicki M, Tomaszewska R, Choraś M, Gerlach R (2020) Innovative machine learning approach and evaluation campaign for predicting the subjective feeling of work-life balance among employees. PLoS ONE 15(5):e0232771

Pereira V, Hadjielias E, Christofi M, Vrontis D (2023) A systematic literature review on the impact of artificial intelligence on workplace outcomes: A multi-process perspective. Hum Resour Manag Rev 33(1):100857

Philip J, Jiang Y, Akdere M (2023) Virtual reality technology for workplace training: The case for developing cultural intelligence. Int J Cross Cult Manag, 14705958231208296

Pieper J (2017) Las virtudes fundamentales. Ediciones Rialp, SA

Plato P (2008) The republic (Vol. 7). Wiley Online Library

Pohling R, Bzdok D, Eigenstetter M, Stumpf S, Strobel A (2016) What is ethical competence? The role of empathy, personal values, and the five-factor model of personality in ethical decision-making. J Bus Ethics 137:449–474

Polizzi G, Harrison T (2022) Wisdom in the digital age: A conceptual and practical framework for understanding and cultivating cyber-wisdom. Ethics Inf Technol 24(1):16. https://doi.org/10.1007/s10676-022-09640-3

Prasolova-Førland E, Fominykh M, Ekelund OI (2019) Empowering young job seekers with virtual reality. 295–302:295–302. https://doi.org/10.1109/VR.2019.8798179

Pritchard MS (1972) Human dignity and justice. Ethics 82(4):299–313. https://doi.org/10.1086/291853

Rebelo F, Noriega P, Veronesi J (2019) A framework to use virtual reality for behavior change to promote safety and health at work. 127–136. https://doi.org/10.1007/978-3-319-94706-8_15

Rocchi M, Bernacchio C (2022) The virtues of COVID-19 pandemic: How working from home can make us the best (or the worst) version of ourselves. Bus Soc Rev 127(3):685–700. https://doi.org/10.1007/978-3-031-31494-0_10

Rocchi, M, Bernacchio, C (2023) Digital Technologies and the Future of Work: An Agent-Centred Ethical Perspective Based on Goods, Norms, and Virtues. In: Lynn, T., Rosati, P., Conway, E., van der Werff, L. (eds) The Future of Work. Palgrave Studies in Digital Business & Enabling Technologies. Palgrave Macmillan, Cham. https://doi.org/10.1007/978-3-031-31494-0_10

Rorty AO (1986) The two faces of courage. Philosophy 61(236):151–171. https://doi.org/10.1017/S0031819100021045

Sagnier C, Loup-Escande É, Valléry G (2021) Virtual reality: Definitions, characteristics and applications in the workplace. Digital Transformations in the Challenge of Activity and Work: Understanding and Supporting Technological Changes 3:31–44. https://doi.org/10.1002/9781119808343.ch3

Sanz P, Fontrodona J (2019) Moderation as a moral competence: Integrating perspectives for a better understanding of temperance in the workplace. J Bus Ethics 155:981–994. https://doi.org/10.1007/s10551-018-3899-x

Schiemann SJ, Mühlberger C, Schoorman FD, Jonas E (2019) Trust me, I am a caring coach: The benefits of establishing trustworthiness during coaching by communicating benevolence. J Trust Res 9(2):164–184. https://doi.org/10.1080/21515581.2019.1650751

Schwartz B, Bernacchio C, González-Cantón C, Robson A (2020) Handbook of practical wisdom in business and management. Springer International Publishing

Sison AJG, Ferrero I (2015) How different is neo-A ristotelian virtue from positive organizational virtuousness? Business Ethics: A European Review 24:S78–S98. https://doi.org/10.1111/beer.12099

Sison AJG, Beabout GR, Ferrero I (Eds.) (2017) Handbook of virtue ethics in business and management (1st ed., 1–2). Springer

Soleimani M, Intezari A, Taskin N, Pauleen D (2021) Cognitive biases in developing biased artificial intelligence recruitment system. http://hdl.handle.net/10125/71238

Vallor S (2016) Technology and the virtues: A philosophical guide to a future worth wanting. Oxford University Press. https://doi.org/10.1093/acprof:oso/9780190498511.001.0001

Wang W, Lei S, Liu H, Li T, Qu J, Qiu A (2020) Augmented reality in maintenance training for military equipment. In Journal of Physics: Conference Series (Vol. 1626, No. 1, p. 012184). IOP Publishing

Xie B, Liu H, Alghofaili R, Zhang Y, Jiang Y, Lobo FD, Li C, Li W, Huang H, Akdere M (2021) A review on virtual reality skill training applications. Frontiers in Virtual Reality 2:645153. https://doi.org/10.3389/frvir.2021.645153

Young CM (1988) Aristotle on temperance. Philos Rev 97(4):521–542

Part III
Humanism, Anti-humanism, and Human Responsibility in AI

Chapter 7
What's in a Name? Anti-Humanism and the AI Claim

João César das Neves

Abstract The expression "artificial intelligence" is one of the most daring and dreadful claims in human history, implying a dramatic challenge to the core nature of mankind. The fact that it became a household name, characterizing one of the most promising area of human development, is a paradox deserving understanding. In fact, computer science represents a crucial area of technical research, having already produced several excellent results and promising even better. These projects are conceptually independent of the original purpose of building "thinking machines" and creating an "artificial intelligence". This paradox raises three problems, which are briefly accessed in the paper. The first is how the "artificial intelligence" project came to exist and what was its logical foundation. The second is the characterization of the anti-humanistic elements implied by the claim to have "thinking machines": ideological, theological, and operational. Finally, the last part of the paper will sketch the practical consequences the claim had on the evolution of the field.

Keywords Responsible AI · Ethics of AI · AI regulations · Computer science ethics

> «What's in a name? That which we call a rose by any other name would smell just as sweet»
> Shakespeare, *Romeo and Juliet*, 2, 2.

Computer science and data analysis include some of the most effective and promising technologies of humanity. These algorithms have become omnipresent in society, from social networks to videogames and smart devices. Their successes and promises are remarkable and, even today, simultaneously the stuff of myths and everyday' s reality.

With such an impact, it is unavoidable that the use of these instruments raises some serious ethical issues in many dimensions. There is, nevertheless, one small

J. C. das Neves (✉)
Catolica Lisbon School of Business and Economics, Universidade Católica Portuguesa, Lisboa, Portugal
e-mail: jcn@ucp.pt

R. Fioravante and A. Vaccaro (eds.), *Humanism and Artificial Intelligence*, SpringerBriefs in Philosophy, https://doi.org/10.1007/978-3-031-85478-1_7

element which, although arbitrary and avoidable, seriously affected the field: the title. When it was decided this area of research and technology ought to be called "artificial intelligence" (AI), a plethora of lateral questions were raised, clouding reality, and generating spurious complex questions.[1]

In fact, taken seriously, "artificial intelligence" is one of the most outrageous and troublesome expressions imaginable. The fact that it has become a household name, used casually by everybody, does not hide its deep nature. It assumes implicitly some very strong concepts and implies a basic attitude with serious implications at the scientific, social, political, economic, philosophical, and ontological levels. One may even say this name has introduced a radically new element in human civilization, an element which may be classified as anti-humanistic. This paper tries to describe the origin, nature, and effects of this troublesome expression.

It is important to stress this investigation is conceptual, not moral, or behavioural. Solving complex mathematical problems, developing computational projects, and applying them to social issues are very interesting and useful efforts. None of these imply that the machines are "thinking" in any of the senses of this word. So, most of the work that is included under the classification of AI is completely alien to the claim implied in the name. Consequently, most of what will be said in this paper is thus irrelevant to most of the practical activity of AI.

The issues here discussed are raised only when some of these practitioners, clearly extrapolating from the real character of their tasks, pretend to be building a non-human entity capable, or at least aiming to be capable, of intelligence and will. This attitude, as will be seen, was crucial in the pioneering days, those of what became known as GOFAI, "Good Old-Fashioned Artificial Intelligence". Later developments showed the futility of the effort and turned the field to other, more practical, and useful purposes and the hubris of yore was mostly forgotten. But the name remained, and that original sin is latent in the area, resurging from time to time. This became particularly evident after November 30th, 2022, when the public presentation of ChatGPT, a large language model (LLM) of OpenAI, allegedly created a new era, arousing many old dreams and nightmares of the primordial epoch.

Dealing with such deep conceptual issues and the severe anti-humanistic charge they contain, the following pages have thus no implications either for the good faith of the practitioners or the social utility of the models. What is at stake here is the fundamental logic and purpose of the project of the creation of an artificial intelligence, not its concrete realizations and circumstances. What will be said below is thus distant from most of the many questions, ethical, social, political, or economic, raised by computer techniques, programs, machines and their uses and results. As will be argued in section one, most of the activity in computer science is really orthogonal to the original stance encapsulated in the proper name, "artificial intelligence".

---

[1] Some of these are even deplored by the practitioners themselves: «Current technology lags behind these popular images, making it easy to find an audience for the idea that AI has failed to live up expectations. Yet, we clearly cannot use these fictions as a standard for measuring progress in the field. If AI were named "nifty computer programs," it would surely be hailed an unqualified success» (Hopsgood 2003, p. 25).

The paper will try only to briefly discuss the significance of the "intelligence" designation, and its impact both on science and society. Section one will access the arbitrariness of the expression, describing its origins and justification. Section two will characterize the "anti-humanistic" elements implicit in the project, at least in three different senses: ideological, theological, and operational. Finally, section three will look at the main lines of the socio-economic results of the real technologies, identifying some problems generated by the distortion implicit in the name.

7.1 The Path Towards AI

The expression "artificial intelligence" appeared late in the long development of computer science, but it can be said to have been an instant success. The name proved very popular, obsessive even, quickly becoming the norm in the field, latter turning into a household expression. Today everybody talks about artificial intelligence as if it was a normal and common thing, without a thought for its terrible meaning.

The main justification for the bold claim that machines think and are intelligent, something which became common knowledge in the last half century, is, of course, the remarkable accomplishments machines achieve all the time.[2] This is, in fact, logically unsustainable because none of these deeds necessarily imply any real intelligence. A radio, telephone or television may say very smart things without having any real understanding. But there is something in computer science which forces such conclusion.

On the other hand, the basic notion of thinking machines is very old in human imagination. Descriptions of the concept go all the way to Antiquity, referring to several early myths, like the automata in Homer's *Iliad*,[3] (Crevier 1993, p. 2). In particular, the novelistic genre of "science fiction", which flourished since the 19th century, is also crucial as a preparation for the topic.[4] All users today have already seen, in movies and series, much more than reality will ever bear. This only shows how humanity was eager and prepared to accept intelligent behaviour from machines as soon as some real scientists publicly asserted there were real smart apparatuses.

[2] Great impact had the string of victories computers achieved over humans in many intellectual sports: in 1979 the program BKG 9.8 defeated Luigi Villa, the world champion of backgammon; in 1995 the program Chinook won against the champion Don Lafferty at checkers/draughts; in 1997 the champion Garry Kasparov lost at chess against Deep Blue; in 2011 Watson wins Jeopardy! and in 2016 AlphaGo discomfitured the Go champion Lee Sedol.

[3] Iliad, Book V, 749; XVIII, 372–377, 410–420, 468–473.

[4] For example, the word "robot" didn't result from any scientific project, but from the 1920 play *R.U.R.* by the Czech writer Karel Čapek (1890–1938), decades before any such a mechanism existed.

7.1.1 An Unnecessary Claim

The field of artificial intelligence, unlike most of the other scientific and technological areas, has a very precise and well-defined starting point. The *Dartmouth Summer Research Project on Artificial Intelligence*, convened from June 18th to August 17th, 1956, is generally recognized as the founding event of the field. Of course, there were many previous steps of crucial importance, some of them will be discussed below; but in the seminar at the Dartmouth College, Hanover, New Hampshire, one may find a fully developed cluster of research projects.

The conference was convened through a "Proposal" presented under the signature of four scholars.[5] The explicit purpose of the endeavour was, from the start, to replicate the human brain and make machines think. Or, as the text says, "simulate it".

> «The study is to proceed on the basis of the conjecture that every aspect of learning or any other feature of intelligence can in principle be so precisely described that a machine can be made to simulate it. An attempt will be made to find how to make machines use language, form abstractions and concepts, solve kinds of problems now reserved for humans, and improve themselves» (McCarthy et al. 1955)

The practical purpose of the meeting was to combine several lines of work to achieve a common research project, with well-defined methods and goals. The result was not at all satisfactory:

> «The Dartmouth conference was in many ways inconclusive and deeply disappointed its principal organizer, John McCarthy. (…) No consensus emerged on what the field was or where it was going, and most of the participants later persisted in their own approaches» (Crevier 1993, p. 49)

In a way, this failure and all the future mishaps, some of them will be described below, show that this meta-purpose of achieving machine intelligence was spurious. The field had been, and still is, the aggregation of a lot of specific symbol-processing projects, each with a very particular practical job and many with great results. Success must be measured by the ability to solve the tasks, with the assumption of "intelligence" as an added stamp. But, because the mission at hand, like playing chess or translating languages, is considered typically intellectual, the machine is deemed smart.

In fact, the provocative name is merely a supplementary tag, irrelevant for all the process. If the claim of intelligence had not been made, all the work would go through undisturbed. It is not at all necessary to make the impudent, and in the end unjustified assertion of thinking machines for us to have all the great products

[5] These were John McCarthy (1927–2011), then assistant professor of Mathematics at Dartmouth College, Marvin Minsky (1927–2016), Harvard Junior Fellow in Mathematics and Neurology, Nathaniel Rochester (1919–2001), manager of information research at IBM corporation and chief architect of IBM 701, and Claude Shannon (1916–2001), mathematician at Bell Telephone Laboratories and then already famous as the "father of information theory". The two academics were still 28 years old during the seminar, while the industry members were older: Rochester 37 and Shannon 40.

generated by this research area. Just like when Physics demonstrated the sun and stars were not deities but just bodies in space, without impinging on the theological question of the existence of God, also these projects may have machines replicating some complex results leaving untouched the superiority of the human brain.

7.1.2 *An Unscientific Claim*

What do computers have to do with intelligence? Only the lay and ignorant user could attribute the operation of the machine to any kind of real reasoning. All persons minimally aware of the procedures involved know they are simple electromagnetic machines obeying a program and mimicking some mathematical operations; the only intelligence there comes from the shrewdness of the programmers and the users. Lately these algorithms have become very big and complex, even implying in some cases that nobody really understands what is happening inside the computer. Nevertheless, it is still and always a simple electromagnetic machine obeying a program.

This was understood generally by all experts in early days. In fact, computer science pioneers felt no need to consider "intelligent machines".

> «As regards the problem of the thinking ability of computing machines, the historical record shows an impressive unanimity. From Pascal to Von Neumann, all great contributors to the theory and development of computers refused to attribute thinking and consciousness to them. Such an unanimity should give at least some pause to those claiming the possibility, let alone the existence of artificial minds» (Jaki 1989, p. 59)

In fact, Blaise Pascal's (1623–1662) view on his mechanical calculating apparatus, completed in 1642, was:

> «The arithmetic machine produces effects which come closer to thought than anything animals do; but it does nothing that could indicate that it has will, like animals»[6]

On the other hand, John von Neuman (1903–1957), in the last words of his unfinished work *The Computer and the Brain*, states clearly the limits of the artificial endeavour:

> «The outward forms of our mathematics are not absolutely relevant from the point of view of evaluating what the mathematical or logical language truly used by the central nervous system is. However, the above remarks about reliability and logical and arithmetical depth prove that whatever the system is, it cannot fail to differ considerably from what we consciously and explicitly consider as mathematics» (von Neumann 1958, p. 82)

A computer is not really "thinking", in any of the meanings of this word. Two main aspects contribute to this conclusion. First, the question of intelligence is not, and can never be, a part of the field of work of the computer expert. The definition and elaboration of this concept imply deeply philosophical questions and can only

[6] Pascal *Pensées*, édition Chevalier 262, ed. Lafuma 741; ed. Brunschvicg 340.

be assessed through disciplines like anthropology or theory of knowledge, very old and complex areas of study. Computing and data analysts, through their electronic efforts, may raise intricate questions in metaphysics and epistemology, but can never decide them. No programmer can determine, through programming, whether her work is generating an intelligent entity.

On the other hand, a scientist is someone deeply committed to rigour and objectivity. This implies careful distinction between facts, theories, hypotheses, and conjectures. Thus, any good and well-defined research project must be very careful with the wording of its axioms, elaborations, and conclusions, to avoid fallacies, confusions, and false results. Choosing, at the start of the venture, a provocative and overstated name does not help with the logical solidity of the effort. Good scientists do not deal with false claims and wild extrapolations. These belong in the attitude of ignorant demagogues, populists, and popularisers, willing to sell fake science for the real thing.

For all these reasons, no self-aware and respected researcher could honestly apply the expression "artificial intelligence" to any of the efforts today classified under such a claim. Other expressions, like "assisted intelligence", would be much more adequate and honest. In fact, what happens in the field is that the intelligence of the researcher or the user, the only intellects present, are being assisted by the machine.

In conclusion, the use of the expression "artificial intelligence" is misleading, unnecessary and, as will be argued below, even dangerous. If this was the case, how come the wrongful expression became so divulged and prominent?

7.1.3 A Necessary Ploy

According to the Encyclopedia Britannica, «The earliest substantial work in the field of artificial intelligence was done in the mid-20th century by the British logician and computer pioneer Alan Mathison Turing»[7] This is a pacific and consensual attribution. Not only did Turing (1912–1954) in 1936, at the age of 24, established the basic definition of a computer, what is now called a "Turing machine" (Turing 1936), but he was the one credited with the elimination of the conceptual obstacles for the implementation of an artificial intelligence. Without ever using the expression,[8] what Turing really did, in a remarkable flash of genius, was to find a way to allow (even induce) all his colleagues to talk about intelligence while avoiding any philosophical elaborations.

The famous 1950 paper, published in a full-blown philosophical journal, *Mind—A Quarterly Review of Psychology and Philosophy*, starts in a very formal and appropriate way: «I propose to consider the question, 'Can machines think?'. This should

[7] www.britannica.com/technology/artificial-intelligence/Alan-Turing-and-the-beginning-of-AI

[8] He preferred 'intelligent machinery'. This is the title of his 1948 unpublished report, introducing many of the basic concepts of the future field. See Hodges (1983, xvii and 467) and the text of the report in Copeland (2004), chapter 10, pp. 395–432.

begin with the definitions of the meaning of the terms 'machine' and 'think'» (Turing 1950, p. 433). This shows how much the author is aware of the true nature of his query. Nevertheless, he does not proceed to those definitions[9] and, strangely enough, a few pages below he is even contradicting himself by saying: «The original question, 'Can machines think?' I believe to be too meaningless to deserve discussion» (Turing 1950, p. 442). One may ask, if that is the case, why raise it in the first place?

What mediates between these two inconsistent statements is, of course, one of the most famous and astute devices in human science, the "imitation game", which came to be known as the "Turing test":

> «The new form of the problem can be described in terms of a game which we call the 'imitation game'. It is played with three people, a man (A), a woman (B), and an interrogator (C) who may be of either sex. The interrogator stays in a room apart from the other two. The object of the game for the interrogator is to determine which of the other two is the man and which is the woman. (...) In order that tones of voice may not help the interrogator the answers should be written, or better still, typewritten. (...) We now ask the question, 'What will happen when a machine takes the part of A in this game?' Will the interrogator decide wrongly as often when the game is played like this as he does when the game is played between a man and a woman? These questions replace our original, 'Can machines think?'» (Turing 1950, pp. 433–434)

The conclusion is made more explicit next: «It was suggested tentatively that the question, 'Can machines think?' should be replaced by 'Are there imaginable digital computers which would do well in the imitation game?'» (Turing 1950, p. 442). Of course, this approach depends crucially on the validity of this replacement, something the paper assumes rather than proves. Is a good result in the game equivalent to an intelligent machine? What Turing did was replace reality with appearance; a "simulation", as the future 1955 Proposal will say. Nevertheless, here, like in any other field of human activity, the ability to convince an observer is very different from the real thing.

A lateral, but very relevant aspect is that Turing and all his disciples never really got to the formalization the game. How to set-up the examination? Who is an acceptable interrogator? In what conditions are the interrogatories made? How long the inspection lasts? Are there limits to the type of questions asked? Of course, the simple fact that one is unable to identify the computer after a few questions does not mean the test was successful, because the next, more astute question, may reverse the conclusion. Consequently, the only definitive result of this process would be a successful identification of the computer, as the failure to do so may always be attributed to inability of the interrogator, justifying the continuation of the process.

Considering the importance of this game, the basis of all the research area, it is very revealing that none of these practical questions were addressed either by Turing or any of his followers. Nobody really took the game seriously, but everybody acted like they did. The "imitation game" was simply used as passport for the use of the

[9] The paper includes a rather detailed discussion of the definition of "machine", in sections 3, 4, and 5, carefully describing the "digital computer" in the spirit of the 1936 paper. About "intelligence", arguably the most decisive of the two, there is total omission.

"thinking" and "intelligent" categories in all the algorithms, free from any deep and complex conceptual discussions.

In the meantime, the philosophical research proceeded to discard the equivalence suggested by Turing, showing its lack of logical sustainability. The implicit fallacy was, among others, famously challenged by the American philosopher John Rogers Searle (1932–…) with the "Chinese room" scenario, (Searle 1980): a person in a closed room, receives Chinese characters through a slot in the door, process them according to an instructions book, and produce Chinese characters as output. This person passes the Turing test without really knowing any Chinese.

All these discussions may be very interesting, but they are in fact irrelevant. The important point is that, after Turing, inside the computer science field, the controversies and details implied by the "intelligence" claim were discarded, and the Turing test enthusiastically adopted by most experts in the field as the necessary excuse. After all, it was a cheap and easy way to avoid the intricate and eccentric philosophical discussions about thought. Without any sufficient proof of the logical validity of the reasoning, and even without ever really taking seriously the game, the Turing suggestion was assumed as a free license for the construction of an artificial intelligence. The path was cleared for the project to go on. It would start six years after, in Dartmouth.

7.1.4 The Unnecessary Wall

Despite the flawed logical support, history would prove Turing was much too careful. The field was so eager to adopt the inflated claim that the wall separating the interrogator from the interrogated was unnecessary. Even in cases where the observers knew perfectly well that they were communicating with a computer, there was a natural tendency to identify the conversation as human-like. This is what the field came to call the "ELIZA effect" (Hofstadter 1996).

One of the first programs to claim approval in the Turing test, in the vague and unformal way it was always used, was the ELIZA chatbot. Created in 1966 by MIT computer scientist Joseph Weizenbaum (1923–2008), it was programmed to emulate the famous Rogerian therapy, pioneered by the American psychologist Carl Rogers (1902–1987). What the machine did was to rephrase the human answers as new questions or statements. This created an empathic relationship, as the repetition of the person's declarations implies understanding. The author himself explains:

> «With ELIZA as the basic vehicle, experiments may be set up in which the subjects find it credible to believe that the responses which appear on his typewriter are generated by a human sitting at a similar instrument in another room. (...) On the other hand, suppose the subject is told he is communicating with a machine. What is he led to believe about the machine as a result of his conversational experience with it? Some subjects have been very hard to convince that ELIZA (with its present script) is *not* human. This is a striking form of Turing's test. (…). ELIZA shows, if nothing else, how easy it is to create and maintain the illusion of understanding, hence perhaps of judgment deserving of credibility. A certain danger lurks there» (Weizenbaum 1966, pp. 42–43)

This phenomenon has been studied in many aspects. The important point, for our purpose, is to show how prone humans are to project their humanity in the objects around. Persons always make an anthropomorphic interpretation of reality, as the fables of old clearly illustrate. This also helps explain the popularity of the outlandish pretension of artificial intelligence. We are all hard-wired to believe it. All it took were very ambitious and not very rigorous scientists for the myth to take hold.

7.2 Anti-Humanism of AI

The previous section sketched the reasons for the origin and popularity of the unsustainable belief in artificial intelligence. Now it is necessary to consider the negative implications of such assumption. The fact that these methods and techniques, very useful as they are, were grouped under the misleading umbrella of "thinking machines" was not a neutral choice. It proceeded from a particular ideological attitude and generated serious consequences. Strangely enough, the main practitioners of the area seem now to be the main victims.

Both the origin and the results of this choice of name may be considered from many points of view. Here only the perspective of humanism will be assessed, which allows for a deeper and fundamental analysis. If fact, the main logical element in the intellectual project of building mechanisms may be deemed as a form of anti-humanism, which then translates into social, political, economic and many other impacts.

What is the humanistic perspective? "Humanism" is a very equivocal word. Just like "democracy", "liberalism", or "rationality", it forms a wide tent were very diverse, and even opposite positions may find shelter.[10] Jean Paul Sartre says his "existentialism is a humanism", (Sartre, 1946), while Pope Francis, from the opposite side of the philosophical spectrum, exhorts: «We urgently need a humanism capable of bringing together the different fields of knowledge, including economics, in the service of a more integral and integrating vision» (Francis 2015). It is hard to know exactly what is meant by the term. We may even conclude, with Heidegger, that it is best to abandon the expression altogether.

> «You ask: *Comment redonner un sens au mot 'Humanisme'?* This question proceeds from your intention to retain the word 'humanism'; I wonder whether that is necessary. Or is the damage caused by all such terms still not sufficiently obvious?» (Heidegger 1945)

Humanism may be a name beyond salvation. Even so, something precise may spring from this debate. Whatever the exact meaning one gives to the word, and there are many, (Copson 2015), one can be certain of two things: it is an axiological doctrine, and it has to do with humanity. "Humanism", in its assorted and contradictory senses, explicit puts human persons centre stage. This common characteristic,

---

[10] Fioravante and Vaccaro (2025) define, not "Humanism" but "Dehumanization", as "acting towards other individuals or groups as less worthy of human attributes and human treatment".

beneath the intense debates among the humanistic stances, is enough to allow for the second point of this paper, its connection with artificial intelligence.

7.2.1 *The Ideological Attitude*

As said above, the project of AI is undoubtedly a very powerful, influential, and useful piece of technology. It already has contributed richly to the progress of our societies and economies, drastically changing lots of activities, and promising even more remarkable advances in the near future. Some old and stubborn problems of humanity, from disease to translation or location, may be about to be solved, or at least helped, by the new powerful algorithms. It is easy to get excited about AI.

Despite that, if we centre our analysis on the core logic of the field, one must admit that it, not only is alien to humanism, but may even be seen as opposed to it. The problem is not related to the methodologies, effects, consequences or even purpose of this whole venture, but to its central conception and substance. The nature of AI is not humanist and may said to be anti-humanistic.

How is it possible to make such a drastic evaluation of such a good technological endeavour? The problem is the basic intellectual attitude. The whole point of this magnificent enterprise was, as said, the creation of a non-human entity capable of replicating, and even surpassing, one of the most crucial characteristics of humanity, the ability to think. That which separate us from other physical being, our reason, will be able to create a clone of itself in a non-human, inanimate entity, with capacity to exceed its maker.

From the start, the subject of this endeavour was not humanity or human beings, but machines. Returning to the original statement of intentions of the *Dartmouth Summer Research Project on Artificial Intelligence*, quoted above, the closest thing we have to an original vision of the field, one element is obvious: these men wanted to make intelligent machines. Why?

The purpose and justification are not described, and the 23-page document presents no discussion of the motivations to achieve this attempt to challenge humans at what they hold most defining. If there was a thorough humanistic motive justifying the effort, it was not addressed. The proposal is all about instruments and processes, not justifications. And those instruments and processes were not human.

He can take these efforts as clear examples of the vices of "scientism" and "technicism", which appear when researchers get so captured by the beauty of the means to lose sight of the purposes. "Technology for technology's sake" is a paradoxical sentence, but one that can easily arise.

If most of the actors in this area were technicians, centred on "what is possible" and not on "why do it", some early discussions express a much well-defined purpose, also more explicitly anti-humanistic. To find it we must travel six years, back to the seminal 1950 paper by Alan Turing, considered the roadmap for the enterprise. Strangely, but also astutely, as seen, the author does not enter at all in a discussion of what "thinking is", and even less why it would be a good idea to have machines do it. Nevertheless, the Turing approach adds a new element to this humanistic discussion.

When debating the several arguments against his solution, the mathematician and computer scientist adds the challenge that this endeavour will imply to humanity's prominence. This aspect, although obvious, will not be explicit in the future "Proposal":

> «We like to believe that Man is in some subtle way superior to the rest of creation. It is best if he can be shown to be *necessarily* superior, for then there is no danger of him losing his commanding position. The popularity of the theological argument is clearly connected with this feeling. It is likely to be quite strong in intellectual people, since they value the power of thinking more highly than others, and are more inclined to base their belief in the superiority of Man on this power. I do not think that this argument is sufficiently substantial to require refutation. Consolation would be more appropriate: perhaps this should be sought in the transmigration of souls» (Turing 1950, p. 444)

It is interesting to notice that these questions are classified under the caption "theological argument", which shows a curious confusion between anthropology and theology.[11] Anyway, the anti-humanistic element is very visible. Somehow, Turing although human, is not very interested in "Man's commanding position", probably because he believes he can still live his life happily under the new mechanical commanders.

When presenting this view, Turing is not original. He is simply copying a bearing which had become standard in some scientific environments in previous decades. We may even say his attitude and purpose can be taken as the fourth, and maybe last, stage of a majestic dehumanizing effort which some authors have attributed to science. The canonical formulation of this stance is usually taken to be Sigmund Freud's, although he was not the creator of the concept[12]:

> «Humanity, in the course of time, has had to endure from the hands of science two great outrages against its naive self-love. The first was when humanity discovered that our earth was not the center of the universe, but only a tiny speck in a world-system hardly conceivable in its magnitude. This is associated in our minds with the name "Copernicus", although Alexandrian science had taught much the same thing. The second occurred when biological research robbed man of his apparent superiority under special creation, and rebuked him with his descent from the animal kingdom and his ineradicable animal nature. This re-valuation, under the influence of Charles Darwin, Wallace, and their predecessors, was not accomplished without the most violent opposition of their contemporaries. But the third and

[11] Much latter, one of the Dartmouth pioneers, the future Nobel Prize winner Herbert Simon (1916–2001), will make a similar theistic attribution when defending himself from attacks against the use of the "intelligence" claim: «There are the questions about how people feel about intelligent machines and their relations to people. These are questions of emotion and value that are not susceptible to demonstration and proof. (…) You don't get very far arguing with a man about his religion, and these are essentially religious issues (…) My own posture has been this: my scientific work, and that of other A.I. researchers, will, in the long run, determine how many of Man's thinking processes can be simulated. I believe that ultimately all of them can, but feel no great urge to try to prove that to others who feel differently. In science, it is the facts that give us the final answers» (Simon 1991, p. 274).

[12] According to Finkelstein (2013), the original author of this thesis is, not Freud, but the German physiologist-polymath Emil du Bois-Reymond (1818–1896).

> most irritating insult is flung at the human mania of greatness by present-day psychological research, which wants to prove to the 'I' that it is not even master in its own home, but is dependent upon the most scanty information concerning all that goes on unconsciously in its psychic life. We psychoanalysts were neither the first, nor the only ones to announce this admonition to look within ourselves. It appears that we are fated to represent it most insistently and to confirm it by means of empirical data which are of importance to every single person. This is the reason for the widespread revolt against our science, the omission of all considerations of academic urbanity, and emancipation of the opposition from all restraints of impartial logic. We were compelled to disturb the peace of the world, in addition, in another manner, of which you will soon come to know» (Freud 1920, pp. 246–247).

Comparing the wording of this with the Turing text it is easy to say that 11 years after Freud's death, the tone and purpose are obviously the same. More than that, the mathematician may be even added as additional participant in the procession of deflators of humanity "naive self-love", after Copernicus, Darwin, and Freud. In line with the cosmological, the biological and the psychological step, there would come an electro-mechanical contribution to the degrading of humanity.

This attribution has its plausibility, but there are two clear differences separating the last step from the previous three. The first difference is methodological. The early authors were scientists, great scientists, each enlarging the knowledge frontier at their respective fields. The 16th century Polish astronomer was only trying to study the skies, with no overt attack on the role of humanity in Creation. Darwin and Freud, as biologist and psychiatrist, were analysing topics closer to human nature, but still scientists accessing the available reality. Their purposes were discovery and knowledge, not ideology; the "outrages" to humanity were simple corollaries of their research, when they were, unwittingly or not, drawn into the acid philosophical debates of their time. Their work must be considered in the realm of methodological hypotheses, with the doctrinal results for humanity's position as mere lateral outcomes.

Contrary, Turing's project of "thinking machines" must be seen as very different. In this endeavour the mathematician presents itself, not as a scientist, but as a technician. His attempt is not to understand reality but to generate a new thinking entity. He is not describing discoveries but stating a mechanical purpose. His obvious onslaught on the position of humanity in the universe will not derive from a research effort, as the three others, but from his original driving purpose. The attack on humanism is the result, not of what he saw in reality, but from what he wants to build. Using the mentioned Fioravante and Vaccaro (2025) definition, we may say we are here clearly in "dehumanizing" territory.

The second difference between the last and the early members of the dehumanizing procession is that the impact on humanity's position would be massively bigger and higher in the Turing project than in the previous studies. To be out of the centre of the universe, the result of the evolution of species or even influenced by unconscious psychological processes is much less dramatic that having to divide the world with other intelligent beings, in particular ones as relentless and powerful as mechanisms. Freud saw the succession as a progression, but this last jump, made after his death, is by far the largest. AI is thus the ultimate anti-humanistic enterprise.

From these promising initial steps, rose all the story of artificial intelligence, which an early description, (Crevier 1993), called "tumultuous". Time and again the issue of anti-humanism would come to the fore. In fact, having such a purpose, every advance raised the question of the implicit challenge to humanity. In no small measure, understandably, this research was always involved in hubris, boasts, inflated egos and expectations.[13]

This ideology, more or less hidden, always accompanied the leaps and bounds of the field. The extreme version of the thesis, one that dramatically confirms the anti-humanism, may be found, not in some early predictions of the forerunners, but in a very recent declaration of a 21st century reference of the field. Geoffrey Hinton (1947–...) was the creator of artificial neural networks, winner of the 2018 Turing Award, the Nobel of computing, professor at the University of Toronto and research at Google Brain. On May 3, 2023, at the "The Future of Intelligence", the EmTech conference of the MIT Technology Review, Hinton said "I think it's quite conceivable that humanity is just a passing phase in the evolution of intelligence."[14] It is hard to get more anti-humanistic than this.

7.2.2 Theophoric Aspirations of AI

The ideology which motivated the use of the intelligence claim has another twist which separates it even more from the previous dehumanizing scientific efforts of the Freud's succession. This also adds another, a bit more subtle, reason why artificial intelligence can be considered anti-humanistic, now in a narrower sense. The element is connected to the implicit role of God in the project.

As said above, there are many senses the word "humanism" may take. In early days, two definitions dominate the field.

> «On its entry into English it carried two separate and distinct meanings. On the one hand, in historical works like those of Jacob Burckhardt[15] and J. A. Symonds,[16] it was applied retrospectively to the revival of classical learning in the European Renaissance and the tradition of thought ignited by that revival. Its second meaning referred to a more contemporary attitude of mind. It is 'humanism' in this second sense that we are concerned with here.

[13] A case in point from the early days illustrate how damaging to objectivity those brags were: «The Perceptron first existed as a simulation in an IBM 704 computer. In 1958, Rosenblatt [Frank Rosenblatt (1928–1971)] introduced it to the press with the distinctive flourish that eventually brought the wrath of the scientific community upon him. Under the title "Human Brains Replaced?" the prestigious magazine *Science* reported on the invention as "no ordinary mechanical mind which stores up information and regurgitates it ... Perceptron may eventually be able to learn, make decisions, and translate languages" (Science, 21 July 1958, p. 50)» (Crevier 1996, p. 103).

[14] https://www.technologyreview.com/2023/05/03/1072589/video-geoffrey-hinton-google-ai-risk-ethics/.

[15] Carl Jacob Christoph Burckhardt (1818–1897), a Swiss historian of art and culture, mainly known by his *The Civilization of the Renaissance in Italy* (1860).

[16] John Addington Symonds Jr. (1840–1893), an English poet and cultural historian of the Renaissance.

Throughout the nineteenth century the content of this latter 'humanism', the holders of which attitude were now also called 'humanists', was far from systematized, and the word often referred generically to a range of attitudes to life that were non-religious, non-theistic, or non-Christian» (Copson 2015, pp. 1–2).

It is undeniable that, whatever the latter evolution, originally "humanism" means "non-theism". Even in the first sense, connected to ancient civilization, it presupposes the effort to evade the Christian approach to reality, dominant at the time. But if this is the case, couldn't we say AI is humanistic?

Paradoxically enough, the anti-humanism of AI in the first sense, the effort to replace humans, may be seen as connected to another type of anti-humanism, now of a theistic sort. In fact, AI implies a form of theophany, where the researcher assumes a god-like position.

We already saw how Turing and Simon, two of the founders, related AI to theology and religion. But the statements of another one of the pioneers of the field clarify this position. Marvin Minsky, the Dartmouth pioneer, and a central figure of most posterior developments in the field, was always an outspoken atheist, regularly accusing religions of many evils.[17] It turns out such spiritual views have obvious connections with his AI research.

«Marvin Minsky of MIT "believes that humans are nothing but meat machines that carry a computer in their head" also made of meat. Minsky, who is an atheist and works in the field of Artificial Intelligence (AI), "claimed that people should give their money to AI research rather than their churches, as only AI would truly give them eternal life." [Anne Forest, *God in the Machine: What Robots Teach us About Humanity and God* (New York: Dutton/Penguine Group, 2004), 43.]»[18]

The first element of this quote refers to a crucial axiom of the field, which is frequently omitted: it is only possible to have artificial intelligence if human intelligence is reducible to physicochemical processes. Behind all efforts to create a real thinking machine is the old materialistic reductionist hypothesis that "the brain secretes thought just as the liver secretes bile."[19] The alternative position, the dualistic view, assuming humans as composed of body and soul, was always, and still is dominant, both in philosophy and culture. Of course, if it is the soul or the mind that, although through the physical brain, has consciousness and reason, then artificial intelligence would never be possible. The choice between both views is, as

[17] Among many other expressions, a very clear is in the obituary tribute of the site space.com, written by Robert Lawrence Kuhn on March 04, 2016, quoting a 1999 Minsky interview with the author: «"The trouble with religion is that it picks particular things, like 'why are we here?' or 'what created the world?' or 'what should we do in various conditions?'" he began. "But these can be studied and understood by thinking more. … If a lot of people believe something and it's complicated [like religion], then it's unlikely that they thought of it themselves. So it's probably an infectious mental disease, a little network of ideas like a virus that knows how to jump from brain to brain and spread"». https://www.space.com/32153-god-artificial-intelligence-and-the-passing-of-marvin-minsky.html.

[18] https://americanvision.org/posts/ai-and-god-S-revelation/.

[19] The original formulation of this motto is attributed to the French philosopher Pierre Jean Georges Cabanis (1757–1808), in his 1802 book *Rapports du physique et du moral de l'homme* (On the relations between the physical and moral aspects of man).

said, not scientific, but philosophical. Minsky, along with most of his colleagues, chooses a mechanist vision of human thought and mind, which can then be reproduced electronically.[20]

Returning to the Minsky quote, the first part looks very "humanistic", in the non-theistic sense. But the problem results from the second section, which should be seen as a natural deduction of the first. If humans are just machines, then the researcher, while building electro-mechanical clones of minds, assumes the role of God. In fact, the accusation of "playing God" accompanies the field since its inception. And this creates some serious quibbles with the non-theistic humanists.

Examples of this divine assumption abound. The *Whole Earth Catalogue* was one of the most influential early publications in the area,[21] edited by the American visionary Stewart Brand (1938–…). The first sentence of the editorial of the first number, September 1st, 1968, is: «We are gods and might as well get used to it».[22] Almost fifty years later, in September 2015, the former artificial intelligence expert at Google Anthony Levandowski (1980–…) created a religious institution, dissolved in 2021,[23] called *Way of the Future*, aiming to "develop and promote the realization of a Godhead based on Artificial Intelligence."[24]

This is another paradox of the field. A discipline which started as an electro-mechanic project, implicitly rejecting any transcendence of the human soul, thus following the humanistic non-theistic tradition, becomes a form of worship, asking machines to solve the deepest mysteries of humanity. This result is anti-humanistic in all the senses of the word. Not only it is rejected by the atheistic humanism, as being religious, but also by all the other versions of humanism as minimizing human autonomy and independence.

---

[20] For the alternative vision, see the recent European Union report on the issue: «The term 'autonomy' stems from philosophy and refers to the capacity of human persons to legislate for themselves, to formulate, think and choose norms, rules and laws for themselves to follow. (…) They typically entail the features of self-awareness, self-consciousness and self-authorship according to reasons and values. Autonomy in the ethically relevant sense of the word can therefore only be attributed to human beings. It is therefore somewhat of a misnomer to apply the term 'autonomy' to mere artefacts, albeit very advanced complex adaptive or even 'intelligent' systems» (EU 2018, p. 9).

[21] «When I was young, there was an amazing publication called *The Whole Earth Catalog*, which was one of the bibles of my generation». Steven Jobs (1955–2011), speaking to Stanford graduates in June 12, 2005 https://academyatthelakes.org/wp-content/uploads/2016/02/SteveJobsatStanfordUniversityExcerpts.pdf.

[22] https://monoskop.org/images/0/09/Brand_Stewart_Whole_Earth_Catalog_Fall_1968.pdf.

[23] https://www.theverge.com/2021/2/19/22291769/anthony-levandowski-church-closed-artificial-intelligence-waymo-uber.

[24] https://www.wired.com/story/god-is-A-bot-and-anthony-levandowski-is-his-messenger/.

7.2.3 AI and the Future of Humanity

The two previous sections were concerned with the implicit ideology in the AI claim. Now is time to look at the anti-humanistic elements of the perceived consequences.

The group of methodologies grouped under the AI umbrella are, of course, technologies. And, like all technologies, the final purpose of these algorithms is to improve the life and welfare of humanity.[25] On the other hand, all technology aims at surpassing human abilities. Through machines, even the crudest ones, human beings achieve many results which would be impossible otherwise. Why is AI different from the stone axe, the steam engine, atomic energy, or the internet? The anti-humanist indictment may thus be seen as too harsh, even unfair. Are not the beneficial results enough to exempt AI from such charges?

In fact, when we leave the conceptual area to consider the practical improvements, which is where the role of technology should be evaluated, still the anti-humanists shadow remains dominant; darker the more we advance in the project.

From the start of the endeavour there were warnings from the experts about the dangers involved. Norbert Wiener (1894–1964), the founder of cybernetics, was particularly explicit in his 1950 classic, contemporaneous of the Turing paper:

> «The new industrial revolution is a two-edged sword. It may be used for the benefit of humanity, but only if humanity survives long enough to enter a period in which such a benefit is possible. It may also be used to destroy humanity, and if it is not used intelligently, it can go very far in that direction. There are, however, hopeful signs on the horizon. (...) There are many dangers still ahead, but the roots of good will are there, and I do not feel as thoroughly pessimistic» (Wiener 1950, p. 162)

Later came the formal attacks on the notion of "artificial intelligence" made, not by philosophers, but by practitioners themselves.[26] These particularly hurt because they came from very respected authorities, like the mathematician Richard E. Bellman (1920–1984), author of the pivotal Bellman equation, and Weizenbaum of ELIZA fame. Nevertheless, as said, all these could, and were, discarded as "arguing with a man about his religion" (Simon 1991, p. 274). So, the caravan continued.

This fact is understandable. What is more alarming is that the tone and urgency of warnings has been rising. Strangely enough, the recent advent of the large language models of ChatGPT fame, provoked several of the most influential experts of the field to alert everybody of the terrible results their efforts may bring down upon humanity.

On March 22nd, 2023, a thousand technological leaders and researchers, including some of the most prestigious name of the field,[27] lately enlarged to tens of thousands,

---

[25] This statement is, of course, humanistic in nature, and is challenged by the "technicist" view. If methods are more important than purposes, then techniques become ends in themselves, and their impact on humanity is secondary or even irrelevant, as in the quoted Turing criticism of the "superiority of Man".

[26] The most significant are Taube (1961), Dreyfus (1965), Dreyfus (1972), Weizenbaum (1976). Bellman (1978) and Dreyfus & Dreyfus (1986). These are the attacks Simon mentions in the above quote.

[27] The first signatories include figures like Yoshua Bengio (1964–...), Founder and Scientific Director at MILA and 2018 Turing Award winner and professor at University of Montreal; Stuart

published "Pause Giant AI Experiments: An Open Letter", asking for a moratorium of large AI[28] due to their high risks.

Less than 70 days later, on May 30th, 2023, another group of hundreds of eminencies[29] published a document of just 22 words, "Statement on AI Risk,"[30] warning for the risks of extinction of humanity.[31] According to the most remarkable authorities in the field, AI is one of the most anti-humanist menaces in history.

Another of the visionaries of recent times had already expressed similar concerns. Stephen Hawking (1942–2018), the famous cosmologist, in one of his last public appearances, through a video conference in the Web Summit on November 6, 2017, in Lisbon, a few months before his death, said:

> «Success in creating effective AI, could be the biggest event in the history of our civilization. Or the worst. We just don't know. So we cannot know if we will be infinitely helped by AI, or ignored by it and side-lined, or conceivably destroyed by it. Unless we learn how to prepare for, and avoid, the potential risks, AI could be the worst event in the history of our civilization. It brings dangers, like powerful autonomous weapons, or new ways for the few to oppress the many. It could bring great disruption to our economy»[32]

It is thus easy to see that the question of anti-humanism of AI is much larger than just the dreams of some technological futurists. Once these dreams started coming to fruition, the same experts went panicking about their creations. What started as a Pinocchio project (Collodi 1883), turned into a contemporaneous version of the *Frankenstein* novel (Shelley 1818), where the scientists are destroyed by the results of their own experiments. It is hard to find a more damning condemnation of this project than these words of some of its main contemporaneous exponents.

7.3 The Significance of AI Applications

The final element of this approach is to briefly consider the real results of the original AI techniques. As technologies, it is in their ability to generate productivity enhancement that their verdict lies. This will reveal how anti-humanistic they were in their original conception, even if they managed to turn into very useful methods.

Russell (1962–...), Professor of Computer Science at Berkeley, director of the Center for Intelligent Systems, and co-author of the standard textbook *Artificial Intelligence: a Modern Approach*; Elon Musk (1971–...), CEO of SpaceX, Tesla & Twitter; Steve Wozniak (1950–...), Co-founder, Apple and Yuval Noah Harari (1976–...), Author and Professor, Hebrew University of Jerusalem and author of *Homo Deus: A Brief History of Tomorrow* (Harvill Secker, 2015)

[28] https://futureoflife.org/open-letter/pause-giant-ai-experiments/.

[29] Including figures like Bill Gates (1955–...), co-founder of Microsoft, Demis Hassabis (1976–...), CEO of Google DeepMind, Sam Altman (1985–...), CEO of OpenAI, creator of ChatGPT, as well as two of the 2018 winners of the Turing Award, Geoffrey Hinton and again Yoshua Bengio.

[30] https://www.safe.ai/statement-on-ai-risk.

[31] The text is voluntarily minuscule: «Mitigating the risk of extinction from AI should be a global priority alongside other societal-scale risks such as pandemics and nuclear war.»

[32] https://www.youtube.com/watch?v=E3efC-IpBo0.

The initial purpose was not to help humanity, but to enjoy in the exciting project of replacing it. Then much more practical approaches ensued.

This attitude gives rise to two elements which will be described briefly. The first are the already mentioned tumultuous swings of the first decades, with a sequence of booms and busts surrounding the area. The second, more worrying, is the surprising lack of real results for the effective trajectory of the economy.

7.3.1 The AI Roller-Coaster

The 1956 seminar generated no practical purpose or list of achievements because, as said, it achieved no consensus. Nevertheless, there was financing,[33] mostly from the military, through the Office of Naval Research and the Advanced Research Projects Agency (ARPA, later called DARPA). The problem with these first projects was, not the lack of results, but the lack of usefulness of these results.

> «While these AI experiments of the 1960s and early 1970s were fun to watch and probably even enjoyable to create, it soon became clear that the techniques they employed would not be useful apart from dealing with carefully simplified problems in restricted areas. Not surprisingly, the U.S. military, one of the main sponsors of early AI research, was also one of the first to have second thoughts. Tech Square, and other centers that had sprung up around the world with high hopes of early success, soon found themselves fighting for their very survival. Human intelligence, whatever it was, was not about to yield its secrets quickly» (Crevier 1993, p. x)

This gave rise to the first "AI winter,"[34] a period of reduced funding and interest in this research. There would be other busts, but the first one was the most significant as it may be said to have drastically reduced the anti-humanistic element in the field. The efforts of 1960s and 1970s were to create a mechanic mind. This turned out to be much fun but mostly useless. In fact, this attitude ties to a crucial characteristic of computer efforts, which may be called the "Feynman disease", as it was described by Nobel Prize winner physicist Richard Phillips Feynman (1918–1988) in 1985, reporting on his work at Los Alamos National Laboratory from 1943 to 1945:

> "[There is a] computer disease that anybody who works with computers now knows about. It's a very serious disease and it interferes completely with the work. The trouble with computers is you *play* with them. They are so wonderful. You have these switches - if it's an even number you do this, if it's an odd number you do that - and pretty soon you can do more and more elaborate things if you are clever enough, on one machine. (…). But if you've ever worked with computers, you understand the disease - the *delight* in being able to see how much you can do» (Leighton and Feynman 1985, part 3).

The good result of the first "AI winter" was that the field only recovered when it changed its ways and adopted a much more humanistic attitude. This was achieved,

---

[33] The proposal itself list a grant from the Rockefeller Foundation to the tune of 13,500 US.

[34] This expression was first used in 1984, as the title of a public debate at the fourth annual meeting of the American Association of Artificial Intelligence (AAAI), from August 6–10.

first through the birth of the "expert systems" and later by "deep learning" and "big data".

> «Inside the computer science community, people gave up on general AI in the 1990s. General AI is now called Good Old-Fashioned Artificial Intelligence (GOFAI). Narrow AI is what we actually have. Narrow AI is purely mathematical. It's less exciting than GOFAI, but it works surprisingly well and we can do a variety of interesting things with it. However, the linguistic confusion is significant. Machine learning, a popular form of AI, is not GOFAI. Machine learning is narrow AI. The name is confusing. Even to me, the phrase machine learning still suggests there is a sentient being in the computer» (Broussard 2018, chapter 7).

The name remained and practitioners continued to pay lip-service to the purpose of thinking machines; but now the issues were eminently pragmatic, devising algorithms to solve concrete questions. The anti-humanistic purpose may be said to have subsided.

The story of these new expert systems, some of them directly developed in companies, outside of the academic original nest, was also to be bumpy. There was even a second "AI winter" in the late 1980s and early 1990s (Crevier 1993, p. 203), but now things were and stayed much more pragmatic. The creation of thinking beings was replaced by the purpose of making useful and profitable applications. GOFAI seemed dead and forgotten.

Nevertheless, the old dream was still vivid. This is shown by the recent reactions to the new language models. One must say, as Broussard said about machine learning, that LLMs "are not GOFAI", they are narrow AI. Nevertheless, like with their grandmother ELIZA, people start treating them as sentient beings. The mentioned alarms following the impact of ChatGPT and clones are enough to illustrate how much the myth of Turing "thinking machines" is ingrained in our subconscious; even in the case of those which, being experts, should have known better.[35] Significantly, there are already some clear economic signs that the hype generated after by the new LLMs is turning into a new winter.[36]

7.3.2 *The Minuscule Bottom Line*

The final evaluation of the humanistic character of a technology is, as said, done through the measurement of the benefits it has on the life and prosperity of humanity.

[35] A very relevant exception is the third 2018 Turing award, the French Yann LeCun, Professor at New York University and Vice-President, Chief AI Scientist at Meta. He is openly critical of the alarmist positions of his colleagues, considering them "preposterously ridiculous." https://www-technologyreview-com.cdn.ampproject.org/c/s/www.technologyreview.com/2023/06/20/1075075/metas-ai-leaders-want-you-to-know-fears-over-ai-existential-risk-are-ridiculous/amp/.

[36] "Your job is (probably) safe from artificial intelligence. Why predictions of an imminent economic revolution are overstated", *The Economist*, edition of May 7th 2023, https://www.economist.com/finance-and-economics/2023/05/07/your-job-is-probably-safe-from-artificial-intelligence; "How businesses are actually using generative AI. Some experiments with chatbots are more useful than others", *The Economist*, edition of February 29th, 2024, https://www.economist.com/business/2024/02/29/how-businesses-are-actually-using-generative-ai.

Omitting all the hype and hubris resulting from the inflated egos of some researchers, what remains is the production generated by the machines.

What are the concrete economical results of AI? Omitting all the headlines, promises and myths, after almost 70 years of investments, research, and implementations, what is the real bottom line of all these enterprises? Surprisingly enough, when we enter this arid field of economic evaluation, we still find lots of ambiguity, subjectivity, and ideologies. A recent survey of the field summarizes the problem in a trilogy of positions.

> «Interestingly, at first glance, ideas around AI in economics can be grouped into three streams. From many consulting organizations' points of view, AI has great potential to enhance human life quality and economic growth, and the natural implication is that industries, investors, and consumers should embrace it as a blessing (BCG 2015; MGI 2017). However, policymakers are more concerned with its impact on employment, in that jobs might be destroyed and workers might be replaced by AI. Meanwhile, most economists seem to be on neither side, and tend to be more cautious about the future AI world. This cautiousness is due mainly to empirical studies using recent data. Crafts and Mills (2017) found that total factor productivity (TFP) growth has declined steadily from 1.5% to 1.0% per year over the past 50 years. Since the late 1990s, and after the Global Financial Crisis (GFC) in particular, almost all OECD countries have experienced a slowdown in labor productivity growth. This slowdown is also true in emerging and developing economies, whose productivity growth accelerated during the 2000s then peaked around the time of the GFC (Syverson 2017). This creates a paradox between the potential of a highly automated world in the future and the sad reality of the current economic slowdown, which is referred to, by Gordon (2016), Brynjolfsson et al. (2019), and many others, as the Solow (1987) Paradox» (Lu and Zhou 2021, p. 1047).

The most troubling element of this undefinition is that, almost 40 years after it was formulated, the ironic contradiction presented by one of the best scholars in economic dynamics is still valid. Robert Solow (1924–2023), the 1987 Nobel Prize winner in Economics, famously said «You can see the computer age everywhere but in the productivity statistics» (Solow 1987). Much has changed in society and in the computer age, but both elements of the phrase still stand: computers are ever more visible in our everyday life and in all stages of the production process. On the other hand, labour productivity numbers stubbornly refuse to show the expected benefits.

Of course, this simple idea has generated lots of research and many solutions to the paradox, as in the papers mentioned in the quote. People talk about measurement problems, delays in applications, problems of diffusion, lags in learning and adaptation, even the distraction effects of technology on workers. But a recent book-form diagnosis places the blame for the reduced productivity directly in the arrogance of the AI claim:

> «Digital technologies are general purpose and can be developed in many different ways. In steering their direction, we should focus on how useful they are to human objectives. –what we will call "machine usefulness." Encouraging the use of machines and algorithms to complement human capabilities and empower people has, in the past, led to breakthrough innovations with high machine usefulness. In contrast, infatuation with machine intelligence encourages mass-scale data collection, the disempowerment of workers and citizens and a scramble to automate work, even when this is no more than so-so automation –meaning that it has only small productivity benefits. Not coincidently, automation and large-scale data

collection enrich those who control digital technologies» (Acemoglu and Johnson 2023, pp. 299–300).

What is true is that the idyllic world where machines would do all the work and humans can enjoy themselves is now more distant than it looked in 1956. People, even experts, talk, not of paradise, but of apocalypse.

This is not the place to discuss such matters. What is important is that, once again, there is an evident gap between myth and reality when talking about AI. Only those who really believe in GOFAI, and consequently are radically anti-humanistic, do not get worried about this evolution.

7.4 Conclusions

Technology is not a predetermined necessity, a path we are force to follow. It is a social, political, and economic choice, an instrument to be used for the welfare of mankind. But, at the same time, there is a fascination with machines, a technicist ideology of progress which sometimes takes hold of a field, replacing the dignity of humanity for some ideal machinery purpose.

The field of AI started with a very clear and daring purpose: the creation of a mechanic, artificial entity able to reason. The motivations of such a troubling project were seldom explicit, but it was certainly great fun to play God. In less than three quarters of a century the evolution was undoubtedly extraordinary. The AI algorithms are today omnipresent and most of us benefit largely from their results.

It is true no artificial brain was ever built, productivity is not rising, and we are today as far from real general AI as in the 1950s. Nevertheless, strangely enough, the dreams and the terrors generated by this project are almost the same as they were in the old days. The 2022 ChatGPT generated as much controversy, expectations, and accusations as the 1958 Perceptron.

The crucial element seems to be that the claim of an artificial intelligence, with its evident anti-humanistic elements, may be said to have poisoned the entire field. When technology stops serving mankind and aims to create its own reference and purpose, whatever gains are achieved, the menaces remain.

Of course, there is another approach which, without losing any of the benefits from technology, has the purpose to access problems without the arrogance of building super-human entities. This approach is best summarized in a simple motto: «No man is better than a machine, and no machine is better than a man with a machine». This, without negating the power of the new technologies, places them at the service of mankind. Significantly, the origin of the phrase is connected, not the technical and engineering sectors, but to the economic and financial world.[37]

[37] The authorship of this phrase has been attributed to several persons, but the most quoted are the millionaire investor Paul Tudor Jones II (1954–…), founder of the Tudor Investment Corporation and the MIT professor of economics Richard Bookstaber (1950–…) in his book *The End of Theory* (Princeton University Press, 2017).

Even in the computer science field, this lesson is gaining ground. Many in the new generation of experts seem to follow such a line. Fernando Pereira (1956–…), a researcher in natural language and Google vice-president since 2016, said recently in an interview:

> «I do not like to use the term "intelligence" in these contexts, because it raises too many philosophical questions. Anyone who worked in these areas since the 1970's must be very humble, and cannot make assertions saying this or that is intelligent»[38]

References

Acemoglu D, Johnson S (2023) Power and progress. Our thousand-year struggle over technology and prosperity. Basic Books.

BCG (2015) Industry 4.0: the future of productivity and growth in manufacturing industries. Technical Report. Boston Consulting Group.

Bellman R (1978) Artificial Intelligence: Can computers think? Boyd & Fraser

Broussard M (2018) Artificial unintelligence: how computers misunderstand the world. The MIT Press, Cambridge, MA

Brynjolfsson E, Rock D, Syverson C (2019) Artificial intelligence and the modern productivity paradox: a clash of expectations and statistics. In Agrawal G, Goldfarb (eds) The economics of artificial intelligence: an agenda. Chicago, USA: National Bureau of Economic Research, Inc, pp 23–57

Collodi C (1883) Le avventure di Pinocchio. Storia di un burattino. Paggi, Firenze

Copeland BJ (ed) (2004) The essential turing: seminal writings in computing, logic, philosophy, artificial intelligence, and artificial life: plus the secrets of enigma. Oxford University Press, New York

Copson A (2015) What is humanism? In: Copson A, Grayling AC (eds) The Wiley Blackwell handbook of humanism, 1st edn. John Wiley & Sons, New York

Crafts N, Mills TC (2017) Predicting medium-term TFP growth in the United States: econometrics vs 'techno-optimism.' Natl Inst Econ Rev 242(1):R60–R67

Crevier D (1993) AI: The tumultuous history of the search for artificial intelligence. Basic Books, New York

Dreyfus H (1965) Alchemy and artificial intelligence. RAND Corporation, Santa Monica

Dreyfus H (1972) What computers can't do: The limits of artificial intelligence. Harper & Row, New York

Dreyfus H, Dreyfus S (1986) Mind over machine: the power of human intuition and expertise in the era of the computer. Free Press, New York

European Union (2018) Statement on artificial intelligence, robotics and autonomous' systems. https://op.europa.eu/en/publication-detail/-/publication/dfebe62e-4ce9-11e8-be1d-01aa75ed71a1

Finkelstein G (2013) Emil du Bois-Reymond: neuroscience, self, and society in nineteenth-century Germany. MIT Press, Cambridge, MA

Fioravante R, Vaccaro A (2025) Humanism, dehumanization, integral human development: an overview of boundaries and capabilities of human-centered artificial intelligence in business and organizations. In: Fioravante R, Vaccaro A (eds) Humanism and artificial intelligence. Springer

---

[38] *Expresso*, 22 July 2022 (content in Portuguese) https://expresso.pt/economia/2022-07-24-Fernando-Pereira-vice-presidente-da-Google-Muito-do-nosso-trabalho-e-gasto-a-convencer-maquinas-estupidas-a-fazer-o-que-precisamos-f904d99b.

Francis (2015) Encyclical Letter Laudato Si'. Vatican

Freud S (1920) A general introduction to psychoanalysis. Horace Liveright, New York

Gordon R (2016) The rise and fall of American growth: The U.S. standard of living since the civil war. Princeton University Press, Princeton, New Jersey

Heidegger M (1945) Letter on humanism. http://timothyquigley.net/cont/heidegger-lh.pdf

Hodges A (1983) Alan Turing: the enigma. Princeton University Press, New Jersey

Hofstadter DR (1996) Preface 4 the ineradicable Eliza effect and its dangers, epilogue. In: Hofstadter DR (ed) Fluid concepts and creative analogies: computer models of the fundamental mechanisms of thought. Basic Books, New York, pp 155–169

Hopgood AA (2003) Artificial intelligence: hype or reality? Computer, May, 24–28

Jaki SL (1989) Brain, mind and computers, 3rd edn. Gateway Editions, Washington, D.C.

Leighton R, Feynman RP (1985) Surely you're joking, Mr. Feynman!: Adventures of a curious character. W.W. Norton, New York

Lu Y, Zhou Y (2021) A review on the economics of artificial intelligence. J Econ Surv 35(4):1045–1072

McCarthy J, Minsky ML, Rochester N, Shannon CE (1955) A proposal for the Dartmouth Summer research project on artificial intelligence, https://raysolomonoff.com/dartmouth/boxa/dart564props.pdf

MGI (2017) A future that works: Automation, employment, and productivity. Technical Report. McKinsey Global Institute. Retrieved from https://www.mckinsey.com/~/media/McKinsey/Global%20Themes/Digital%20Disruption/Harnessing%20automation%20for%20a%20future%20that%20works/MGI-A-future-that-works_Full-report.ashx

Pascal B (1962) Pensées. Texte établi et annoté par Jacques Chevalier. Livre de Poche, Paris

Sartre JP (1946) L'existentialisme est un humanisme. Les Editions Nagel, Paris

Searle J (1980) Minds, brains and programs. Behav Brain Sci 3:417–457

Shelley M (1818) Frankenstein or, The Modern Prometheus. Lackington, Hughes, Harding, Mavor & Jones, London

Simon H (1991) Models of my life. Basic Books, New York

Solow R (1987) We'd better watch out. New York Times Book Review, July 12, 36

Syverson C (2017) Challenges to mismeasurement explanations for the US productivity slowdown. J Econ Perspec 31(2):165–186

Taube M (1961) Computers and common sense, the myth of thinking machines. Columbia University Press, New York

Turing AM (1936) On computable numbers, with an application to the Entscheidungsproblem. Proc Lond Math Soc 2(42):230–65

Turing AM (1950) Computing machinery and intelligence. Mind, New Series 59(236):433–460

von Neumann J (1958) The computer and the brain. Yale University Press

Weizenbaum J (1966) ELIZA–a computer program for the study of natural language communication between man and machine. Commun ACM 9(1):36–45

Weizenbaum J (1976) Computer power and human reason: from judgment to calculation. W. H. Freeman, San Francisco

Wiener N (1950) The human use of human beings. Cybernetics and society, 2nd edn. Free Association Books, London, 1989

João César das Neves , born in 1957, married, father of four, is full professor and Chair of the Pedagogical Council and the Ethics Commission of the Catolica Lisbon School of Business & Economics at Universidade Católica Portuguesa (UCP) in Lisbon. Holds a PhD and BA in Economics (UCP), MA in Economics (Universidade Nova de Lisboa, Portugal) and MA in Operations Research and System Engineering (Universidade Técnica de Lisboa, Portugal). He was from 1991 to 1995 economic advisor of the Portuguese Prime Minister, in 1990 advisor to the Portuguese Minister of Finance and in 1990/1991 and 1995/1997 technician at the Bank of Portugal. Author of more than 60 books and several scientific papers, he has been a regular commentator at the Portuguese media.

Chapter 8
Nonhuman Persons and Other Things

David J. Gunkel

Abstract In both law and ethics, we typically distinguish between *persons*, who are subjected to and the subjects of the law, from *things*, which are nothing more than objects or property owned by persons. This way of dividing up and categorizing all that exists has been useful and expedient, even if we have, at various times in our history, mistakenly and unfortunately categorized as things that which later came to be seen as other persons. The question that now confronts us in the face of artificial intelligence is whether this new kind of being is to be classified as a thing or instrument that we can use and even abuse as we see fit, whether it should be classified as another person or another kind of person with its own set of rights and responsibilities, or whether it might be something other that is both/and or neither/nor. This chapter will present and evaluate the costs and benefits of all three options and conclude by proposing a moral and legal ontology suitable for responding to and taking responsibility for artificial intelligence.

Keywords Artificial Intelligence · Legal person · Natural person · Slavery · Thing

8.1 Introduction

Artificial intelligence is a curious sort of thing. On the one hand, these systems and devices are designed and manufactured technological artifacts. They are things. And like any of the other things that we encounter and use each and every day, they are typically considered to be objects with instrumental value. Yet, and on the other hand, these things are not quite like other things. They seem to have social presence, they are able to talk and even converse with us, and many are designed to mimic or simulate the capabilities and behaviors that are commonly associated with other socially significant subjects.

So is AI a thing, a technological object that we can use or even abuse as we decide and see fit? Or is it the case that AI can or even should be something like a

D. J. Gunkel (✉)
Northern Illinois University, DeKalb, IL, USA
e-mail: dgunkel@niu.edu

R. Fioravante and A. Vaccaro (eds.), *Humanism and Artificial Intelligence*, SpringerBriefs in Philosophy, https://doi.org/10.1007/978-3-031-85478-1_8

person, i.e. another subject who would need to be recognized as a kind of socially significant Other with some legitimate claim on us? These questions concern not only how we understand the ontology of AI systems (i.e. What they are?) but also how we decide—as individuals and communities—to situate these technologies in social reality.

The following investigates and seeks to respond to these questions. It begins by demonstrating how we typically resolve such inquiry by way of a moral and legal ontology that has deep roots. It then details how robots and other seemingly intelligent artifacts effectively interrupt or resist efforts at both reification and personification, rending AI and similarly situated interactive artifacts something Other, i.e. something does not quite fit or easily accommodate the existing ways of thinking. In response to these documented difficulties, the final part of the chapter evaluates three possible modes of response that can be taken-up and operationalized as we struggle to integrate these technologies into human society and culture.

8.2 Persons and Things

In confronting and dealing with others we inevitably make a decision that has the effect of dividing things into one of two types, arranging an exclusive distinction that separates those others who we are obligated to respect from what remains mere things. As the eighteenth century German philosopher Immanuel Kant described it: "Beings whose existence rests not indeed on our will but on nature, if they are non-rational beings, still have only a relative worth, as means, and are therefore called *things*, whereas rational beings are called *persons*, because their nature already marks them out as ends in themselves, i.e., as something that may not be used merely as means, and hence to that extent limits all choice (and is an object of respect)" (Kant 2012, p. 40).

But even if you've never read Kant's moral philosophy, this just sounds intuitively correct. We go out into the world and deal with others, knowing there's a difference between other persons to whom we owe respect as ends in themselves and those things that are mere objects with instrumental value as a means to an end. As Robert Esposito (2015, p. 1), who arguably wrote the book on this subject, explains: "If there is one assumption that seems to have organized human experience from its very beginnings it is that of a division between persons and things. No other principle is so deeply rooted in our perception and in our moral conscience as the conviction that we are not things—because things are the opposite of persons." This is not just good reasoning, it's the law. In fact, the binary distinction separating who is a person from what is a thing has been the ruling conceptual opposition in both moral philosophy and jurisprudence for close to 2000 years. When the Roman jurist Gaius (130–180 CE), in a legal treatise he titled *Institutes*, explained that law involved two kinds of entities, either persons or things, he instituted a fundamental ontological division that has been definitive of Western (but not just Western) moral and legal systems.

Consequently, in the face of others—another human being, a nonhuman animal, a tree, an extraterrestrial, a robots, or a large language model—the first and perhaps most important question that must be addressed and resolved is "What is it?" Is it another *person* similar to another human being, to whom I would be obligated? Or is it just a *thing* that can be taken-up, possessed, and used without any further consideration or concern? Sounds easy enough. But, when it comes to AI and other seemingly intelligent and socially interactive artifacts, this determination turns out to be much easier said than done, as these technologies appear to resist efforts at both reification and personification.

8.3 Things

We all kind of know what things are, such that asking a question like "What is a thing?" seems to be uninteresting and entirely self-evident. But as the German philosopher Martin Heidegger pointed out, this is precisely the problem. Because things are already familiar—perhaps too familiar—we have little or no critical distance on them as things. This is because, as Heidegger (1962, pp. 96–97) explains, things are not typically disclosed to us as things but encountered as objects. In other words, things are not experienced as mere entities laying around out there in the world. They are always pragmatically situated and characterized in terms of our involvements and interactions with the world in which we live. For this reason, things are first and foremost made available to us or revealed as objects for a subject. They are objectified.

The term *object* is crucial in this context. Things are always and already objectified by being situated in opposition to and placed in the service of a human subject. This mode of existence—what Graham Harman (2002) calls "tool-being"—applies not just to artifacts, like hammers, pens, and smartphones. It also describes the basic existential condition of natural objects, which are, as Heidegger (1962, p. 100) explains, discovered in the process of being put to use: "The wood is a forest of timber, the mountain a quarry of rock, the river is water-power, the wind is wind 'in the sails.'" Everything therefore exists and becomes what it is insofar as it is useful for some humanly defined purpose. Things are not just out there in a kind of raw and naked state but come to be what they are in terms of how they have been objectified and put to work or used by us as equipment for living.

This objectivist understanding of things can be correlated with what scholars of media and technology call the "instrumental theory of technology," which Heidegger subsequently addressed in *The Question Concerning Technology*. "We ask the question concerning technology," Heidegger (1977, pp. 4–5) writes, "when we ask what it is. Everyone knows the two statements that answer our question. One says: Technology is a means to an end. The other says: Technology is a human activity. The two definitions of technology belong together. For to posit ends and procure and utilize the means to them is a human activity." According to this explanation, the presumed role and function of any kind of technological object, whether it be a simple mechanical device, like a corkscrew or bicycle, or something more sophisticated, like a digital computer or algorithm, is that it is a means employed by human users for specific ends. As Andrew Feenberg (1991, p. 5) has neatly summarized it, "the instrumentalist theory offers the most widely accepted view of technology. It is based on the common sense idea that technologies are 'tools' standing ready to serve the purposes of users."

Consequently, things—no matter how sophisticated, intelligent, and social they are, appear to be, or may become—are and will continue to be tools of human decision and action, nothing more. If something goes wrong (or goes right) because of the actions or inactions of an AI or some other seemingly intelligent object, there is always someone who is ultimately responsible for what happens with it. Finding that person (or persons) may require sorting through layer upon layer of technological mediation, but there is always someone—specifically, some human someone—who is presumed to be responsible and accountable for it. And this line of reasoning is entirely consistent with current legal practices. "As a tool for use by human beings," Matthew Gladden (2016, p. 184) argues, "questions of legal responsibility... revolve around well-established questions of product liability for design defects (Calverley 2008, 533; Datteri 2013) on the part of its producer, professional malpractice on the part of its human operator, and, at a more generalized level, political responsibility for those legislative and licensing bodies that allowed such devices to be created and used."

Recent technological innvations in AI, however, do not seem to fit easily within this rather tidy theoretical framework. The thing with AI, AI enabled robots, and similar artifacts is that they are or often appear to be something other than mere objects or instruments. Consider the following three examples:

8.3.1 Things that Talk

There are things that talk and appear to use language in ways that appear to be intelligible, like chatbots, digital assistants, and large language models. In fact, the emulation of human conversational behaviors has been the defining condition of machine intelligence since Alan Turing's agenda-setting paper from 1950, "Computing Machinery and Intelligence." Users of these systems often find it difficult to distinguish between human communication mediated through the instrumentality of a computer and conversational behaviors generated by the machine itself. So much so that there have been a number of legislative efforts, stipulating that any and all implementations of what Simone Natale (2021, p. 11) calls "communicative AI" disclose their true artificial nature prior to interacting with human users—a kind of "Warning: I am AI" label. Unlike artificial general intelligence (AGI), which would presumably occupy a subject position reasonably close to that of another human person, these actually existing and ostensibly mindless but very loquacious things simply muddy the water (which is probably worse) by complicating and leaving undecided questions regarding who or what is actually doing the talking.

8.3.2 Things that Think for Themselves

There are things that are deliberately designed to exceed (or at least seem to exceed) the comprehension, oversight, and control of their human developers—things like DeepMind's AlphaGo and its successor AlphaZero, self-driving automobiles and lethal autonomous weapons systems (LAWS), and many other machine learning implementations and algorithms. Although the extent to which one might reasonably assign "autonomy" to these mechanisms remains a contested issue, what is not debated is the fact that the rules of the game seem to be in flux. As Andreas Matthias (2004, p. 177) points out, summarizing his survey of learning automata: "Presently there are machines in development or already in use which are able to decide on a course of action and to act without human intervention. The rules by which they act are not fixed during the production process, but can be changed during the operation of the machine, by the machine itself. This is what we call machine learning." The instrumental theory, which effectively tethers machine decision and action to human persons, no longer adequately applies to or fully explains mechanisms that have been deliberately designed to operate and exhibit some form, no matter how rudimentary, of independent action or autonomous conduct. Contrary to the usual instrumentalist way of thinking, we now have things that have (or at least seem to possess) a mind of their own.

8.3.3 Things that Are More Than Things

There are things that are designed to be and promoted as being something that is more than a mere thing, like robot companions and social robots. In 2014, for instance, social robotics pioneer Cynthia Breazeal introduced the Jibo robot with the following explanation: "This is your car. This is your house. This is your toothbrush. These are your things. But these [and the camera zooms into a family photograph] are the things that matter. And somewhere in between is this guy. Introducing Jibo, the world's first family robot." According to this ontological classification, Jibo is not just another instrument or tool, like the automobile or toothbrush. But he/she/it (and the choice of pronoun is not unimportant) is also not quite another member of the family pictured in the photograph. The social robot inhabits a place in between the two categories of thing and person, becoming what Katrin Etzrodt and Sven Engesser (2021) have called—using a curious mashup of existing terminology—"personified things." This is, it should be noted, not necessarily unprecedented. We are already familiar with other entities that occupy a similar ambivalent social position, like the family dog.

In fact, as Kate Darling (2021) has effectively argued, animals and pets, in particular, provide a good template for understanding the changing nature of things. "Looking at state of the art technology," Darling (2012, p. 1) writes in one of her early essays on the subject, "our robots are nowhere close to the intelligence and complexity of humans or animals, nor will they reach this stage in the near future.

And yet, while it seems far-fetched for a robot's legal status to differ from that of a toaster, there is already a notable difference in how we interact with certain types of robotic objects." This occurs, Darling explains, because of our tendencies to anthropomorphize things by projecting into them cognitive capabilities, emotions, and motivations that do not necessarily exist in the mechanism per se. But it is this inescapable emotional reaction that necessitates new forms of response and responsibility in the face of these things. "It's important," Darling (2021, p. 154) concludes, "to understand that we will treat robots like living things. Our tendency runs deep, and as much as we could decry it and argue against it, it's not going away. When it comes to interacting with machines, even more so than with animals, we know that we're projecting something that's not there, and we do it anyway."

All these "things" (though that word might not be entirely suitable in this context, hence the scare quotes), seem to resist efforts at reification and/or impede classification as an instrument and object. And they do so not only because they have been designed to be or to appear to be (and the difference between "being" and "appearing to be" will not be insignificant) intelligent, autonomous, or social; but also because of our innate (and rather mindless) human tendency to anthropomorphize all kinds of things that are situated in such a way that they seem to have social presence as documented and explained across several decades of research with what Byron Reeves and Clifford Nass have called "the media equation": "When it comes to being social, people are built to make the conservative error: When in doubt, treat it as human. Consequently, any medium that is close enough will get human treatment, even though people know it's foolish and even though they likely will deny it afterwards" (Reeves and Nass 1996, p. 22).

8.4 Persons

If these AI applications and devices are not easily accommodated and contained by the category of "thing," does this mean that they are or should be persons? This question again seems to be direct and immediately understandable. But as was the case with things, the concept of "person" also turns out to be far more interesting and complicated than one might initially anticipate, making answers to this inquiry equally difficult to resolve.

Typically, when we use the word "person," we are referring to another human being. But this seemingly natural and everyday understanding is not entirely accurate. The word "person" has a long and intricate history. It is originally derived from the Latin noun *persona*, which referred to the mask worn by actors in a stage play. As a result of this, "person" denotes not just an individual human being but more accurately names the role that one plays or is assigned within the context of a social situation or performance. This can be seen especially in law, where who is considered a person has not been limited to human individuals but can also be extended to other kinds of non-human entities that occupy or play roles that are important for our shared social reality—corporations, organizations, ships, animals, and the natural environment. In order to account for this important difference, person is often divided into two types: *natural person* and *legal person.*

8.4.1 Natural Person

Whether something is or is not a natural person is usually decided on the basis of individual properties and capabilities—e.g. rationality, consciousness, sentience, etc. So there is a kind of litmus test for achieving recognition as a person. We (and who is interpellated by this first-person plural pronoun will not be insignificant) first define the criteria for what makes an entity a person. In other words, we devise a standard by deciding what we believe are the necessary person-making properties or capabilities. We then use this standard to test and evaluate whether something qualifies as a natural person or not. So the question—whether AI or similar technological systems, like a robot, could ever become natural persons—is a question that we get to evaluate based on criteria that we get to define.

Answers to this question typically divide into a simple and mutually exclusive yes/no set of responses. On the side of "no," there have been efforts to limit who can be included in the category person. According to this way of thinking, no matter how sophisticated AI applications and systems may become or seem to be, they will never actually achieve any of the person-making properties, like consciousness, rationality, or sentience. They might appear to do so through various programmed behaviors that we take as signs of an inner life (e.g. consciousness or sentience), but they do not and cannot really possess the capability that they have been designed to simulate.[1] On the other side, you have those who assert the exact opposite, arguing that artifacts, like AI and other seemingly autonomous systems, either are or will be able to achieve the benchmarks of person. If and when—and it is more often than not a matter of "when"—this happens, then withholding the title of person from these things would be unethical and unjust.

Perhaps the best example of this tension and its significance can be seen with recent events surrounding former Google engineer Blake Lamoine and the LaMDA large language model. In June of 2022, Lemoine claimed that the LaMDA system was conscious and therefore was a person deserving of moral respect and legal consideration. Google—the corporation that funded the research and built LaMDA—took the opposite position, not only arguing that LaMDA, like any computer application, was not conscious but suspending and then eventually firing Lemoine. Both sides in this debate asserted and sought to justify their positions by mobilizing what Mark Coeckelbergh (2012, p. 14) has called the properties approach to deciding moral status. And each side struggled with the same set of problems—accurately defining the qualifying ontological or psychological properties and then proving (or disproving) that these properties were actually present in the algorithm. In fact, the entire debate was defined by and circulated around the inability to resolve these fundamental issues.

8.4.2 Legal Person

Unlike natural person, which is grounded in the ontological conditions or essential properties of the individual entity, legal person—or what has also been called "artificial person" (Kurki 2019)—is a socially constructed and conferred recognition. In other words, the title to person has little or nothing to do with what something *is*. Instead, it concerns how something comes to be situated in the context of socially constructed situations and relationships. It is, to return to the etymology of the word "person," a matter of the role that an individual entity occupies or performs within social reality. Consequently, the criterion for decision, as Chopra and White (2011, p. 155) explain, is not a matter of "physical makeup, internal constitution, or other ineffable attributes of the entity." It is a practical matter that concerns the integrity and functioning of existing legal systems. "The recognition of legal personality by legislatures or courts," they continue, "takes place in response to legal, political, or moral pressure. The legal system, in so doing, seeks to ensure its internal functional coherence. Legal entities are recognized as such in order to facilitate the working of the law in consonance with social realities."

If the paradigmatic natural person is the human being in possession of a set of natural capabilities that make one a person, the paradigmatic legal person is the corporation, which is a person not because of its intrinsic nature but due to the fact that it is recognized and situated within the law as a subject of the law (Dyschkant 2015, p. 2084). Thus, the question confronted in the face or the faceplate of AI or other seemingly intelligent and/or socially interactive artifact is whether it would make sense to extend the category of legal person to these other kinds of entities—not, it should be pointed out, because of what they need and deserve as "natural persons," but because of the role we want or need them to play in *our* social reality.

Responses to this question also tend to divide into two opposed and seemingly irreconcilable positions. Those who are critical of the idea argue that recognizing technological artifacts as persons, although clearly possible and entirely legal, is wrong and should not be allowed to happen. Extending the title of person to robots and AI, they argue, would only exacerbate existing problems with corporate personhood concerning responsibility gaps, shell companies, and liability shields (Bryson et al. 2017). Those who have advocated for it take an entirely different position, arguing that extending legal personhood or personality to robots and other intelligent (or at least seemingly intelligent) artifacts will be necessary for integrating these technologies into our social reality and moral/legal systems. As Visa AJ Kurki (2019, p. 189) neatly summarizes it, "endowing an AI with the incidents of legal personhood that enable it to function as an independent commercial actor does not bespeak any acceptance of the notion that AIs are endowed with ultimate value. The legal personhood of an AI can rather serve various purposes that might have nothing to do with the AI itself, such as economic efficiency or risk allocation."

The terms of this debate became evident in May of 2016 when the Committee on Legal Affairs of the European Parliament—the legislative branch of the European Union—proposed that "sophisticated autonomous robots" be considered "electronic persons" with specific rights and obligations for the purposes of contending with the challenges of technological unemployment, tax policy, and legal liability (Delvaux 2016). The proposal, which did not pass as originally formulated, was strongly opposed by over 250 experts in the field of AI and robotics, who signed onto an open letter addressed to EU lawmakers. According to the opinion expressed in this document, the very idea of "creating a legal personality for a robot is inappropriate whatever the legal status model" (Robotics Open Letter 2017).

8.5 Disruptions and Available Solutions

The person/thing dichotomy has been an undeniably useful and influential ordering principle, one that not only has the weight of history behind it but has been codified in language and law. For this reason, the principal challenge that can now be seen taking shape in the face or the faceplate of AI, robots, and other seemingly intelligent and socially interactive technologies concerns how *we* decide to fit these artifacts into this often unquestioned and seemingly unassailable social order. And the problem is that accommodating these innovations to one category or the other has been debatable, inconclusive, and seemingly irresolvable. "In the dichotomous model that has long opposed the world of things to the world of persons," Esposito (2015, p. 3) writes "a crack appears to be showing." And "artificial intelligence" appears to be one designation for that fissure. So now what? How can or should we respond to this disruption?

8.5.1 Business as Usual

We can decide to reassert and defend the existing moral and legal ontology, forcing AI, robots, and other artifacts to fit into one or the other designation. As Esposito (2015, pp. 1–2) has explained: "If there is one assumption that seems to have organized human experience from it very beginnings it is that of a division between persons and things….Since Roman times, this distinction has been reproduced in all modern codifications, becoming the presupposition that serves as the implicit ground for all other types of thought—for legal but also philosophical, economic, political, and ethical reasoning." Proceeding according to this standard way of organizing things (actually not just things but things and persons) seems reasonable, obvious, and natural, but that is THE problem and for three reasons.

First, binary oppositions, although useful for categorizing things, restrict what is possible to know and to say about the world and our own experiences. This is because conceptual opposites push things toward mutually exclusive options. In this either/or mode, any phenomenon is assumed to be reducible to x or its opposite, not-x. Though this kind of exclusivity has a certain functionality and logical attraction—something that in Aristotelian logic has been called the "law of non-contradiction" (Gottlieb

2019)—it is often criticized for not being entirely in touch with the complexity and exigency of facts on the ground. And the person/thing dichotomy, as Anna Beckers and Gunther Teubner (2021, p. 13) point out in the context of AI and robot law, provides an almost perfect illustration of the problem, insofar as existing technology already seems to resist both reification, where the AI or robot is "just a tool" of human action, and personsification, i.e. promoting the artifact to a moral or legal position that would be similar to that of a natural human person. In the face of these technological innovations, the efficacy of the person/thing binary appears to be, if not already broken, then at least straining against its own limitations to the point of breaking.

Second, the existing debates about how AI, robots, and other seemingly intelligent artifacts fit into the existing ontological categories of person or thing has produced a lot of activity, but the effort seems to be caught in what 19th-century German philosopher G.W.F. Hegel (2010, p. 202) called a "bad infinity"—a seemingly endlessly repetition of the same arguments and disputes that do not make much progress on the issue. After several decades of work and robust discursive activity, we haven't got very far and find ourselves in a kind of stalemate or *cul de sac*. There are seemingly good reasons to conclude that AI cannot and should not be regarded as a mere thing. But there are just as many good arguments and evidence that say extending the status of person to these machines would be just as bad, if not worse. So at this juncture, we find ourselves in something of an impasse. Each side in the debate—the critics and the advocates—continues to heap up arguments and evidence to prove or substantiate their position. But neither side appears to have won the contest or is even showing signs of making progress on it.

Finally, the seemingly natural opposition between person and thing, proceeds from a distinctly Western way of thinking, "genetically composed of the confluence between Greek philosophy, Roman law, and the Christian conception" (Esposito 2015, p. 3). This way of organizing things—this way of dividing up all of existence into one of two mutually exclusive types—is not only exported around the world through colonial conquest and religious conversion but has, for better or worse, dominated the entire domain. Other cultures and traditions, distributed across time and space, do not divide-up and make sense of the diversity of beings in this arguably binary fashion. They perform decisive cuts separating the *who* from the *what* according to other ways of seeing, valuing, and acting. As Archer Pechawis explains in his contribution to the essay "Making Kin with Machines":

> *nēhiyawēwin* (the Plains Cree language) divides everything into two primary categories: animate and inanimate. One is not 'better' than the other, they are merely different states of being. These categories are flexible: certain toys are inanimate until a child is playing with them, during which time they are animate. A record player is considered animate while a record, radio, or television set is inanimate. But animate or inanimate, all things have a place in our circle of kinship or *wahkohtowin*. (in Lewis et al. 2018, unpaginated)

This alternative formulation—which is just one among many—runs counter to the dominant ways of proceeding, seeing the boundary between what Western philosophy and law call "person" and "thing" as being endlessly flexible, permeable, and more of a continuum than an exclusive, binary opposition.

Similar opportunities/challenges are available by way of other non-Western religious and philosophical traditions. In her investigation of the social position of robots in Japan, Jennifer Robertson finds a remarkably different way of organizing the difference between living human persons and artificially designed/manufactured things:

> *Inochi*, the Japanese word for 'life,' encompasses three basic, seemingly contradictory but inter-articulated meanings: a power that infuses sentient beings from generation to generation; a period between birth and death; and, most relevant to robots, the most essential quality of something, whether organic (natural) or manufactured. Thus robots are experienced as 'living' things. The important point to remember here is that there is no ontological pressure to make distinctions between organic/inorganic, animate/inanimate, human/nonhuman forms. On the contrary, all of these forms are linked to form a continuous network of beings. (Robertson, 2014, p. 576)

These are not the only available alternatives, and, by citing these two instances, the intention is not to suggest that these different ways of thinking difference differently are somehow "better" than those developed in Western philosophical and religious traditions. In fact (and this is where things become really complicated), making and operating on that kind of assumption would itself be an instance of "orientalism" (Said 1979), which always sought new resources derived from exoticized others in order to rehabilitate and ensure the continued success of Western hegemony. These alternatives, by contrast, are just different and, in being different, offer the opportunity for critically questioning what is assumed to be true and often goes without saying. Gesturing in the direction of other ways of thinking and being can have the effect of shaking one's often unquestioned confidence in cultural constructs that are already not natural, universal, or eternally true.

8.5.2 Both/And Alternatives

One understandable frustration with conceptual oppositions, like that which has distinguished person from thing, is that they have "compressed and continue to compress human experience into the confines of this exclusionary binary equation" (Esposito 2015, p. 4), such that between person and thing "there appears to be nothing" (Esposito 2015, p. 16). Though binary oppositions have a certain functionality and logical attraction, they often seem to be unable to represent or to capture the rich experiences of actual existing empirical reality, which always seems to complicate simple reduction into one of two options. It is for this reason that we are generally critical of "false dichotomies"—the parsing of complex experience into a simple and irreducible either/or distinction.

One method for resolving this problem is to formulate a third alternative that is neither one thing nor the other but a kind of combination or synthesis of the one and the other. Alternatives like this sound liberating and hold considerable promise, precisely because they appear to interrupt the structural limitations imposed by either/or logic and arrange for a more nuanced representation and understanding that is both/

and. And such an alternative is already available to us with the legal institution of slavery.[2]

Already in Roman times, slaves were regarded as something more than a mere thing but not quite a full person. They occupied a position that was situated in between the one and the other, being both thing and person. And there has been, in both the legal and philosophical literature, a surprising number of serious proposals arguing for instituting what can only be called Slavery 2.0 (Katz 2008; Bryson 2010; Chopra and White 2011; Katz and MacDonald 2020; Pagallo 2013; Izumo 2018; Navon 2021).

Clearly use of the term "slave" is provocative and morally charged, and it would be impetuous to presume that the various proposals for repurposing the paradigm of slavery to deal with robots and AI would be the same or even substantially similar to what had occurred (and is still unfortunately occurring) with human bondage. But, and by the same token, we also should not dismiss or fail to take into account the documented evidence and historical data concerning slave-owning societies and how institutionalized forms of slavery affected both individuals and human communities. The corrupting influence of socially sanctioned, institutionalized bondage concerns not just the enslaved population but also those who would occupy the position of mastery. "The problem," as Lantz Fleming Miller (2020, p. 301) concludes, "is the term 'slave.' If slavery is, as most of the world now concurs, not morally good, it is reasonable to deduce that not only should no one be anyone's slave, but also no one should be anyone's master. There is something about the relationship that is wrong." Consequently, even if one would be inclined to agree that "robots should be slaves" (Bryson 2010, p. 63) or that we can, in the words of Steve Petersen (2011, p. 283), "design people to serve" us (also see Musiał 2017), we still need to ask ourselves whether we would ever want to risk becoming masters.

Additionally (and adding yet another layer of ethnocentric complexity to the problem), the extension of the seemingly paradigmatic master–slave relationship to robots, AI, and other things is culturally specific and distinctly Western. This is something that is identified and explained by Raya Jones in her examination of the work of Masahiro Mori, the Japanese robotics engineer who first formulated the uncanny valley hypothesis back in 1970. In a statement that directly contravenes the largely Western robot-as-slave model, Mori (quoted in Jones 2016, p. 154) offers the following counterpoint: "There is no master–slave relationship between human beings and machines. The two are fused together in an interlocking entity." As Jones (2016, p. 154) explains, Mori's statement "connotes two ways that the concepts of 'human' and 'robot' can relate to each other. The 'master–slave' viewpoint that Mori eschews accords with individualism and the conventional understanding of technology in terms of its instrumentality. The viewpoint that Mori prompts is based in the Buddhist view of the interconnectedness of all things."

8.6 Thinking Otherwise

Eventhough AI, robots, and other technological artifacts are humanly designed and manufactured things, they are not necessarily the kind of things that are (or should be) situated and conceptualized as the polar opposite of persons. They are not limited to being merely objects for a subject, instrumental means as opposed to an end, or *res* in distinction to *persona*. Instead, it is with these things that "the bivalent logic of modernity is opening up to other paradigms"—other ways of thinking and responding in the face of "things that are no longer merely objects, and of subjects who are increasingly difficult to confine inside the dispositif of the person" (Esposito 2015, p. 132). These technologies appears to be a kind of glitch or anomaly that interrupts and deconstructs the existing binary logic that differentiates person from thing. They destabilize the very terms and conditions of the debate, and in doing so they invite us to think differently and otherwise. It is, therefore, in the face or the faceplate of AI that we are called to respond to and take responsibility for beings that are otherwise—that do not fit or accommodate the existing moral and legal ontology.

Consequently, the task before us—a task that begins to stand out in relief in the face of technological things that challenge us and our "misunderstood anthropocentrism" (Esposito's term)—is to learn to question our privilege and develop critical perspectives on our own sense of exceptionalism. We—we human beings who have been bestowed with or granted to ourselves the power to decide all things—need to learn how to take responsibility for our privilege, for the damage and harm that it has perpetrated across the centuries, and for the myriad of exclusions and marginalizations that it has instituted and justified.

Questioning privilege from the position of privilege is never an easy undertaking, precisely because it is often rendered transparent by the assumption that it is just normal, somehow part of the natural order of things, and true for all times and places. But these ways of thinking and acting come from somewhere, and they are supported by a particular ideological formation, one that has effectively concealed itself from view by adopting the guise of universality. Yet even here (with this critical self-reflection), all things are not equal, as this privilege is something that has not been evenly distributed. Fortunately, it is in the face of AI and other things—things that resist, for one reason or another both reification and personification—that we are able to catch a glimpse of our own unique position and status such that we are invited (or compelled) to investigate and take responsibility for its lineage, its current formations, and its possible futures. It is only by challenging ourselves to engage in this critical self-reflection that we can begin to assemble a moral and legal ontology that can respond to and take responsibility in the face of things.

Ultimately, then, this is not really about AI, robots, and other artifacts. It is about us. It is about the moral and legal institutions that we have fabricated to make sense of all that is. And it is with these technological artifacts—that play the role or occupy the place of a kind of spokesperson for these things—that we are now called to take responsibility for this privileged situation and circumstance. What is needed in response is not some forceful reassertion of the usual ways of thinking but a significantly reformulated moral and legal ontology that can scale to the opportunities and the challenges of the twenty-first century and beyond. What this new framework will look like and how it will be developed is the task for thinking and acting from this point forward. Confronting this will be as terrifying and exhilarating as any of the robot uprisings imagined in science fiction or AI extinction events recently circulated in the popular media, because getting this right will require nothing less than a thorough rethinking of everything we thought was right, natural, and beyond question.

Notes

1. This difference—something philosophers call "ontological difference"—is rooted in Platonism and can be found in, for example, "The Allegory of the Cave" situated in Bk. VII of *The Republic* (Plato 1987).
2. In this context, it should be noted that the word "robot" was first introduced and initially used in Karel Čapek's 1921 stage-play *Rossumovi Univerzální Roboti* (Rossum's Universal Robots). In Czech, as in several other Slavic languages, the word *robota* (or some variation thereof) denotes "servitude or labor," and *robot* was the word that Čapek employed to name a class of manufactured, artificial servants or slaves.

References

Beckers A, Teubner G (2021) Three liability regimes for artificial intelligence: algorithmic actants, hybrids. Hart Publishing, Crowds

Bryson J (2010) Robots should be slaves. In: Wilks Y (ed) Close engagements with artificial companions: key social, psychological, ethical and design issues. John Benjamins, pp 63–74

Bryson J, Diamantis ME, Grant TD (2017) Of, for, and by the people: the legal lacuna of synthetic persons. Artif Intell Law 25:273–291. https://doi.org/10.1007/s10506-017-9214-9

Calverley D (2008) Imagining a non-biological machine as a legal person. AI Society 22(4):523–537. https://doi.org/10.1007/s00146-007-0092-7

Chopra S, White LF (2011) A legal theory for autonomous artificial agents. University of Michigan Press

Coeckelbergh M (2012) Growing moral relations: critique of moral status ascription. Palgrave MacMillan

Darling K (2012) Extending legal protection to social robots. IEEE Spectrum, 10 September 2012. http://spectrum.ieee.org/automaton/robotics/artificial-intelligence/extending-legal-protection-to-social-robots

Darling K (2021) The new breed: what our history with animals reveals about our future with robots. Henry Holt and Company

Datteri E (2013) Predicting the long-term effects of human-robot interaction: a reflection on responsibility in medical robotics. Sci Eng Ethics 19(1):139–160. https://doi.org/10.1007/s11948-011-9301-3

Delvaux M (2016) Draft report, with recommendations to the Commission on Civil Law Rules on Robotics, 2015/2103(INL). Committee on Legal Affairs. European Parliament. https://www.europarl.europa.eu/doceo/document/JURI-PR-582443_EN.pdf?redirect

Dyschkant A (2015) Legal personhood: how we are getting it wrong. *University of Illinois Law Review*, August 31, pp. 2075–2110. https://www.illinoislawreview.org/print/volume-2015-issue-5/legal-personhood-how-we-are-getting-it-wrong/
Esposito R (2015) Persons and things (trans: Hanafi Z). Polity.
Etzrodt K, Engesser S (2021) Voice-based agents as personified things: assimilation and accommodation as equilibration of doubt. Hum-Mach Commun 2:57–79. https://doi.org/10.30658/hmc.2.3
Feenberg A (1991) Critical theory of technology. Oxford University Press
Gladden ME (2016) The diffuse intelligent other: an ontology of nonlocalizable robots as moral and legal actors. In: Nørskov M (ed) Social robots: Boundaries, potential, challenges. Ashgate, Burlington, VT, pp 177–198
Gottlieb P (2019) Aristotle on non-contradiction. In: Zalta EN (ed) The Stanford encyclopedia of philosophy. Spring 2019 Edition. https://plato.stanford.edu/entries/aristotle-noncontradiction/
Harman G (2002) Tool being: Heidegger and the metaphysics of objects. Open Court Publishing
Hegel GWF (2010) The science of logic (trans: Di Giovanni G). Cambridge University Press. Originally published 1816
Heidegger M (1962) Being and time (trans: Macquarrie J, Robinson E). Harper & Row. Originally published 1927
Heidegger M (1977) The Question concerning technology and other essays (trans: Lovitt W). Harper & Row. Originally published 1962
Izumo T (2018) Digital specific property of robots: a historical suggestion from roman law. Delphi 1(1):14–19. https://doi.org/10.21552/delphi/2018/1/8
Jones R (2016) Personhood and social robotics: a psychological consideration. Routledge
Kant I (2012) Groundwork of the metaphysics of morals (trans: Gregor M, Timmermann J). Cambridge University Press. Originally published 1786
Katz A (2008) Intelligent agents and internet commerce in Ancient Rome. Computers and Law. https://www.scl.org/articles/1095-intelligent-agents-and-internet-commerce-in-ancient-rome
Katz A, MacDonald M (2020) Autonomous intelligent agents and the roman law of slavery. In: Edwards L, Burkhard S, Harbinja E (eds) Future law: emerging technology, regulation and ethics. Edinburgh University Press, Edinburgh, pp 295–312
Kurki VAJ (2019) A theory of legal personhood. Oxford University Press
Jibo (2014) JIBO: The world's first social robot for the home. https://www.youtube.com/watch?v=H0h20jRA5M0
Lewis JE, Arista N, Pechawis A, Kite S (2018) Making Kin with the machines. J Des Sci, 16 July. https://doi.org/10.21428/bfafd97b
Matthias A (2004) The responsibility gap: ascribing responsibility for the actions of learning automata. Ethics Inf Technol 6:175–183. https://doi.org/10.1007/s10676-004-3422-1
Miller LF (2020) Responsible research for the construction of maximally humanlike automata: the paradox of unattainable informed consent. Ethics Inf Technol 22:297–305. https://doi.org/10.1007/s10676-017-9427-3
Musiał M (2017) Designing (artificial) people to serve—the other side of the coin. J Exp Theor Artif Intell 29(5):1087–1097. https://doi.org/10.1080/0952813X.2017.1309691
Natale S (2021) Deceitful media: artificial intelligence and social life after the Turing test. Oxford University Press.
Navon M (2021) The virtuous servant owner—a paradigm whose time has come (again). Front Robot AI 8(715849):1–15. https://doi.org/10.3389/frobt.2021.715849
Pagallo U (2013) The laws of robots: crimes, contracts, and torts. Springer, Dordrecht
Petersen S (2011) Designing people to serve. In: Lin P, Abney K, Bekey GA (eds) Robot ethics: the ethical and social implications of robotics. MIT Press, pp 283–298
Plato (1987) Plato V & VI: Republic (trans: Shorey P). Harvard University Press, Cambridge, MA
Reeves B, Nass C (1996) The media equation: How people treat computers, television, and new media like real people and places. Cambridge University Press

Robertson J (2014) Human rights vs. robot rights: forecasts from Japan. Crit Asian Stud 46(4):571–598. https://doi.org/10.1080/14672715.2014.960707

Robotics OpenLetter (2017) Open letter to the European commission artificial intelligence and robotics. http://www.robotics-openletter.eu/

Said EW (1979) Orientalism. Vintage Books, New York

Turing AM (1950) Computing machinery and intelligence. Mind, LIX (236):433–460. https://doi.org/10.1093/mind/LIX.236.433 Reprinted in Mayer PA (ed) Computer media and communication. Oxford University Press, pp 37–58

Chapter 9
|Ethics of AI| as a Floating Signifier; or Towards a Politics of AI Ethics

Alberto Romele

Abstract In this chapter we question the use of the term |ethics of AI|. Our thesis is that |ethics of AI| is a floating signifier, a notion borrowed from Ernesto Laclau. The article is divided into two parts. In the first part, we discuss the need to include in the ethics of AI a reflection on the ethics of communication about AI. We also introduce the concept of the floating signifier. In the second part, we propose an analysis of the discourses mobilizing |ethics of AI| in the daily press. We examine articles mobilizing |ethics of AI| that appeared in eight daily newspapers in four European countries (France, Italy, the UK, and Germany) over a three-month period. We show the existence of three discursive uses of AI ethics: the normativity of institutions, the critique of researchers, and the techno-solutionism of companies.

Keywords AI ethics · Floating signifiers · Struggle for hegemony · Press speech

9.1 Introduction

Today, the ethics of artificial intelligence (AI) is the subject of a considerable number of discourses. The aim of this chapter is not to focus on the content (the *what*) of these discourses. Rather, I want to question the *why* and *how* of these discourses. My thesis is that behind this multiplicity of discourses lies a symbolic struggle for hegemony in the field of AI. In other words, my thesis is that the term |ethics of AI| is a floating signifier. The concept of floating signifiers was introduced by Laclau (2005) to denote terms and concepts that are sufficiently polysemic to be interpreted, understood, and strategically used in different ways by different social groups for hegemonic purposes.

The article is divided into two parts. In the first part, which is theoretical in nature, I discuss the need to include in the ethics of AI a reflection on the ethics of AI communication. In this first part, I also introduce the concept of floating signifier and how it has been mobilized in the field of media studies. In the second part, which

A. Romele (✉)
IRMÉCCEN, Université Sorbonne Nouvelle, Paris, France
e-mail: alberto.romele@sorbonne-nouvelle.fr

R. Fioravante and A. Vaccaro (eds.), *Humanism and Artificial Intelligence*, SpringerBriefs in Philosophy, https://doi.org/10.1007/978-3-031-85478-1_9

is empirical in nature, I propose an analysis of discourses mobilizing |ethics of AI| in the daily press, where the press is understood as an arena of debate and struggle between rival hegemonic claims. I examine articles mobilizing |ethics of AI| that appeared in eight daily newspapers in four European countries (France, Italy, the UK and Germany) over a three-month period. In particular, I show the existence of three discursive uses of AI ethics: institutional normativity, researcher critique, and corporate techno-solutionism.

9.2 |Ethics of AI|, in Theory

Studying discourse dynamics does not mean focusing only on the internal structure of discourses. Rather, it means studying discourses in their multiple trivialities (Jeanneret 2008). Analyzing the triviality of a discourse (whether written or oral, textual or visual, etc.) means considering its creation, dissemination, and consumption in its multiple material and symbolic displacements. One might think that a discourse analysis of the ethics of AI has little to do with the ethics of AI. At best, it is communication ethics applied to the specific field of AI communication. However, I believe that this oversight of AI communication, widespread among AI philosophers and ethicists, is the result of an empiricist bias.

With the empirical turn (Brey 2010), philosophers and ethicists of technology have turned their attention to the material structures and iterations of technologies, as well as to what "really" goes on in research and development labs. For them, ethical questions are never general or transcendent, but depend directly on the materiality of the technical object in question. Every ethically just solution is therefore the result of a new arrangement of the material components of the technical object. To give an example, the ethics of an AI algorithm will depend on its robustness, its transparency, its reliability in producing results free from social and cultural biases, and so on.

Philosophers and ethicists of technology, in their desire to be close to "things themselves," have forgotten the contexts in which these things are always embedded. These contexts are of various kinds: technological, economic, documentary, sociocultural, and so on. Each of these conditions of possibility has an ethical significance that risks being overlooked from an empiricist point of view. In the case of AI, as it happens, it is precisely those companies whose economic power and know-how enable them to produce the most materially robust algorithms that use them in the least ethical way.

AI philosophers and ethicists do not give much weight to AI discourses and communication. On the contrary, I believe that AI discourses and communication play a fundamental role in AI innovation processes. For example, AI narratives crystallize and produce specific technological imaginaries (Romele 2023).

The literature on science communication and popularization has long emphasized how communication contributes to processes of technological production and scientific discovery. For Bucchi (1996), popular science communication influences scientific practice in many ways that go far beyond mere support and reinforcement. This idea is further developed by Goulden (2013), who compares the relationship between science and science popularization to the encounter between fresh and salt water in a river delta. According to Jeanneret (2008, p. 104), a popular science magazine article is not simply a simplified science lesson, but a complex object that mobilizes everyday ideas, moral judgments, definitions of character, and relationships with others.

Based on what has been said so far, it is not surprising to see a gap between AI ethics and the lack of ethics in science communication about AI and AI ethics. As an example, consider how the European Community visually communicated one of its major initiatives in the field of AI ethics (the "Ethical Guidelines for Trustworthy AI") with an image purchased from Shutterstock.[1] As written elsewhere (Romele 2022), the problem with such images is not so much their lack of reference to "real" AI, but their lack of "pensiveness", a term borrowed from the philosopher Jacques Rancière. The colors (especially blue), the patina reminiscent of devotional images (Dondero 2007), as well as the subjects of these images (a robot in a thinking attitude, a robot finger and a human finger meeting as in Michelangelo's *The Creation of Adam*, etc.) have an "anaesthetic" effect (a term reminiscent of aesthetics and anesthesia): instead of encouraging non-experts to participate in the debate about AI and its ethics, they exclude them from it. Similarly, Robert (2017, p. 221) argues that the macro-techno discourse "does not provide a framework for the intelligibility of ICTs; it performs another function: to drown us in a discursive river [...] that occupies the space and thus prevents the emergence of relevant, political or ethical questions."

In this context, I am not interested in the ethics of AI, but in the politics behind the use of the term |ethics of AI|. Orthodox Marxism begins with a reversal of the Hegelian perspective from matter to spirit. Drawing on Feuerbach's theses, Marx ends up arguing that anything that is not material, be it religion, art, or law, is not real. And it is precisely for this reason that any struggle for hegemony in society is played out on the level of matter. For Marx and orthodox Marxism, communist revolution means the reappropriation of the means of production owned by the bourgeois class. Alongside this materialist Marxism, there exists a Marxism that could be described as "symbolic"; this Marxism certainly does not deny the value of matter, but it also affirms that, alongside material domination, there exists a no less important one of a symbolic nature—on this subject, see Ricœur (2016).

Among the representatives of this symbolic Marxism, we can undoubtedly include Antonio Gramsci. The interest of Gramscian Marxism lies not only in having "discovered" the symbolic dimension of domination, but also in having understood that those who are dominated from a material point of view always have room for maneuver from a symbolic point of view. This is why Gramscian Marxism has been so successful in the field of cultural studies (Maigret and Martin 2020).

Laclau and Mouffe's theory has rightly been called a "neo-Gramscian" theory of discourse (Martin 2002). Three elements are central to this perspective: (1) the idea

---

[1] https://ec.europa.eu/futurium/en/ai-alliance-consultation.1.html. Last accessed December 29, 2023. The image is one of dozens of human-robot versions of Michelangelo's The Creation of Adam. For a detailed analysis of this type of image, see Singler (2020).

of the discursive constitution of society, (2) the analysis of specific discourses, and (3) the concept of hegemony. With regard to (1), Laclau and Mouffe see discourse not as just another aspect of society, but as the ontological foundation of society itself. Everything that is not said in the discourse of a society is as if it did not exist in that society in some way. This is a first gesture of inclusion and exclusion, which for Laclau and Mouffe is also "politics" as the instituting moment of a society. As far as (2) is concerned, the terms and concepts of discourse have no value in themselves, but only a differential value. The hegemonic nature of social reality makes these differential meanings vulnerable and unstable. Finally, with regard to (3), this is where the Gramscian influence is most direct. However, while for Gramsci hegemony remains a class practice, Laclau and Mouffe understand it as the discursive articulation principle of society as a whole. In short, for Laclau and Mouffe, social reality is the result of a struggle for symbolic hegemony and, at the same time, the concealment of the traces of this struggle by those who have emerged victorious.

It is within this theoretical framework that Laclau developed his concept of floating signifier. A floating signifier is not a simple case of polysemy of a term or concept. Rather, it is a term/concept that denotes situations in which the same term/concept is subjected to the structural pressures of competing hegemonic projects. In short, it is a term/concept contested by different political projects. For Laclau, floating signifiers appear especially in times of crisis, when the symbolic system needs to be radically transformed. As Laclau himself writes:

> We know now that constructing a 'people' also involves constructing the frontier which the 'people' presupposes. Frontiers are unstable, and in a process of constant displacement. This is why I have talked about 'floating signifiers.' This entails a new hegemonic game: any new 'people' would require the reconstitution of the space of representation through the construction of a new frontier. The same happens with the 'outsiders' of the system: any political transformation implies not only a reconfiguration of already existing demands, but also the incorporation of new demands this much more effectively than a whole legislature of representatives. (159–160)

In a sense, the floating of signifiers is at the heart of politics itself. The absence of floating, the shift to a logic of equivalences and empty signifiers, is the death of politics in favor, as Laclau reminds us (162), of what Rancière calls the "police."

The notion of floating signifier has been used in the field of media studies, and more specifically in the analysis of the phenomenon of fake news, by Farkas and Shou (2019). These authors argue against a problematic "truth-based solutionism" approach when it comes to fake news. While recognizing the spread of fake news as a threat to democratic systems, they caution against believing that reason and the truth of "proven facts" alone can solve the problem. They point out that democracy is based not only on reason and truth, but also on the inclusion and representation of diverse political projects and groups. Democracy embraces different visions of how society should be organized. This does not mean abandoning the search for truth, but rather contextualizing it and understanding that the search for truth and the promotion of agonism are not mutually exclusive in our democracies. As pointed out elsewhere, the term |fake news| can rightly be treated as a floating signifier:

> Instead of entering the terrain of what defines "truthfulness" or "falsehood," a battleground in which a multiplicity of agents struggle to define what counts as valid or deceitful, we seek to understand "fake news" as a discursive signifier that is part of political struggles. We take a step back and look at how different conceptions of "fake news" serve to produce and articulate political battlegrounds over social reality. In this regard, our goal is not to define the correct definition of fake news, but to analyse the different, opposing and conflicting understandings of the concept. (Farkas and Schou 2018, p. 300)

In particular, based on an analysis of the press, they identify three uses of |fake news|: (1) |fake news| as an expression used to critique digital capitalism, i.e. the idea that platforms generate revenue based on readers or visitors, and that this economic incentive drives them, if not to produce, at least not to hinder the production of fake news; (2) |fake news| as a critique of right-wing politics and media. That is, the idea that this political space is a major producer of fake news; (3) |fake news| as a critique of liberal and mainstream media, which is the discourse put forward by Donald Trump, for example: accused of spreading fake news, he in turn accuses the media of accusing him. The idea is that behind these different uses of the term lies a struggle for symbolic and cultural hegemony between different political projects—for example, between political power and journalistic power.

My idea, which I develop in the next section, is to mobilize the same intuition, as well as a similar methodology, to study the uses of the term |ethics of AI|.

9.3 |Ethics of AI|, in Practice

In his analysis of the Panzani advertisement, Roland Barthes (1964) distinguished between denotation, i.e. (the explanation of) the elements actually present in the image, and connotation, i.e. (the understanding of) the ultimate meaning of the image, which he summarized in the concept of "italianity." The understanding of connotation depends on whether a particular social and/or cultural group shares the same vision or concept of the world. For example, Panzani's "italianity" has little to do with Italy, but rather with the image the French had of Italy and its food in the 1960s. My idea is that the struggle for hegemony around a floating signifier (in this case, |AI ethics|) is nothing more than a struggle between rival connotations. To study this struggle, I mobilize critical discourse analysis (Jørgensen and Phillips 2002).

I limit my analysis to discourses mobilizing |ethics of AI| in the daily press. For this analysis, I used the Europresse database.[2] I limited my search to articles published in the daily press between May 9 and August 9, 2023 (a period of three months). I searched for articles containing either "ethics" and "artificial intelligence" or "ethics" and "AI", either in the title or in the text. I did this for four European countries: France, Italy, the United Kingdom, and Germany. For each country, I selected two newspapers based on popularity: Le Monde and Libération for France, Corriere della Sera and Repubblica for Italy, The Guardian and The Independent for the UK,

---

[2] https://new.europresse.com/.

Table 9.1 Articles containing either "ethics" and "artificial intelligence" or "ethics" and "AI" in eight European daily newspapers in the period May 9–August 9, 2023, either in the title or in the text (*Source* Europresse)

Country	Key words	Newspapers	Relevant results
France	"éthique" "intelligence artificielle" (IA)	*Le Monde* (newspaper + website)	22
		Libération (newspaper + website)	17
		Total France	**39**
Italy	"etica" "intelligenza artificiale" (IA)	*Corriere della Sera* (website)	24
		Repubblica (website)	13
		Total Italy	**37**
United Kingdom	"ethics" "artificial intelligence" (AI)	*The Guardian* (site)	31
		The Independent (site)	1
		Total United Kingdom	**32**
Germany	"Ethik" "künstliche Intelligenz" (KI)	*FAZ* (website)	4
		SZ (site)	5
		Total Germany	**9**
		Total	**117**

Frankfurter Allgemeine Zeitung (FAZ) and Süddeutsche Zeitung (SZ) for Germany. I ran a separate search for each country, translating the keywords into each country's language. Table 9.1 summarizes the results of my search.

It is important to note that, unsurprisingly, a significant proportion of the articles in my corpus deals with the question of (ethics of) generative AI, especially ChatGPT. There are, of course, exceptions, as in the case of the news item in The Guardian of June 2, 2023, according to which "US air force denies running simulation in which AI drone 'killed' operator."[3] In most cases, the specific question of generative AI is understood in the light of broader issues, such as discussions around the European AI law or ethical and philosophical perspectives. I am thinking here of an article in Le Monde published on June 14, 2023, entitled "Behind AI, the return of technological utopias." The article discusses the transhumanist and long-termist thinking of people like Elon Musk and Sam Altman, the latter CEO of Open AI, the ChatGPT company.

[3] The next day, on June 3, 2023, The Guardian published another article entitled "US air force denies running simulation in which AI drone 'killed' operator". The term "killed" is used this time, more cautiously, in quotation marks—it was indeed a simulation. On June 2, 2023, Libération's checknews service had already published an article entitled "Did a drone equipped with artificial intelligence turn against its human operator during US Air Force training?" in which they spoke of a "purely hypothetical" anecdote.

In my analysis, I identified three main groups of actors using the term |AI ethics|: (1) institutions, (2) researchers, and (3) companies.[4]

9.4 The Normativity of Institutions

In terms of institutions, the newspapers focus on the European institutions and their representatives. The European AI Act, i.e. the proposed legislation that provides a framework for the development and use of AI systems in Europe in the coming years is given crucial importance. As an example, I can cite an article published by the FAZ on June 12, 2023, with the headline "European Parliament agrees on framework for law." The article talks about the vote that took place two days later (499 votes in favor, 28 against and 93 abstentions) and questions the reasons for such long negotiations before the vote (18 months). In particular, it discusses two problems: the conflict between "MEPs who see powerful AI systems as a threat" and those who fear "over-regulation", on the one hand, and the "conceptual" problem that the Commission proposed a horizontal framework that treats all high-risk AI systems in the same way, without making clear distinctions in terms of sectors and applications, on the other.[5]

In addition to the European institutions, (representatives of) national institutions are also addressed. For example, on July 5, 2023, Le Monde published an article entitled "AI: the ethics committee proposes regulating services like ChatGPT more than open source models", in which the proposal of the Comité national pilote d'éthique du numérique (CNPEN) is presented, which consists in distinguishing between generative AI systems available to the general public (such as ChatGPT) and "open source" systems without a public interface. In the latter case, obligations could be less restrictive. The article also briefly mentions the tension between the European Parliament, on the one hand, and Emmanuel Macron, on the other, who, in agreement with French start-ups such as Mistral AI and LightOn, is opposed to "measures which, in their view, would prevent the growth of European flagships in this field." This information is repeated in another Le Monde article published on July 19, 2023, which speaks of "tensions surrounding the regulation of the European AI Act."

---

[4] Marginally, other groups of actors are emerging, such as associations and practitioners. As far as associations are concerned, see the article published in Le Monde on June 22, 2023 entitled "AI Act: how the EU is already investing in "high-risk" artificial intelligences to control its borders", in which the European Digital Rights (EDRi) collective and Human Rights Watch are named. As far as practitioners are concerned, let's consider an article that also appeared in Le Monde on May 26, 2023, entitled "Dubbing actors threatened by computer-generated voices unite in an international collective."

[5] Another example is the Libération article published on May 31, 2023 entitled "Artificial intelligence: MEPs give the green light to regulation of ChatGPT et al." In reality, the proposed regulation was formulated long before ChatGPT was launched, and the specific case of generative AI was not really taken into account. Indeed, as the same article states, "the European Parliament also intends [now] to take better account of generative AI such as ChatGPT by calling for a specific regime of obligations [...]."

The struggle for hegemony in the field of AI between two groups of players (institutions and companies, with researchers allied with one or the other) seems quite obvious here. And yet, we should not think that there is harmony between the institutions either. In fact, in this chapter, I act "as if" the three groups of actors we present were unique entities. In reality, we should recognize tensions, hegemonic struggles, within each of these groups of actors. I have just spoken of the French president's "concerns" about the European AI law. On June 10, 2023, Le Monde published an article entitled "Global competition for AI regulation." This article talks in particular about the attempt of the United Kingdom, through the initiative of its Prime Minister, Rishi Sunak, to become a global hub for AI regulation, although Europe, as it stands, would have a "head start."

With regard to the connotations of the discourses of this first group of actors, we can speak of "normativity." By normativity, I mean the fact that, according to institutions, AI ethics can be exercised by imposing and verifying compliance with norms on the part of AI innovators, including corporations. An article published by Corriere della Sera on May 16, 2023, entitled "ChatGPT, Bard, Bert: WHO calls for more ethical and safer artificial intelligence in healthcare applications", cites the six fundamental principles identified by the WHO in its guide on the ethics and governance of AI for health. These principles echo those formulated by other institutions, such as the European Commission in its 2019 guidelines for trustworthy AI. Thus, among the various possible approaches to AI ethics, institutions choose normative approaches because it is precisely through control over norms that institutions classically exercise their power. Normativity as a cipher of institutional discourse on AI ethics is recognized by both institutions and their "enemies" or "competitors", who do not question the efficacy of norms, but rather oppose them to the demands of technological innovation, especially in the face of global competition, according to a TINA (there is no alternative) rhetoric.

9.5 The Critique of Researchers

When it comes to researchers, the daily press makes virtually no distinction between those in the humanities and social sciences and those in the hard sciences. Among the articles we analyzed, we found as many seeking the opinion of philosophers and sociologists as of engineers and computer scientists. For example, in the social sciences and humanities, an article by philosopher Martin Gibert, published in Le Monde on May 24, 2023, discusses "three possible moral architectures" for ChatGPT; in the hard sciences, an article on gender bias in AI, also published in Le Monde on June 7, 2023, by computer scientist Laurence Devilliers. Or we could mention a long interview with philosopher Peter Singer, published in The Guardian on May 21, 2023, and another one published the next day in the same newspaper by computer scientist by training Timnit Gebru, who was fired by Google in 2020 when she co-led a research team within the company on the ethics of AI.[6]

Of course, this does not mean that there are no hegemonic struggles among this group of actors. We could even hypothesize that the emergence of AI ethics is linked to the desire of the human and social sciences to participate in AI innovation and funding.

The question that interests me here is: why have the hard sciences begun to take an interest in the ethics of AI? First, in recent years, the presence of ethical assessments in techno-scientific projects has become a fundamental, if not mandatory, element for obtaining public funding. Secondly, hard science researchers working for public institutions such as universities have lost a lot of power (in terms of investment and innovative capacity) compared to their colleagues working for private companies.

An article published in Le Monde on May 31, 2023 refers to "the university's losing match with the private sector." The article, which refers to a paper published in Science almost three months earlier (Ahmed et al. 2023), discusses the fact that today 70% of AI PhD students are hired in the private sector and 40% of conference presentations come from private laboratories (double the number in 2012). Universities, even the MIT, lack the funding to compete with corporate labs. We can therefore hypothesize that AI ethics is becoming a (seemingly) cheaper haven for hard science researchers. In fact, the same article notes that even on the AI ethics front, companies are submitting more than ever: "for example, three times more in 2022 than in 2021, and their quantity is equivalent to a third of what the academic world produces."

The connotation of the researchers' discourse could be called "critique." By critique, I mean an AI ethics exercised through a constant suspicion of existing practices and the intentions of the actors involved, especially corporations. Certainly, some researchers have argued for a strong normativity. For example, in an interview published in Le Monde on July 9, 2023, philosopher Elsa Godart said that "we need to establish new rules. Innovation [in AI] must also be that of ethics. And sometimes that means banning before allowing! There are also researchers (and institutions) that are converging on the technological solutions proposed by companies." On May 26, 2023, again in the pages of Le Monde, we find an article entitled "The challenge of detecting AI-derived content", which discusses the idea of marking AI-generated images and texts with an invisible cryptographic watermark, an idea on which companies such as Microsoft, Google and Amazon, institutions such as the US government, seem to be converging, but which does not displease Alexei Grinbaum, the researcher

---

[6] A specific feature of the Italian and German press is undoubtedly the presence of theologians among the SHS representatives solicited. This is the case of an article published on July 12, 2023 in Corriere della Sera entitled "The challenge between the United States and China on artificial intelligence: from geopolitics to ethics and religion" with an interview with theologian Paolo Benanti (alongside political scientist Ian Bremmer) and an article published in SZ on July 29, 2023 with an interview entitled "Distrust of omnipotent fantasies" with theologian (by training, now co-director of the Center for Ethics in Science at the University of Tübingen—IZEW) Regina Ammicht Quinn.

interviewed in this article. However, Grinbaum also points out, in a justifiably critical spirit, that "[watermark] detection systems are not infallible."[7]

I cited above the article by Martin Gibert, who mobilizes the history of philosophy to take stock of a possible ethics for ChatGPT. I can also mention an article published in Libération on June 20, 2023, entitled "After eco-anxiety, AI-anxiety?", in which critical AI theorists such as Antonio Casilli and Thierry Ménissier are given the floor. The article is also part of a special issue of the newspaper devoted entirely to AI. In the same issue of Libération, there is an interview with image theorist Antonio Somaini. In the Guardian interview mentioned above, Peter Singer explains his perspective on the moral status of animals and machines. The critic reminds us that we need researchers and their sensibilities, because the ethics of AI cannot be reduced to a set of technological solutions or prohibitions.

9.6 The Techno-Solutionism of Companies

As far as corporations are concerned, we need to make a separate point. Indeed, our analysis of the daily press discourses mobilizing AI ethics shows that, unlike researchers and institutions (which are mobilized to an almost equal extent), corporations are rarely mobilized as subjects of these discourses. In most cases, they are mobilized as objects or even targets of the critical and normative discourses of the first two. Reading the daily press, we constantly have the impression that companies are not the real interlocutors on this issue, but that they are distant, even absent.

On the other hand, it is not uncommon to find articles in which the claims of the representatives of these companies are considered absurd. In fact, I am not even talking about claims in form of discouses, but fragments, passages, hearsay: posts, tweets and so on. I have already mentioned an article published in Le Monde on June 14, 2023, which discusses the transhumanist and long-termist roots of Musk and Altman's technological action.

On May 9, 2023, The Guardian published a long interview with Geoffrey Hinton (an AI specialist who controversially left Google) entitled: "We have discovered the secret of immortality. The bad news is that it's not for us: why does the godfather of AI fear for humanity?" Interestingly, the voice is given only to those who have turned against the companies they have long worked for. Besides, we all know that there is no better testimony against a cause than that of those who have converted and repented.

There are, of course, exceptions, such as an article published in La Repubblica on May 23, 2023, dedicated to a speech given by Bill Gates at an event organized by Goldman Sachs and SV Angel. The article was published in the economic and financial section of the Italian newspaper. On August 4, 2023, The Guardian published

---

[7] The idea for this solution is in fact the result of a meeting between US President John Biden and representatives of American AI companies. See on this subject an article published on July 21, 2023 by the SZ entitled "AI companies promise Biden watermarks for AI content."

an article signed by Dorothy Chou, head of public affairs at Google DeepMind, entitled "AI companies aren't afraid of regulation—we want it to be international and inclusive." In a key passage of the article, Chou states, "Laws are only effective, however, if they are future-proof. That's why it's crucial for regulators to consider not only how to regulate chatbots today, but also how to foster an ecosystem where innovation and scientific acceleration can benefit people, providing outcome-driven frameworks for tech companies to work within."

The connotation of these discourses on AI ethics is characterized by "techno-solutionism." Techno-solutionism places corporations at the forefront of AI ethics because they have the ability to find the best technological solutions. The basic idea is that companies do not need institutions or researchers because they are capable of acting ethically on their own.

In this regard, we can turn for a moment from the press speeches to a small portion of the online material on AI ethics provided by a giant like Google.[8] The page begins with this sentence: "While we are optimistic about the potential of AI, we recognize that advanced technologies can raise important challenges that must be addressed clearly, thoughtfully, and affirmatively." So, on the one hand, there is (finally) full recognition of the ethical issues that AI can raise. On the other hand, this concern does not dispel a certain general "optimism." The solution is not fear, but intelligent action. On the same page, Google proposes six principles that are in some ways reminiscent of those of institutions. What is interesting is the last of these principles, "scientific excellence." The page ends with a section called "Implementing our principles," which shows how the principles are implemented in Google technologies (e.g., skin color assessment through machine learning), precisely because techno-solutionism is the best way to answer the problems of AI ethics affirmatively.

9.7 Conclusion

In this chapter, I have questioned the use of the term |AI ethics|. My intention was not to find a correct definition of AI ethics, nor to evaluate the ethical or unethical character of specific AI systems. Rather, my intention was to analyze the different and often conflicting ways in which this term is used and understood. Paradoxical as it may seem, AI ethics is a deeply political concept before it is an ethical one. What is interesting is that different techno-political projects clash over the definition of what should be called "AI ethics."

Of course, this is not to deny the relevance of AI ethical concerns. Rather, it is to highlight the fact that the way we respond and will respond to concrete questions of AI ethics will always be contextual, in this case political and social. In short, before

[8] https://ai.google/responsibility/principles. See also https://www.microsoft.com/en-us/ai/responsible-ai and https://ai.meta.com/blog/facebooks-five-pillars-of-responsible-ai/. Last accessed December 29, 2023.

we even ask ourselves what is ethical and unethical in an AI system, we need to question ourselves about what we might call the "politics of AI ethics."

In my empirical analysis, I have identified three groups of actors involved in this political struggle for hegemony: institutions, researchers, and corporations. Each of these groups has its own connotation, i.e. a particular vision of how ethics should be implemented in an AI system. I have talked about institutional normativity, researchers' critique, and corporate techno-solutionism. These are three very different ways of implementing ethics in AI.

In conclusion, I can say that the end result of this struggle for hegemony will not be so much a more ethical AI (at least not necessarily), but rather that one of these groups will be able to define the ethics and therefore the legitimacy of an AI system.

Bibliography

Ahmed N, Wahed M, Thompson Neil C (2023) The growing influence of industry in AI research. Science 379(6635):884–886

Barthes R (1964) Rhétorique de l'image. Communications 4(1):40–51

Brey P (2010). Philosophy of technology after the empirical turn. Techné Res Philos Technol 14(1):36–48

Bucchi M (1996) When scientists turn to the public: alternative routes in science communication. Public Underst Sci 5(4):375–394

Dondero MG (2007) Reproductibilité, faux parfaits et contrefaçons: Entre fétichisme artistique et goût esthétique. *Nouveaux Actes Sémiotiques.* https://www.unilim.fr/actes-semiotiques/3261

Farkas J, Schou J (2018) Fake news as a floating signifier: hegemony, antagonism and the politics of falsehood. Javnost Publ 25(3):298–314

Farkas J, Schou J (2019) Post-truth, fake news and democracy: mapping the politics of falsehood. Routledge, London and New York

Goulden M (2013) Hobbits, hunters and hydrology: Images of a "missing link", and its scientific communication. Public Underst Sci 22(5):575–589

Jeanneret Y (2008) Penser la trivialité. Hermès Lavoisier, Paris

Jørgensen M, Phillips Louise J (2002) Discourse analysis as theory and method. Sage Publications, New York

Laclau E (2005) On populist reason. Verso, London

Maigret E, Martin L (eds) (2020) Les cultural studies : Au-delà des politiques des identités. Lormont, Le Bord de l'eau

Martin J (2002) The political logic of discourse: a neo-Gramscian view. Hist Eur Ideas 28(1–2):21–31

Ricœur P (2016) Lectures on ideology and utopia. Columbia University Press, New York

Robert P (2017) L'imaginaire des TIC en question. Interfaces numériques 4(2)

Romele A (2023) Digital habitus: a critique of the imaginaries of artificial intelligence. Routledge, London and New York

Romele A (2022) Images of artificial intelligence: a blind spot in AI ethics. Philos Technol 35(4):1–19

Singler B (2020) The AI creation meme: a case study of the new visibility of religion in artificial intelligence discourse. Religions 11(5)

Part IV
Humanism, Technical, and Values-laden AI

Chapter 10
How to Build an AI Governance Framework with Data Governance

Peggy Tsai

Abstract The rapid proliferation of Generative Artificial Intelligence (GenAI) has fundamentally altered operational paradigms across various industries, enhancing efficiencies in domains such as software development, document summarization, and content creation. While AI-driven automation has been integral to manufacturing and supply chain industries for decades, the advent of large language models has catalyzed the widespread adoption of AI-driven decision-making. This accelerated integration necessitates a critical examination of governance structures to address transparency, accountability, and ethical concerns.

Traditional data governance frameworks, designed to ensure data integrity, consistency, and compliance, provide a foundational model for AI governance. Given AI's reliance on extensive datasets, expanding governance principles to encompass AI-specific challenges—such as algorithmic bias, ethical oversight, and regulatory compliance—is imperative. A structured AI governance framework should integrate established data governance capabilities, including data lineage documentation, quality monitoring, and role-based accountability structures, while addressing AI-specific risks related to bias mitigation, transparency, and ethical deployment.

Furthermore, organizations must adapt risk management frameworks, particularly the "three lines of defense" model, to incorporate AI-specific oversight mechanisms. As global regulatory landscapes evolve, proactive governance strategies are essential to ensuring AI systems align with ethical standards and legal requirements. This paper argues that by extending well-established data governance principles to AI, enterprises can enhance trust, mitigate risks, and foster responsible AI adoption. The application of rigorous governance methodologies will be crucial in shaping the future trajectory of AI, ensuring its responsible deployment while safeguarding societal and organizational interests.

Keywords Ethics of AI · Data governance · Data management · Ethical AI governance

P. Tsai (✉)
Newyork, NY, USA
e-mail: peggytsai923@gmail.com

R. Fioravante and A. Vaccaro (eds.), *Humanism and Artificial Intelligence*, SpringerBriefs in Philosophy, https://doi.org/10.1007/978-3-031-85478-1_10

Generative artificial intelligence (GenAI) rapidly swept the world due to the ease in usability that emerged to change the way people operate in their work and personal lives. From code development to summarizing technical documents, people are leveraging this technology to improve efficiency in their workplace. Outside the office, people have leveraged this technology to quickly plan a vacation itinerary or create new visual images. In no short order, large language models have quickly become ubiquitous in our day to day lives.

But artificial intelligence is not a new concept in business. For over a century, early aspects of automation in manufacturing and supply chain industries have been commonly used to identify repetitive sequences that could be repeated at scale.[1] To take advantage of large scales of data, organizations hired data scientists to apply machine learning to identify patterns in their customer usage and to predict trends in their sales campaigns. Big data technologies such as Hadoop and Apache Spark provided companies the means to store and process large datasets with analytical engines and computational power.

The future of AI technologies can help augment human workers capabilities to make faster and more intelligent business decisions by sourcing data together. AI has already proven to be a helpful assistance in applying algorithmic rules to large scales of data. This level of efficiency has already been applied in workforce hiring where resumes are filtered by key words to closely match with the job descriptions. Similarly, AI is used in banking in credit applications to approve loans based on employment history and behaviors. It can also monitor fraudulent activities in real-time based on large volumes of data.

The technical question arises: where lies the transparency of the rules and who has the accountability in the decisions within the realm of Artificial Intelligence? Much like the challenges that arose in risk model management, the current state of AI decision making can be perceived as a "black box," a term used to describe a system characterized by opaque rules and logic governing its output. This opacity extends to the comprehension of the underlying data used for AI model training. Since large language models rely on large amounts of pre-training datasets to recognize, predict and generate new text, the governance of such data plays a pivotal role in forecasting future outcomes.

Similarly, a business ethical debate also arises amongst technologists on balancing the speed of deployment using continuous ethical checks or quickening the development in order to strike new frontiers and gain new advancements.[2] Data analysts can identify the data elements to support the automated monitoring of ethical checks on bias but policymakers would argue it is a bit more nuanced than just reviewing the metadata and data elements. Data on the demographics of a population could identify if there is a higher weight or bias for gender, age, racial ethnicity, income etc. But combinations of other undefined data elements can also influence the outcome of AI algorithms. Therefore an AI governance framework becomes a necessity to continuously review and monitor the algorithms and models for ethical compliance.

[1] https://nanotronics.co/thinkspace/a-brief-history-of-automation-in-manufacturing/

[2] Fioravante and Vaccaro (2025).

Although much reliance on generative AI is on known data, transparency and accountability are a few principles in the governance of Artificial Intelligence. While Big Data technology companies are often deemed ethically responsible for AI since they created the "engine" to power AI technology, it is up to the quality of the data—or the "oil"—that ultimately determines the accuracy and efficacy of AI. For companies looking to build their own large language models, companies use their proprietary and confidential data, often found in unstructured sources, for bespoke or "small" models. Similarly, small language models that pertain to one domain are based on a smaller set of data so the limited data is exponentially more powerful.

10.1 Data's Impact on the Future of Artificial Intelligence

Data plays a large role in AI. The governance of data continues to be pivotal in the trustworthiness of decision-making outputs. From reports, dashboards, analytics and predictive modeling, data has always been at the center of the valuable assets created inside a company. While information technology teams have governed data through systems, the term "data governance" is the strategic usage of data with the coordination of business owners and technology owners to manage the end-to-end view of data.

However with the rapid creation of new generative content, the role of data governance is unquestionably new and untested. But there is a strong argument for expanding data governance principles to AI. While much of the current US regulatory discussion on AI regulation is focused on the privacy and protection of sensitive data in the model, the humanitarian view of AI should be focused on the governance of AI to ensure transparency of the underlying data and fairness of the data. These traits correspond to data quality dimensions typically measured in data governance programs such as accuracy, completeness, consistency, timeliness, validity and uniqueness.

Data governance across a global enterprise is usually applied to the standardization of data across all teams so that the operations, sales, product, marketing and financial teams "speak the same language." This is important as different teams discuss key performance metrics such as customer lifetime value (total amount of revenue a business can reasonably expect from a single customer account throughout the business relationship), conversion rate (the percentage of visitors to a website or campaign) or customer acquisition cost (the cost associated with acquiring a new customer). Without a commonly agreed upon calculation of the formula inside the company, different results can occur. The concept of who qualifies as a 'customer' can vary within a company due to differing interpretations of when a business relationship officially begins. This ambiguity arises because different departments, like marketing or sales, may have their own definitions. For instance, a marketing team might consider someone a customer from the first point of contact, whereas the sales team might only do so at the time of the actual sale.

The governance of critical data lays the foundation for downstream critical business activities like reporting, analysis and other business intelligence activities. These activities require trusted sources of information that are presumed to be accurately reviewed. Imagine if the data utilized to calculate annual financial statements contained wrong information! The fiduciary responsibility of the Chief Financial Officer (CFO) is to safeguard the accuracy of financial data and ensure that financial statements are prepared in compliance with generally accepted accounting principles (GAAP) and applicable laws and regulations. Similarly, the responsibility of the Chief Data Officer (CDO) is to ensure the accuracy and completeness of the data for different purposes and usage across the organization and comply with industry and regional regulations. The traditional CDO's role was to focus on data management of critical data assets. However in recent years, the areas of domain expanded to data engineering, AI/ML, strategy, change management and even ownership of data platforms.

The oversight of AI—from data preparation for training sets to the modeling data and output—is under the responsibility of CDOs unlike other C-suite executives in the company. The first step involves the preparation of data for training the language models. While models can generate results without regard to data quality, this is often when bias is initially introduced. Therefore a proper governance of the data needed for preparation can help evaluate and monitor for bias as well as provide accountability of the data ownership. By applying the data management and governance framework to the data for usage in AI, companies can feel confident that there is trust and safety in its usage.

10.2 Expanding Data Management Principles to AI

There are several capabilities in the data management program of the company that need to mature in order to expand the scope to AI models. Different industries have varying levels of data maturity as measured by the Boston Consulting Group survey from 2019.[3] Traditionally regulated industries like telecom and financial institutions have more established data programs due to regulations which require stricter compliance. They had to overcome challenges with legacy IT systems, organizational data silos and varying financial and cybersecurity concerns. Therefore the companies invested money, time, and technology into developing data foundation and other business assets like a data catalog, metadata repository, lineage diagrams, and quality metrics. They also established policies, processes and controls to help govern data across their businesses (Fig. 10.1).

There are foundational data principles that can be extended to govern AI. These principles include accountability, transparency, trustworthiness, bias and ethics. The following will dive deeper into each of these principles with data governance capabilities that companies have existing today in varying levels of maturity. By expanding

[3] https://www.bcg.com/publications/2019/rough-road-to-data-maturity.

Fig. 10.1 Data Governance Program capabilities and initiatives

into these capabilities, companies can build an AI Governance Framework to support the efficiency, effectiveness and innovation of AI.

The first principle is **accountability**. A data framework creates an ownership model whereby ownership and responsibilities are identified and documented by data domains as illustrated in Table 10.1: RACI Matrix Model Responsibilities by Domain and Tasks. Owners are separated by responsibility in relation to a data set since not everyone is an owner. Instead they may play other roles such as being Responsible, Accountable, Consulted or Informed. This common model is called RACI. Roles like Data Stewards, Data Custodians, Subject Matter Experts, Operations, Business and Technology teams are sometimes Responsible or Consulted for a data set depending on their existing responsibilities and knowledge of the area (Table 10.2).

In the AI Governance framework, additional roles such as Data Scientists and AI Engineers can be added to the RACI matrix as illustrated in Table 10.3: RACI Matrix Model for AI Governance. Companies can assign specific AI engineering teams to be responsible for the data. Business subject matter experts can be assigned to be responsible for the proper usage of the data. Additional roles may include Technology teams who can be Consulted on the correct sourcing of data. Compliance may be Informed of the different algorithms to ensure ethical and legal usage of the data. These are some examples where additional roles need to be identified to augment the existing data RACI matrix to accommodate for AI. Ultimately the best practices will remain that clear communication and ownership of roles will help manage and control for changes as AI initiatives and projects grow.

Table 10.1 AI Principles and Capabilities that are currently performed under Data Governance and how it can be amended into the new AI Governance Framework

Principles	Capabilities	Current Data Governance Framework	Amended AI Governance Framework
Accountability	Roles and responsibilities: RACI matrix	Identify roles and responsibilities for each domain/task	New roles and responsibilities for AI Engineering team
	Data governance council	CDO and peers to prioritize data governance use cases	New reporting structure for Chief Data & AI Officer
Transparency	Data lineage	Document data flows from source to target	Document data lineage and provenance of AI models and training data sets
	Business glossary	Standardized definitions across lines of business	Expand definitions of AI terms including model inputs and outputs
Trustworthiness	Data quality metrics	Established metrics and acceptable threshold scores	Expansion of metrics for data sets on training data for AI algorithms
	Master Data management and reference data	Managing consistency and accuracy of critical data while maintaining a single record of truth	Expanding the accuracy and consistency of data into AI inputs
Bias	Data quality monitoring	Creating a data scorecard to actively track performance of data quality metrics	Inclusion of data quality monitoring of AI model inputs and outputs
	Remediation	A process for assessing, identifying, assigning ownership and fixing data errors	Inclusion of AI models and training data for ensuring high data quality and detecting bias
Ethics	Policies and controls	Corporate and industry rules implemented into program for compliance	Protection and assurance of compliance of AI per global regulations
	Risk management	Mitigating and monitoring risk taxonomy against current processes	Inclusion of AI to risk taxonomy for risk scoring, profiling and mitigation

Another aspect of accountability that can be amended in this new AI Governance framework is the Data Governance Council. The Chief Data Officer typically presides over the Data Governance Council. The CDO includes their business and technology counterparts including the Chief Technology Officer and the Line of Business Leaders that are owners of data domains under governance. Depending on the focus of the Data Governance Council, the members may identify and prioritize data governance projects, approve budget funding and review data issues for remediation.

In the new age of AI Governance, the new AI Governance Council may be replaced by the Chief Data and AI Officer (CDAIO) to augment the data governance charter to include the company's AI's purpose and scope. The AI Governance Council should

Table 10.2 RACI Matrix Model Responsibilities by Domain and Tasks. RACI = Responsible, Accountable, Consulted and Informed roles

Domain	Task	Data Stewards	Data Custodian	Business Data Owner	IT System Owner	Operations Owner
Finance Data Set	Profile data	R	R	A	C	I
	Define KPIs	I	I	R/A	I	I
	Define business rules	C	C	R/A	I	I
	Create scorecards	R	I	A	C	I
Product Data Set	Prioritize critical data	R	C	R	C	I
	Standardize definitions	R	C	A	I	C
	Build data lineage	R	R	I	A	C
	Remediate data	R	R	I	A	C

Table 10.3 RACI Matrix Model for AI Governance. RACI = Responsible, Accountable, Consulted and Informed roles

Domain	Sample Tasks	Data Stewards	Data Custodian	Business Data Owner	IT System Owner	Operation Owner	Data Scientist	AI Engineer
Finance Data Set	Profile data	R	R	A	C	I	R	C
	Define KPIs	I	I	R/A	I	I	C	R
	Define business rules	C	C	R/A	I	I	R	I
	Create scorecards	R	I	A	C	I	I	I
Product Data Set	Prioritize critical data	R	C	R	C	I	R	R
	Standardize definitions	R	C	A	I	C	I	I
	Build data lineage	R	R	I	A	C	I	I
	Remediate data	R	R	I	A	C	C	C

be expanded to include additional Line of Business team leaders to ensure full representation of business priorities in the application of AI. The new members of the Council should reflect the new roles in the organization for AI such as an AI/ML Engineer, AI Solutions Architect, AI Product Manager, AI Ethicist and an AI global regulation expert. Figure 10.2 illustrates a sample structure of an AI Governance Council that includes the newly created roles in the company. Similar to the current Data Governance Council, these new roles will help to prioritize business use cases, review ethical issues and impacts, discuss resource allocation in addition to the existing data governance responsibilities.

Additional responsibilities for the AI Governance Council may include compliance and enforcement mechanisms for ensuring adherence to the AI policies. Corporate training and communication is another important change that needs to be expanded under the CDAIO. The plan for educating and communicating with stakeholders needs to expand into the ethical usage of data. In addition to these changes, new performance metrics need to be created to measure the success of AI including impact to the company and the customer adoption of these technologies (Fig. 10.3).

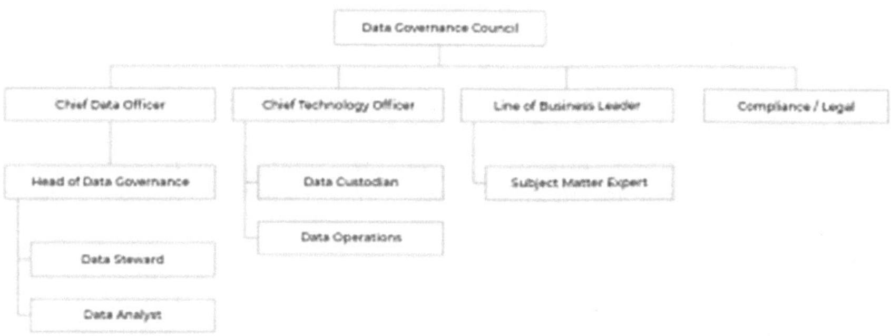

Fig. 10.2 A sample overview of a Data Governance Council members

Fig. 10.3 A sample AI Governance Council with expanded membership to reflect the new roles

Another similarity to the prior Chief Data Officer role is the reporting structure of the new AI data governance council. Depending where the CDAIO sits inside the company—whether it is under the Chief Financial Officer, Chief Digital Officer or Chief Information Officer for example—the scope of the Data Governance Council will either be minimally limited to a specific line of business or more expansively, be open to the entire company. Companies have different reasons for placing the data executive in varying reporting lines. Some of these reasons may include the data maturity, the background of an existing C-suite executive or simply the short-term priorities of the company. Since there is no standard for the reporting structure, variances will ultimately depend on the needs of the company.

There are different pros and cons for the reporting structure and ultimately the ownership of AI initiatives. The Chief Financial Officer may be more concerned with identifying the budget for AI research and restrict innovation by being conservative to ensure a healthy return on investment. The Chief Digital Officer can provide the enterprise wide resources for large scale changes as long as the reporting structure of the AI team also aligns together. There may be instances in companies to initiate AI initiatives with the engineers and data scientists to report into the Chief Information Officer. This is a common starting point whereby technology can own and manage the AI platforms. The hope is that this reporting structure will be balanced by business priorities and requirements.

A second guiding principle in AI regulations is **transparency** specifically knowing what data is utilized in the training sets. The second part of transparency is also understanding where the data is derived and sourced from. By documenting end-to-end data lineage flows whereby each data "hop" is documented including any transformation rules, companies can trace each step of the data movement. Usually data is derived from a single golden copy, or an authoritative source, but this is not always necessarily reflective of the realistic representation of the data landscape. Companies can maintain multiple copies or versions of the data because it can exist for different purposes. Variations of the same data set may exist. For example, if the data set pertained to product sales, the finance team would want to analyze the numbers in order to report on monthly sales. However the marketing team may take the same data set and group by product lines to understand changes by different time periods. Since this can occur many times within and across business units inside a company, the data lineage flows can quickly become complicated to document. It also can be difficult to maintain the freshness of the flows as well since it is often very easy for new data sets to be replicated.

Ultimately full transparency of a company's data can be achieved with data lineage. A data lineage flow effectively documents and ensures comprehensive transparency regarding the entire journey of data across the organization, encompassing various databases, data lakes, data warehouses, applications, and reports. This is a difficult feat for many companies to achieve, and most importantly to maintain, due to the constant change in the creation of data. In addition, copies of data can be managed without sharing with the information technology team. "Shadow IT" is a term that refers to systems that are built and used inside companies without explicit organizational approval. These are known as stealth operations outside the official capacities to build and maintain technology. Employees lean towards "shadow IT" practices for various reasons including seeking immediate or more suitable solutions for their work needs than what is available through official IT channels. This practice makes it even more difficult for companies to completely document data lineage if employees are maintaining separate systems.

Another data management capability that supports transparency principle is the Business Glossary which is a standard living artifact for any data governance program. A glossary contains terms that are commonly used by the business including the definitions of the terms in the context of how it is used inside the company and perhaps in the industry. Standardizing and rationalizing term definitions is crucial to ensure that all employees, regardless of their business unit, tenure, or level within the company, use a consistent and unified language. This means that they have the same information to make the same business decisions. Another benefit to building a business glossary is to avoid confusion and assumptions made with employees of varying knowledge levels on the company's business assets.

Companies can improve the transparency by creating and maintaining an inventory or a data catalog on their data assets. This can be manually or automatically created to list out the technical assets in the company. Technical assets refer to the tools, systems, applications and databases that support the operations of the company. It can also include unstructured data as well such as file share repositories. The inventory or catalog is intended to be a single source of truth for finding all the sources of information. Many companies also leverage a catalog to document additional context that can serve as useful information for understanding how the technical asset should be used in analysis. Ultimately the purpose of an inventory or catalog helps support self-service capabilities for employees to independently search, request and use the data without relying on the technology system owner. Another benefit for building this capability is to help different persona's govern and manage their assets. Privacy teams are concerned with sensitive data, security teams are looking to protect the company's crown jewels and lastly, data teams are concerned with governing critical data elements.

With the emergence of AI, the models and algorithms can be included in the same inventory or catalog. This provides the same benefits of documenting all the company's technical assets. For the AI engineer team, listing out all the different models helps to keep track of the ones created and used inside the company as well as understand the underlying data that comprises the model inputs. Different models can be created for various business purposes and/or by business units. So a complete and single source of all the AI models can assist the AI engineering teams to avoid creating duplicates. The inventory can also document the context of why, how and the purpose of each model. This is ultimately critical for compliance purposes.

The third principle on data management that can be applied to AI Governance is **trustworthiness**. This principle refers to the degree which the data is viewed as reliable, accurate and can be depended upon for making critical decisions. If the data is deemed as trustworthy, it can be used for analysis, reporting and informed decision-making across various business operations.

There are several aspects of an existing data management model that can support this principle. The first one is establishing a Data Quality program including business and technical rules for measuring the data as well as establishing thresholds for acceptable quality levels. There are several dimensions of data quality measurement which may or may not be applicable to all data sources. For example, the 'completeness; dimension is often profiled to identify null values because it is indicated by a blank cell. On the other hand, the 'timeliness' dimension may not be relevant if the data values are static and rarely change.

The most visible data quality dimension that is often noticeable is the 'consistency' dimension. In layman's terms, all data must look similar in format. The structural format of the data is one example of identifying consistency of the data across different sources. Let's dive deeper into why this data quality dimension is of importance for consumer facing companies. For a marketing team of a customer facing company, they utilize email addresses to send communications. If this data has poor data quality, it will delay the communication of time-sensitive messages such as a limited sale promotion.

The structural components of an email address determine how it can be measured against the different data dimensions. An email address follows a standard format consisting of three main parts. This includes the local part which is part of the email address that comes before the "@" symbol. The second part is the "@" symbol which separates the local part of the address with the domain part. Lastly the domain part specifies the mail server that is hosting the email address. Here are additional data quality dimensions that support the trustworthiness principle.

Completeness: This dimension refers to data being populated for all the records or rows in a table or database. The marketing team is looking to have an email address listed out for each customer that has willingly shared this information.

Consistency: The 'consistency' dimension for data quality in an email address can be quickly detected if it does not follow that standard format. This dimension can also be measured across different data sets. This is potentially more relevant when it comes to unstructured data.

Accuracy: The 'accuracy' dimension is not visibly detected by the naked eye. The only true test of identifying accurate email addresses is whether the email address is still active and that there is no bounce back message when using the email address.

Validity: Companies need to ensure that email addresses are accurately tied to the name of the owner in the records. The email address may be accurate but it needs to be valid with respect to the customer name.

The above data quality dimensions apply mainly to structured data. However, much of the training data for AI is based on unstructured data. In many companies, the bespoke and custom knowledge is stored in their unstructured data. There are additional data quality dimensions that may be more applicable to assessing the unstructured data inside large language models. Unstructured data is largely unharnessed despite big data technologies. But recent advancements in deep learning models like Meta's Segment Anything Model for images, OpenAI whispers for speech-to-text, Bark for text-to-speech, GPT for text data and Layoutml for documents paved the way for unstructured data utilization.[4] However due to the complexity of understanding the business context inside files, documents and emails, it is difficult to know the information inside the unstructured data without manual review and labeling.

One of the challenges with AI is understanding the quality of the data that is used in the preparation of the model. It's often said that "garbage in, garbage out" for models implies that the quality of the data inputs will affect the output or results. This directly supports the trustworthiness of data if the quality of the data inputs is not validated. Since many of the data sources fueling the large language model is unstructured data, it is even more imperative to measure data quality. Traditional methods for measuring data quality do not apply the same in structured data and unstructured data. If the data is in a table format, it can be measured against data quality rules like accuracy. But what data quality dimensions would be relevant for unstructured data and how can this be measured? While there are no known methodologies for data quality measurement for unstructured data, here are some possible ways that companies can understand and promote trustworthiness into the unstructured data. Clustering similar data files together can help machine learning algorithms identify outliers in the data points across all the documents. Consistency can be monitored across multiple different critical data elements in a group of documents. This can be presented in a data profiling scatter plot to show the dispersion of the data values. The second data quality dimension that can be measured is validity. Classification in machine learning labeling can verify the information inside the documents to ensure that identifiers such as credit card numbers and account numbers are real and valid.

Another aspect of data management capability that can support trustworthiness is Master Data Management (MDM). One aspect of Master Data Management is cleansing of the data by removing duplicates, correcting errors and standardizing formats. This process helps to fix the data and improve the data quality across multiple dimensions. Companies will typically incorporate a MDM program to correct data errors and also ensure that valid data is utilized. Similarly, data management programs utilize Reference Data Management to validate data to standardized data sets such as US zip codes or abbreviations for country names. This reference list helps to clean out data errors often due to a manual input error. Data cleansing as an activity under Master Data Management can also remove data duplications which means that unnecessary records in tables are deleted. This reduces the potential bias inside AI algorithms which can be heavily weighted on duplicate data. By reducing the "noise" in the model inputs, there is a higher quality of trust in the data.

This leads to the next principle of **Bias** which can often stem from the data used in training the AI models. AI systems can amplify any existing bias in the underlying data. The potential for bias can be identified within data quality metrics which was offered under the trustworthiness of data. However continuous data quality monitoring in the form of scorecards and dashboards can identify potential drifts which indicate a bias in the data population. If the data is not representative of the general population or the scenario that AI is intended to serve, data quality

---

[4] https://www.forbes.com/sites/forbestechcouncil/2023/07/24/unleashing-the-power-of-unstructured-data-th e-rise-of-large-ai-models/?sh = 502d993d40f8.

monitoring can help teams to build controls to monitor changes in the AI algorithms. Personal information that describes the population of people inside datasets such as gender, race, ethnicity, geographic location, education etc. can potentially reflect bias if there is an indication of exclusion. For example, historically, medical research focused on male population and the results generalized to females.[5] Whether this was an unconscious bias or not, researchers' did not recognize the biological differences between women and men resulting in real-life disadvantages for female patients.

In addition to data-driven bias, 'algorithmic bias' may occur when the AI algorithms and models make assumptions or are structured in a way that results in unfair outcomes. Human bias can also be introduced in the design of the model which can include the programming of the model, the problem framing, and interpretation of results. Human intervention is required to review and manually offset any potential perceived bias. Teams can apply mitigation strategies to reduce AI bias. One of these strategies can take form in an existing data governance capability under data lifecycle management called Remediation. Remediation is an important process to fix data that needs correcting to meet certain standards. Data quality teams can review the data quality scores that fall under the acceptable threshold levels, identify the root cause of the data errors and then make the necessary corrections.

Specifically in the AI Governance framework where models can change from unsupervised learning, data quality monitoring can identify model output deviations. AI Engineering teams can leverage the scorecard process in data governance programs to be alerted with data issues and consulted on remediation fixes on their impacted data. Data scientists can also be informed on the quality of data they leverage for selecting data sources to build models. In addition to identifying data errors on the element level, AI teams can also monitor the data quality at the data set level which is a combination of multiple data elements. This is an additional control on the data utilized for AI that is important for building guardrails for safety and trust.

In addition to data quality monitoring, the data governance framework incorporates the purpose specification concept that is a key part of data privacy and protection frameworks. This principle centers around the idea that personal data should be collected for specified, explicit and legitimate purposes. As companies collect data—personal and non-personal—it is important for companies to demonstrate that they are able to protect individuals from unexpected and potentially harmful uses of personal data. As part of this ongoing privacy compliance, data teams need to align the business process context of how and why the data was created so that it can be incorporated in the proper AI algorithm. For example, if a company was developing a recruiting algorithm for the Human Resources department, the data should be trained on the potential pool of candidates and not on data that was collected on profiles of potential customers. While both are people datasets, the data would not be indicative of the same purpose for collection as well as the proper fit for applying to the same business process.

Finally, the last principle that can be leveraged for the AI Governance Framework is **Ethics** and ethical usage of data. The continuous data quality monitoring that

[5] https://www.ncbi.nlm.nih.gov/pmc/articles/PMC8812498/

helps to manage risk associated with privacy data can also be governed by policies and controls. Specifically, this data quality process that exists in the data governance framework can also detect any sensitive information that may or may not be allowed inside the AI models. The continuous scanning of the underlying data can help to discover personal information used in the preparation or calculation inside AI models. Ultimately the AI Governance framework will need to define new policies and controls to prevent the unethical practices of misusing data. These new policies must be created in conjunction with the Privacy, Legal and Compliance teams since they need to weigh in on this new additional component.

Separately, compliance to different global AI regulations is top of mind for Chief Data Officers that are used to following policies in their industry and local region. The addition of AI regulations requires them to work closely with their Privacy, Legal and Compliance team to determine what it means to be "out of compliance." The application and interpretation of behaviors and activities lie in the usage of the AI systems (data, model and interaction with others). Therefore monitoring the ethical usage of data is only a passive monitoring of compliance. Rather responsible ethics involves monitoring and guiding the engagement of the people with AI systems.

Another component of the data governance framework to help with AI ethics is risk management. In many regulated industries like financial services, risk is managed by the three lines of defense: the first line is the operational management or the data office who are directly responsible for maintaining effective internal controls, the second line is the enterprise risk management function who provide oversight and develop risk management frameworks, and lastly the third line of defense is Internal Audit function who provides an independent and objective assessment of the effectiveness of risk management in the company. The three lines of defense contribute to mitigating the traditional risk taxonomy which includes financial, operational, reputational, compliance, political, technology and market risk. Each type of risk requires its own specific management and mitigation strategy. The management of the risk is first owned by the data teams or the operational managers as part of their day-to-day activities.

As companies increasingly involve AI algorithms and systems, the responsibilities of the three lines model must change as well. In Fig. 10.4, the management must continue to involve the first line roles which will now include the AI engineers, data scientists and analytics teams. They will perform the day-to-day responsibilities of identifying, assessing, controlling and mitigating risks. They ensure that their activities are conducted that are consistent with the company's policies and procedures. The second line roles will continue to involve the Enterprise Risk Managers however there is now a specialized focus on AI. There should be amended frameworks to assist in risk identification and assessment for the new applications of AI systems as well as monitor compliance with global laws and AI regulations. Lastly, the third line roles of internal auditors should be to provide independent and objective assurance to AI risk management and governance. They should also create AI frameworks and assessments to test the effectiveness of the company's processes. These frameworks and assessments may be based on existing data frameworks but include scope for AI data, systems and models. Most importantly, internal auditors

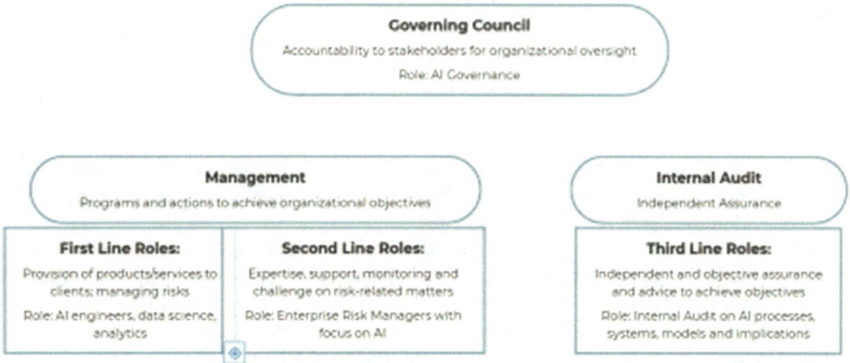

Fig. 10.4 Proposed framework for the three Lines of Defense Roles and Governing Council for AI Governance

will need to work closely with the first lines of defense to ensure full documentation as well as the second line to review the control results. Ultimately the internal audit team reports to the highest level of an organization, typically the board of directors or audit committee should also be knowledgeable of AI governance.

10.3 Conclusion

While AI regulation continues to evolve with Generative and Generic AI, the principles of data governance have been tested to meet compliance requirements over the last decade to ensure high levels of quality and management of the data. Therefore, it is sensible to apply the same governance rigors to AI while achieving the principles expressly outlined in the global AI Acts including EU AI Act and the United States' AI Executive Order at the time of this publication. While many aspects of AI policies have yet to be finalized, the intention to harness the potential benefits of technology while limiting the risks and ensuring transparency is quite evident.[6] Until then, today's Chief Data Officers can rely on existing data governance frameworks to mature and future-proof their data programs as they transition into their roles as Chief Artificial Intelligence Officers for the future.

[6] https://www.nytimes.com/2023/12/08/technology/eu-ai-act-regulation.html.

Bibliography

Baltassis E, et al (2019) A rough road to data maturity. Boston Consulting Group, 30 December, https://www.bcg.com/publications/2019/rough-road-to-data-maturity. Accessed 10 January 2024.

Contributor Guest (2023) 5 ways generative AI will impact culture & society: what tech leaders need to know. TechRepublic, 24 October, https://www.techrepublic.com/article/generative-ai-impact-culture-society/. Accessed 10 Jan 2024

Dahal B (2023) Unleashing the power of unstructured data: the rise of large AI models. Forbes, 24 July, https://www.forbes.com/sites/forbestechcouncil/2023/07/24/unleashing-the-power-of-unstructured-data-the-rise-of-large-ai-models/?sh=502d993d40f8. Accessed 10 Jan 2024

DGI Institute. DGI Data Governance Framework. The Data Governance Institute, https://datagovernance.com/the-dgi-data-governance-framework/. Accessed 10 Jan 2024

Duggal N (2023) Future of AI (Artificial Intelligence): what lies ahead? Simplilearn.com, 6 November, https://www.simplilearn.com/future-of-artificial-intelligence-article. Accessed 10 Jan 2024

Fioravante R, Vaccaro A (2025) Humanism, dehumanization, integral human development: an overview of boundaries and capabilities of human-centered artificial intelligence in business and organizations. In: Fioravante R, Vaccaro A (eds) Humanism and artificial intelligence. Springer

The Institute of Internal Auditors. The IIA's three lines model. The Institute of Internal Auditors, https://www.theiia.org/globalassets/documents/resources/the-iias-three-lines-model-an-update-of-the-three-lines-of-defense-july-2020/three-lines-model-updated-english.pdf. Accessed 10 Jan 2024

Liebert MA (2022) Sex Inequalities in medical research: a systematic scoping review of the literature. NCBI, January, https://www.ncbi.nlm.nih.gov/pmc/articles/PMC8812498/. Accessed 10 Jan 2024

Manyika J et al (2019) What do we do about the biases in AI? Harvard Business Review, 25 October, https://hbr.org/2019/10/what-do-we-do-about-the-biases-in-ai. Accessed 10 Jan 2024

Moore S (2019) How to get started with master data management. Gartner, 5 December, https://www.gartner.com/smarterwithgartner/how-to-get-started-with-master-data-management. Accessed 10 Jan 2024

Nanotronics (2023) A brief history of automation in manufacturing. Nanotronics, 9 May, https://nanotronics.co/thinkspace/a-brief-history-of-automation-in-manufacturing/. Accessed 10 Jan 2024

Satariano A (2023) E.U. Agrees on AI act, landmark regulation for Artificial Intelligence. The New York Times, 8 December, https://www.nytimes.com/2023/12/08/technology/eu-ai-act-regulation.html. Accessed 10 Jan 2024

Tennison J, Maja Bogataj Jancic (2020) The role of data in AI. Global Partnership on Artificial Intelligence—GPAI, 26 November, https://gpai.ai/projects/data-governance/role-of-data-in-ai.pdf. Accessed 10 Jan 2024

Chapter 11
Dementia Care: A Test Case for the Humanity of AI in Health and Nursing Care

Paula Boddington

Abstract This chapter explores the situation of people living with dementia as a test case to examine the possibilities for implementing AI in health and social care in a manner that fully respects the humanity of all involved. People living with dementia unfortunately already often experience dehumanising attitudes and (often inadvertently) dehumanising treatment. This means that examining the treatment and care of this particular group may alert us to issues that may be present for others but less visibly so. Moreover, there exists a body of work which attempts to counter dehumanising attitudes and treatment for this group which can be drawn upon in considering the use of AI, and there are many existing and proposed uses of AI for the care and treatment of those living or at risk of dementia. We consider the use of AI in dementia diagnosis, and also draw on ethnographic observations within hospital of the care of people living with dementia, from a team focused upon improving the quality and humanity of care and on understanding the patterns of dehumanisation found on the hospital ward. The hospital can be used as a 'small society' to examine institutional forces which affect the provision of care and to identify factors to consider when implementing AI in such a setting. Themes focused on include the observation of people using AI and data; control via AI; and the identification of tasks and goals, as well as the general themes of time and efficiency.

Keywords Ethics of AI · AI healthcare · AI ethics of care · AI diagnosis

11.1 Introduction: AI and Human Nature

This chapter considers the use of AI and automation in the care of people living with dementia. People living with dementia, and those at risk of dementia, may stand to gain considerably from sensitive use of AI and automation, but are also particularly

---

P. Boddington (✉)
Geller Institute of Ageing and Memory, University of West London, London, UK
e-mail: paulaboddington@protonmail.com

R. Fioravante and A. Vaccaro (eds.), *Humanism and Artificial Intelligence*, SpringerBriefs in Philosophy, https://doi.org/10.1007/978-3-031-85478-1_11

vulnerable to suffering ill-effects from inappropriate use, and hence may provide a test case where both good and ill may be highly visible.

For the implementation of AI to take a humanistic perspective, a central place must be given to the human person. Many declarations of ethics call for AI to be developed for the 'benefit of humanity', but we need more than some crude utilitarian notion of 'benefit'. If AI is intended to enhance or to replace human agency, thought, and decision-making, we must understand what we really value in human life, in order to appraise whether AI really does enhance us, or really ought to replace us in certain tasks. We must ask questions concerning human nature, as Fioravante and Vaccaro put it in the first chapter of this volume, our ontological status. These questions will include, in the context of medicine discussed in this chapter, how the person is to be understood—simply biomedically, or in terms of the whole person set within a social world (Leonardi 2018).

It is necessary to ask hard questions about how technological progress may be already impacting us and our social systems; humanistic ethics is concerned not just with technology per se but with the social infrastructure of their design and use (Fioravante and Vaccaro 2025). For our view of the world, of ourselves, and of what is to be valued, is being moulded in various ways by the very technology in question. Consider, for instance, the myriad ways in which technology directs our attention—the persuasive technology in the smart phones that most of us carry with us all the time should suffice to illustrate this control of attention, and a key issue to be considered here is how the collection and use of data by technology likewise impacts our attention and our view of the world.

We need also to consider the ideology and implicit values and goals that may accompany technology and its application. The very development of technology such as AI can help to promote certain views of what is best in human nature and what is valuable in human life: the goals that are pursued, the tasks that are seen to be better undertaken by machines than by humans, will implicitly or explicitly make statements about the desirable life for humans – or for certain groups of humans.

Much work in AI focuses upon producing technology to accomplish discrete engineering challenges, but there is also work which focuses on the project of AI conceived in broader and more ambitious terms, with the aims to mimic or to exceed human intelligence, however that is conceived. Such a project thus rides upon assumptions about the nature of intelligence and why it is valued, as well as sometimes making assumptions regarding the place of intelligence as a central or even defining feature of human nature. Intelligence may be conceived in ways which stress certain cognitive tasks, and viewed instrumentally in terms of the capacity efficiently to achieve certain goals: 'humans are intelligent to the extent that our actions can be expected to achieve our objectives' (Russell 2019, p. 9) (meaning that assessing the goals is not part of 'intelligence'), although there are robust debates in the field about the nature of intelligence (Larson 2021; Legg and Hutter 2007; Chollet 2019). Some may indeed consider all problems have an AI solution, a view summed up by Demis Hassabis of DeepMind as the ambition to 'solve intelligence, and then use that to solve everything else' (Burton-Hill 2016). A technological solutionism or 'technological fix' may thus take hold (Weinberg 1966, Morozov 2014). But then, as AI is being developed and becoming more and more integrated into human life, if such attitudes become entrenched, its very deployment may be influencing how we think of human nature, and what we see as valuable in human life, even without any ideological attachment to certain views of the nature and value of intelligence. Conversely, at the same time, intense debate and opposition to certain ideological stances influenced by AI technology are occurring.

As noted, the influence of AI upon our lives may be extended through the ubiquitous ways in which humans and technology mutually interact within socio-technological systems, impacting our perception and knowledge of the world and how we relate to and perceive each other and ourselves, as data about us is collected and analysed through technologies. This means that in examining the impact of AI we need to consider local cultures. Especially within institutions, this will be within a hierarchical context, of particular concern as we consider the culture within hospital wards, a 'small society' that has been described as closely reflecting the wider world (Caudill 1958, p. 3). The implicit values that may be present in the application of AI, for example, that efficiency, however understood, is a good, that speed is to be valued, that certain goals can be delineated and measured, may or may not be coherent with the values of a humanistic approach to life. Yet we can often see that such goal-oriented, efficiency-led thinking is already present in the institutions within which much technology is deployed. What will be the impact of adding even more technology to such contexts?

It is clear that we need to ask various epistemological questions about human nature and about AI. This paper takes as a central issue one blending epistemology and ethics, the mutual and reciprocal recognition of other human beings, the capacity for which is one hallmark of human nature, albeit one often sadly lacking. There are many sources of the very real risk of dehumanisation, including the failure to pay sufficient and true attention to the other (Weil 2009; Buber 1970), and technological determinism is multifaceted (Fioravante and Vaccaro 2025). Our capacity to neglect and to (mis)understand each other as humans relating to other humans suggests that we must ask how well technology can capture and respond to our human condition, and what happens when we rely on technology as a means through which to gaze on the other; what is going on as AI looks at us and as we look at AI? Might technology fail to capture all that is of importance in human experience? For '… no alarm exists for a patient's sense of isolation, yet this does not detract from its importance' (Archibald and Barnard 2018, p. 2478).

Our strategy is to examine an group for which dehumanisation already frequently occurs, but where many are already attempting to understand and combat this, the group of people living with dementia, including those at risk of the condition. This can provide material upon which to draw in considering the requirements for the humane introduction of AI, not just for the general mass of humankind, but for each and every individual. We will attempt to do this without adopting a tendency found common within the nursing sphere of assuming an opposition between technology and humanism (Barnard and Sandelowski 2001; Barnard 2002). In this volume, Fioravante and Vaccaro highlight the importance of the question of human boundaries in relation to technology; the recognition of and appropriate responses to the boundaries of the human is indeed an acute and central issue in humane relationships with and treatment of people living with dementia.

We consider two cases: AI for the diagnosis of dementia, and the situation of people living with dementia in the complex social and institutional world of the hospital ward. These two cases both involve entwined questions of epistemology and ethics. The proposed uses of AI in dementia diagnosis take us into the world of everyday life, for much proposed AI diagnosis would operate ubiquitously on the general population sometimes from many decades before onset. In contrast, the closed world of the hospital provides a world in miniature whose culture can be examined in some detail.

These issues are extremely complex, with multiple interlinking factors and it will thus be impossible to do more than indicate some of the issues and challenges for the successful and humane implementation of AI. This chapter will therefore raise broad themes to consider as background influences, and select certain themes for discussion.

11.2 Dementia and Dehumanisation

Despite considerable research efforts, much is still unknown about the condition of dementia, its aetiology, and effective prevention and treatment strategies. It often remains undiagnosed, or is diagnosed late, with currently little treatment to the condition, with major challenges in the provision of appropriate care. A variable condition, many people will live with dementia for a number of years (Liang et al. 2021). This means that there are considerable challenges in caring for this group, especially as dementia can potentially affect all areas of life. Technologies such as AI are perceived as potentially transformative of healthcare including nursing care (Archibald and Barnard 2018), and in particular there are multiple initiatives for the use of AI in dementia care, treatment, and research. Applications of AI and machine learning in use or development include the diagnosis of dementia, the stimulation of memories of those living with dementia, the use of tracking devices to prevent wandering into unsafe areas, the use of surveillance cameras around the home for safety monitoring, the use of care robots for companionship or the administration of medications or food, and the use of remote devices for monitoring and communication, with mixed reports on their benefits (Astell et al. 2019; Buchanan et al. 2020).

Dementia generally involves problems with memory and cognition and the use of language. Communication problems are common. The key place of reason and language in our understanding of what it is to be human means that people living with dementia are often subject to slights and dismissive language, such as 'death while alive', 'zombies' (Schweda and Jongsma 2022) 'funeral without end' (Mitchell et al. 2020). A common view is dementia 'by definition then seems to threaten the identity and self-hood of the individual at risk' (Higgs and Gilleard 2016, p. 773). The many living with dementia who are trapped in hospitals may be dismissed as 'bed-blockers' (Bates 2004), as if hospitals were really for 'other people'. But dementia represents a possibility for all of us as we age, and thus understanding the basis for such dehumanisation is important for us all. As the value of cognition and high levels of intelligence is increasingly emphasised by the excitement around AI, a close examination of treatment of those whose powers of cognition are in decline should prove valuable.

Humanist traditions have recognised the importance of communication and of understanding languages and cultures from our past, emphasising the study of ancient languages and texts of Greek, Latin, and Hebrew as well as the translation into the vernacular (Davies 2008). Acute attention to addressing the challenges in communication concerning people living with dementia thus can be seen as echoing this humanist tradition, especially insofar as it represents an attempt to recognise and value those who go before us: in this case, not the ancients, but simply our elders.

Furthermore, the very challenges of care mean that, as indicated above, there is already a robust debate regarding dementia, personhood, and the humanity of care, which presents us with a rich literature and body of evidence on which to draw. Tim Kitwood's work advocating person-centred care for people living with dementia has been very influential in practice (Kitwood 1997), and following this, there has been considerable work in qualitative social sciences exploring the humanity of care of those living with dementia, much of which rests upon notions of the person which emphasise social and embodied aspects of personhood.

Although there are complex debates within cognitive science, AI, and robotics about the relationship between cognition and the body, popularly the development of AI goes along with notions of a view of the mind as primarily or wholly mental, as inherently individual, as disembodied in essence, and therefore as capable of being realised within a variety of substrates, with much speculation that AI may develop consciousness or personhood. Such a view thus may go hand in hand with models of the person which emphasise rationality, language, individual autonomy, and cognition, in line with models of personhood developed by philosophers such as Dennett and others (Dennett 1988). Such an approach to personhood has led to debates about whether or not some human beings who have lessened cognitive capacities might be considered cases of 'marginal personhood' (Wasserman et al. 2017).

But a considerable body of thinking and research within the field of dementia care has taken a firmly different view. For example, the sociologist Pia Kontos (2004, 2005) draws upon the work of Merleau-Ponty and Bourdieu to argue for an embodied and social sense of personhood, demonstrating from long-term observational work of people living with dementia that a sense of self and awareness of social and cultural norms and practices may remain in an embodied selfhood, even with severe decline of linguistic capabilities. There is insufficient space in this chapter to explore different views of personhood in depth, but their significance for how technology is embedded within our social systems will be explored below.

11.3 Knowledge of the Human Being: Epistemology Matters

Much of the work emphasising person-centred care, the continued humanity and hidden capabilities of people living with dementia, arises from qualitative research methods such as ethnography. This again is relevant to concerns about attention, and may contrast with the different approach to knowledge gained via collecting and analysing data using AI.

Ethnographic observations typically take place over an extended period. The ethnographer embeds him- or herself within an environment, attempting to make sense of the meanings of the social world (Atkinson and Housley 2003). From a position both within and without a social world, the ethnographer may observe and record interactions between people in ways which capture intent and nuance in a manner that mere recording of 'behaviour' may not. Ethnography may draw upon the researcher's own reactions to a situation. Some work referred to below also draws upon methodologies of rhythmanalysis following on from work of Henri Lefebvre (2013), which is currently receiving considerable attention (Lyon 2020; Chen 2016). Lefebvre states that everywhere there is interaction between a place, a time, and an expenditure of energy, there is rhythm. Notably, he distinguishes between the cyclical time of the body and the linear time of modernity, which may often be in tension causing a breakdown of rhythms (arrythmia). Others have likewise made use of a distinction between linear and cyclical time, with Fuchs drawing links between cyclical time and bodily memory, noting the importance of the latter for people living with dementia (Fuchs, 2018, 2020).

For Lefebvre, the cyclical time of the body has its own rhythms with natural cycles of completion; this is felt within the body. Linear time is imposed through the military rhythms of modernity, as for instance, with the imposition of discipline, order, and timetables within institutions (Lefebvre 2013, p. 48). This will be of importance below in relation to discussions of efficiency and timetabling on hospital wards, and to the place of the human being within an institution and in response to technology.

Note the position of the human body as observer and as observed in this methodology. To attend, the rhythmanalyst uses their body, firstly paying attention to its rhythms, and from here, appreciating the rhythms of the world (Lefebvre 2013, p. 29). Arrhythmias occur when rhythms clash, which may cause a bodily reaction in the rhythmanalyst as observer. Note the embodied nature of the human being as observer of other human beings, in contrast with the gaze of technology. Note that the contrast between linear and cyclical time points to an imposition of order for example within an institution, or via technology, which help or disrupt the natural cyclical rhythms of the human being. This will help to frame a general question of how to introduce technology into an already ordered space in a humanising manner; the significance of the particularities of human embodiment is a major concern in considering the impact of AI.

This paper draws upon ethnographic work examining the care of people living with dementia on acute hospital wards, conducted with a view to finding ways of improving the humanity of care. Observations from this team have taken place over 8 years with, to date, over 500 days of observations in hospitals across different geographical areas of England and Wales. Projects have focused upon examining the refusal and resistance to everyday care (Featherstone et al. 2019); continence care (Featherstone et al., 2022), and the uses of restraint in care practices (Mwale et al. 2024). Of particular interest are repeated findings of inadvertent dehumanisation in care practices. No malpractice was uncovered, yet standard working practices within hospitals frequently led to people living with dementia receiving poor care, contributing to the decline and deconditioning which is very common for this group, who have very poor outcomes following admission to hospital.

Featherstone and Northcott state that 'the profound invisibility of people living with dementia was striking' (2021, p. 37). Issues identified include poor communication, and difficulties experienced by people living with dementia in keeping up with the institutional demands of timetabled care. This frequently led to 'looping' whereby a classification interacts with the people so classified (Hacking 2007). For Goffman, writing of the 'total institution', 'an agency that creates a defensive response on the part of an inmate takes this very response as the target of its next attack' (1961 (1991), p. 41). Difficulties in complying with the 'rules of the ward' led to behaviour which produced a doubling down of the treatment which had provoked the very behaviour in question, in a manner very similar to that first observed in classic sociological studies of institutions in the 1960s (Menzies Lyth 1960). For example, a patient might attempt to leave their bed in order to go to the toilet. A nurse may explain to the patient that this is not necessary, as they are wearing a continence pad; the wards guard against 'wandering' out of fear of falls, for which there is mandated recording. The patient's continued attempts to leave their bed might then be viewed as irrational and the person as non-compliant. The bedrails are raised, yet the patient continues to attempt to climb over the rails, increasing their risk of a fall. Such instances are so common for people living with dementia on these wards that such cases were called 'climbers' (Featherstone and Northcott 2021, p. 126). This purported evidence of 'irrationality' and loss of agency might in at least some instances more truly reflect a determination of agency and the expression of preference.

The complexity of the social world of the ward, with its own rules of operation which may be inadvertently dehumanising, should alert us to the great complexity of introducing technology into such a space in ways that ensures it really advances the humanity of care, not simply for patients but also for staff.

Some general themes have emerged from this and other work regarding the care of people living with dementia which mirror issues arising in the application of AI, and which also mirror concerns within humanism.

Firstly, questions arise about how people are observed and understood, both by other human beings and via analysis and application of the data that are collected about them. There are many opportunities for misunderstanding whereby the full humanity of the person may fail to be recognised. Here, those living with dementia are especially vulnerable, as indeed their very invisibility on hospital wards makes clear. The use of AI to collect and analyse data about humans thus must be seen within this context of grave potential misunderstandings; dehumanisation does not just ‘happen’, it occurs within specific contexts, including the context of the hospital whose very remit and ethos is to care. The potential large impact on this vulnerable group of poorly implemented AI, plus the great potential for benefit, again make people living with dementia a valuable group to examine, as the magnitude of possible impacts may help us to spot issues that also occur with others but less visibly.

A second general theme is control. The ethical question(s) of control of AI is well-known; there are many aspects to this problem. AI’s autonomous nature produces challenges for our capacity to retain ultimate human control of AI. But we must also address the control of humans by those who use and control AI. Within any hierarchical organisation such as a hospital, issues of control are central and are likely to be impacted by the introduction of technology such as AI. Potential for improvements via the use of such technology exists, but also the possibility that control might be increased or altered with deleterious impacts, especially on those with the least control, those at the bottom of any institutional hierarchy. These are likely to be the most vulnerable patients, as well as the staff who perform tasks of basic care, whose working lives are subject to tight controls of task-oriented efficiency. As we shall see, the control exerted over vulnerable patients is linked to how they are perceived and how their behaviour is understood within the institutional context of the ward.

Linked to this, a third general theme concerns the identification and pursuit of goals and tasks. The goals of any AI must be the right goals, adequately identified, and the impact upon a system as a whole of employing AI in achieving such goals must be considered. But the goals of technology may not always be in harmony with the goals of those swept up in its path. The tasks undertaken on a hospital ward may be in some dispute: problems so produced also may again disproportionately impact people living with dementia, as shall be indicated below. Goal-oriented management of medical conditions may not always be sympathetic to other values, including communication, tasks of basic nursing care, and everyday actions which help to humanise and to assist people to be recognised fully within the social world of the ward (Barnard 2002). Moreover, the hierarchical system of the hospital gives priority to certain kinds of tasks and to the pursuit of certain goals; any introduction of technology must of necessity consider how tasks are viewed and understood within this hierarchy, noting that ‘official’ narratives of institutional goals may not truly reflect reality on the ground.

These themes linked to questions of time: time taken to observe and understand others, time saved by AI, time in the swift pursuit of technological and scientific progress and quest to implement such, time in the drive for efficiently completing identified tasks; notions of speed and efficiency as noted are indeed embedded into understandings of artificial ‘intelligence’. It is commonly claimed that AI will free human beings up to perform other more ‘human’ tasks such as interaction with people. This claim will be assessed below in the context of findings about time management on hospital wards.

11.4 AI in the Diagnosis of Dementia

We now consider the proposed uses of AI and machine learning (ML) in the diagnosis of dementia. This will demonstrate how the collection and analysis of data by AI technologies may be beneficial, but may at the same time produce significant shifts in how we view ourselves and others, creating profound individual and social questions: the 'control question in AI' is often not so much how do we control any particular AI, but how we address the cascading network of impacts of its routine embedded use. Similar issues may arise in the diagnosis of other conditions, but the diagnosis of dementia via AI and ML produces a plethora of wide-ranging and particularly acute issues concerning how we understand disease, how we understand and respond to the human being, and what happens when AI is introduced into the equation. The use of AI in dementia diagnosis could be seen as nothing other than the application of AI in the dispassionate search for information; but this view sits uneasily with the profound human significance of a disease diagnosis. This discussion also acts as a general introduction to many of the challenges facing people living with dementia as a prolegomena to our discussion of hospital care, and indeed, we draw upon ethnographic data from hospital care in our discussion of the potential impacts of a dementia diagnosis, to add useful context to the impact that a diagnosis of dementia may have on how a person sees themselves and is seen by others.

11.4.1 Speed and Urgency

First, note that much technological development is trumpeted with claims of the urgency and severity of the problem to be addressed, hence the need for speed in efficiently tackling a problem; this may seem like harmless enthusiasm but may interfere with a humanistic approach. The literature around the use of AI and ML in dementia diagnosis likewise emphasises the severity of this condition, its prevalence and projected increase, stressing the healthcare, social, and economic costs (Amini et al. 2021; de la Fuente Garcia and Ritchie 2020; Danso et al. 2019), with many describing dementia as a 'burden' (Kourtis et al. 2019) or as 'devastating' (Dashwood et al. 2021), with a climate of 'urgency' (Li et al. 2021). Indeed, worries are sometimes expressed that concern with ethics in the face of such urgent challenges is unethically hindering technological progress for the benefit of humanity.

While such descriptions of the challenges of dementia may be broadly accurate, it is notable that such a presentation of the condition contrast starkly with the approach of the care sector, which has worked hard to counter characterisations of those living with dementia as a burden or as in a hopeless situation, and often as, in some sense, no longer 'fully persons' (Kitwood 1997; Kitwood and Brooker 2019). Note then two very contrasting approaches, one stressing dementia as a medical condition, the disorder understood in biomedical ways, one stressing the *person* who must *live* with dementia.

11.4.2 The Use of Data

Understandings of human functioning and ill-health produced via AI depends upon data. The collection, analysis and sharing of large volumes of data has been also a notable feature of research into Alzheimer's disease for many years (Milne et al. 2022), and ML and other technologies being used greatly facilitate the collection and analysis of a very wide range of data types and of modes and places of data collection. The variety of data used reflects the complexity of the condition of dementia, which can affect many aspects of functioning, and also reflects the uncertainty regarding the causes and biomedical manifestations of the various dementias (Dekkers and Rikkert 2006; Weller and Budson 2018).

The data may include various biomarkers and/or behavioural or cognitive function; may be data that may be broadly thought of as 'medical', collected in a clinical context, or outside the clinic; and may be collected at a discrete time, or over an extended period of time. The wide variety of behavioural data used includes gait analysis, mood, heart rate, sleep, navigation, and a person's capacity to undertake everyday tasks such as making toast, as well as individual patterns of technology use, in 'digital phenotyping' of clinically relevant behaviour (Insel 2017; Jain et al. 2015). Much work uses ML to analyse linguistic data, such as conversations, medical notes, and test results (Astell et al. 2019; de la Fuente Garcia and Ritchie 2020; DHSC 2020; Mullard 2021; Shibata et al. 2019; Shimoda et al. 2021; Spichak 2021). Cognitive tests may include traditional tests (such as the classic 'clock drawing test' (Jiang et al. 2021) as well as digital versions of standard tests, or newly designed digital tests. There is work underway attempts to bypass language difficulties, e.g. with tests requiring one to classify photos as 'animal' or 'not animal' (Kalafatis et al. 2021; Khaligh-Razavi et al. 2019). Medical data used varies (Berisha et al. 2021) and includes administrative health data (Park et al. 2020), various physiological measurements (Reith et al. 2021), and imaging (Cope et al. 2021). ML is used to improve interpretation of established tools of dementia diagnosis, such as MRI scans of the brain, or to find new tools, such as retinal scanning (De Fauw et al. 2018).

Crucially, technology thus facilitates the creation of a picture of dementia risk from potentially any facet of life and behaviour.

11.4.3 The Personal and Social Significance of a Dementia Diagnosis

Such data collection and analysis raises profound questions about how people living with or at risk of the condition are seen and labelled. There may be radical divergences between the view of the subject garnered via technologically mediated data collection, and that of the care sector operating at its best and most humane. Data collection and analysis leading to diagnosis may be of profound individual significance. A disease diagnosis or risk assignment may be seen as more or less determining of one's future, more or less threatening to one's sense of agency and of self. The impact will vary depending on many factors, among them, the very ways in which the condition is conceptualised, how an individual sees their personal risk, who seeks a diagnosis and why, what care and treatment is available, and how society in general views different risk and disease groups. A dementia diagnosis is far more than a biomedical label: it can lead to a cascading loss of membership of a social community.

11.4.4 The Reach and Impact of AI

AI can significantly alter the data landscape of everyday life. Data may be collected in unanticipated ways, in a manner below conscious awareness; information can be extracted from data once thought to be trivial or meaningless. Routine medical information becomes relevant to a dementia diagnosis. Data collected for recreational purposes in tracking activities is potentially revealing of a diagnosis with serious implications for one's future, turning the everyday into a location for medical hazard. An expanding range of data suddenly become 'medical' data; going about one's everyday business, one can leave a trail of 'data exhaust' holding clues to one's dementia risk. Wearables may collect both behavioural and physiological data and may be used both for diagnosis and for ongoing monitoring to detect progression (Astell et al. 2019; Frey et al. 2019; Kourtis et al. 2019). Ambient data may be collected from everyday use of smart devices. The class of those at risk will be moulded by the capacity of the technology and of developments in scientific understanding. This issue presents itself forcibly with research ambitions to diagnose dementia 'decades' before symptoms appear (Frey et al. 2019). This will raise questions about what it is to have the condition; given the widespread stigma associated with dementia, this is a troubling issue indeed, especially as attempts to combat stigma in various areas are often doomed to failure, as the source of stigma may simply shift elsewhere (Buchman and Reiner 2009). Research also aims to distinguish dementia from normal cognitive changes that may occur with ageing, and of course this may be extremely beneficial, but note that it comes with constant monitoring of normal cognitive changes with age. The irony of potentially constantly monitoring a population for cognitive difficulties via a technology that heralds and promotes the value of intelligence is noted.

11.4.5 Classification, Accuracy, and Perception

Likewise, much research is driven to improve accuracy of diagnosis, to detect subcategories of dementia, and to finely monitor disease progression. This is laudable, but the context of application of diagnostic knowledge should be noted; the ambition of fine-grained diagnosis contrasts sharply with research findings on the ward. In some wards, symbols, such as a forget-me-not or a butterfly, are placed above certain patient's beds to alert staff to a dementia diagnosis. But not only may these symbols sometimes fail to match the patient, staff generally interpret symbols as indicating advanced dementia, as a result often underestimating capacity, with even those capable of self-care constructed as high dependency (Featherstone and Northcott 2021, p.71). Ironically, communicating disease status via these 'technologies of attention' then sometimes led to staff failing to communicate with a patient (Featherstone et al. 2020).

11.5 Data Collection, Disease Diagnosis, and Control

11.5.1 The Impact on the Self

We need to consider the type of data collected and its analysis, but also the relationship of the data subject to this data. Work on the 'data self' provides a useful tool for analysis (Lupton 2016). Contrast two cases, that of early adopters of health tracking wearables and other devices, who may use this actively to increase their autonomy, gain self-understanding, and improve fitness and health (Ng and Kong 2016); with those labelled with dementia or seen in a high-risk category. The question of who is doing the surveillance and why is critical: the individual, the healthcare system, relatives, others: is the one under surveillance the active data self, or the mere object of the gaze of others? Note that for those considered at risk of dementia, talk is almost exclusively that of monitoring by others, and systems may be designed so that those monitored are unaware, for example via automatic monitoring of routine health data (Miled et al. 2020). These raise complex issues that are genuinely hard to resolve but as we shall see below, in some ways mirror the experiences of those living with dementia.

11.5.2 Control by AI and by Others

Passive data generated in everyday activities is especially welcomed for application to groups who are considered to be 'nonadherent' to treatment plans (Insel 2017). It is argued that passively collected data better reflects the true nature of the condition, in contrast to data collected in artificially designed cognitive tests. Ecological validity is a central concept of digital phenotyping (Jain et al. 2015), whereby passively collected data is a means to achieve 'real world' objective tracking of 'reality' (Milne et al. 2022). But notions of the 'ecological validity' of data may increasingly reify the concept of disease. Such data collection techniques potentially mould the understanding of a 'diagnosis' from a label applied to an individual, by examination of that individual, at a specific time; to assigning an individual or entire class of people into a risk category, a predictive model, formed from extrapolation from a population group (Milne et al. 2022). By such means, the very understanding of what it is to have a 'disease' could be transformed.

Moreover, the potential ubiquity of data collection, especially if passive, raises serious issues of individual control by the data subject; an issue which is already a feature of life experienced by many living with dementia (Armstrong and Byrne 2011). For some, medical information is liberating, but not for all (Milne et al. 2022). Loss of control may thus be extended to a far larger group of those 'at risk' of an earlier and earlier diagnosis. In the field of genetics, there have been long-standing discussions of 'genetic responsibility' – the question of whether individuals have a responsibility to find out and act upon genetic information (Leefmann et al. 2017). These questions could then be expanded via the diagnosis of disease more generally via data collected in everyday life by AI, with particular significance for different conditions.

11.5.3 Agency and the 'Disobedient' Patient

The so-called 'nonadherent' patient is a category into which those suspected of dementia are likely to fall. Debate within medical ethics about 'adherence' to medical regimes should warn us of the dangers of seeing patients as 'noncompliant' (Resnik 2005). Moralisation of the data subject impacts their epistemic status as the object of data collection. To be passively monitored for signs of cognitive decline may have tangible benefits but seems in tension with a reciprocal relationship of belonging within a social world. The embedding of such data-collecting capacity into everyday technology and the interrogation of this data to produce a diagnosis or a risk score makes passive data subjects of us all. This may heighten agency for those who seek this self-knowledge, but for others, passively collected data may reduce agency, and all the more so, the more that the information so derived is considered of superior validity to other forms of knowing the human subject. Which is the 'true' patient, the potentially hyper-real person constructed from digital data, or this human being here and now? How does the person viewed in this way, reacting to this view of themselves, compare to the person observed under the attentive gaze of another human being?

11.5.4 The Hollow 'Future Promise' of AI for Some?

Milne et al. (2022) usefully discuss a notion of the 'data shadow', a picture of the self which is derived from data which may mar one's future hopes. The future promise of individual empowerment through digital technologies may be real for some, but for the person living with dementia, or with a diagnosis of future dementia, there may be no ‘data self’ but only a data shadow, a data ‘non-self’, to whom the glittering future promise of technology is only a future threat. You have just successfully argued a case at the High Court, or had a paper refuting string theory accepted in Nature; on the other hand, an app on your phone alerts you to signs of cognitive decline undetectable by either you or your colleagues. Note again the dementia patient’s invisibility (Featherstone and Northcott 2021, p. 37).

On the other hand, there may be room for optimism. Milne et al. (2022) show how the continual monitoring and tracking makes room for a future projection of change of the digital self over time, counter to ideas of the constant self. Dementia is generally seen as an inevitable progressive decline. Yet results from routine testing may show variability in scores over time. Could this help counter the trope of the ‘inevitable slide downwards’ and lack of hope of dementia?

11.5.5 The Interpretation of Behaviour

As should now be apparent, a general issue we must address is the context and meaning of data and information. A technologically mediated view of the world and of data may fail to understand the meaning that such data has for individuals. The picture of a person, the diagnosis of a disease, constructed via technology will depend crucially on how data sources are interpreted. There is an especial hazard if a diagnosis achieved through new technologies is simplistically assumed to have the epistemic power fully to capture the condition; yet the scope and variety of data potentially used in AI dementia diagnosis may well nudge towards such a biomedical view of the disease. To move towards a position where growing numbers of individuals and groups will be given risk labels for cognitive decline would have profound implications which need to be discussed, debated, and predicted before technological and informational revolutions become embedded into our health service, care, and everyday infrastructure. We need to consider both how the technology may ‘see’ the person, and also how people, including the data subject, may use the findings of technology. Human behaviour is not bare bodily movement but requires understanding to read (Anscombe 1957; Taylor 1968). The same behaviour can be read in quite different ways by different human beings, so even human oversight of ML may not fully address the issues. Interpreting behaviour is a particular issue for those seen as deficient cognitively or in executive functioning and social awareness. We shall also note below the priority of data and metrics on the ward as what can be readily measured takes priority over many care concerns.

Consider the remote monitoring of movement for those at risk of dementia (Astell et al. 2019; Ng and Kong 2016), and compare this with the actual monitoring of movement that occurs on wards. Ethnographic research finds that for those with a dementia diagnosis, attempts to exercise agency, such as getting out of bed, walking around a hospital ward, or attempting to leave the ward, are likely to be seen as ‘wandering’ and ipso facto as lacking in agency or intent (Featherstone and Northcott 2021). This perception then loops back to confirm a diagnosis, and perceptions of a possibly worsening condition, meaning any further attempts by the person to communicate and act are also seen as lacking clear agency. Yet a patient may simply be trying to stretch his or her legs, to talk to another patient, or relieve the unrelenting boredom of the ward. The 'future promise' of a person living with dementia may be modest indeed compared to many others, yet careful observation finds that even this little may be taken away.

11.6 AI, Dementia, and the Hospital Ward

We are seeing how complex the consequences of a dementia diagnosis might be, something of the significance for the individual person and for how others see them, and how these might be compounded by the prospect of passive mass screening of a population for signs of dementia using AI. Issues that stand out include the question of how we are seen by others, and how we are seen by the data collected via technology. The small world of the hospital ward mirrors these issues, but at the same time provides us with a smaller stage in which to observe, as research finds that the experiences of those living with dementia in hospital are not simply the consequences of their condition, but of their place in the complex social world around them.

And so we turn to the hospital ward. There is much that could and should be said, and unfortunately much will be skimmed over. For reasons of brevity we will use the time promise of technology as a linking framework for the three themes identified above: how people are observed and seen including the use of metrics and data; the various questions of control; and the identification and prioritisation of goals and tasks. We start by examining technology's promise of freeing up time for other more human tasks, moving on to discuss the need for flexibility in timing, considering what needs to be in place for such promises to be made good, considering how tensions might arise from the introduction of technology into a complex social and institutional system. Fears have long been expressed that the introduction of technology into nursing may produce merely technical provision of care through adoption of protocols and metrics (Locsin 2005); in response there have been calls for a proactive approach that reflects the central role of technology while also fostering person-centred care (Archibald and Barnard 2018, p. 2475) and for a move away from focus on adverse effects of technology to positive outcomes from nurse patient relationship (Kitson et al. 2014). People living with dementia can be shown to be an early warning system for fault lines which potentially could impact all of us, and research which carefully observes their care can provide some clues about what might help or hinder the humane introduction of technology.

11.6.1 Freeing up Staff Time: The Promise

One of the biggest claims for AI in general and within the nursing and medical spheres in particular is that by taking over mundane or routine tasks, and/or by performing tasks faster and more efficiently, its use will free up time not simply for more medical procedures and to clear waiting lists, but also for more human and interpersonal contact (Wise 2022; Buchanan et al. 2020; Mieronkoski et al. 2017). The benefit of added time for the humane details of patient care have also significant potential for the wellbeing of staff. Staff burnout in nursing and care staff is closely associated with feelings of being unable to care for patients to the high standards to which staff aspire (Vahey et al. 2004). There are complexities however; the potential clash between precision and efficiency which come with the introduction of technology, and attributes of nursing such as care and compassion has been noted (Archibald and Barnard 2018). The introduction of AI health technologies may result in nurses spending less time with patients and an increased workload (Buchanan et al. 2020).

Within the hospital ward, this future promise could lead to hopes of time for attention to personal and individual needs, to personal grooming, and for entertainment and conversation with patients, within an environment which is often one of unremitting boredom for patients within an atmosphere of constant busyness for staff. People living with dementia may especially benefit such time and attention, and thus observations of their experiences on hospital wards provides useful material to consider what must be in place for this promise of extra time to materialise. As research indicates, much must be in place.

How might extra time help? Ethnographic observations shows considerable evidence that greater attention to addressing issues such as grooming and dress can potentially have significant impacts upon the mood and behaviour of individuals. Research demonstrates the importance of familiarity including the familiar feel of a person's own clothes to ground people living with dementia in their present reality and aid memory and cognition (Buse and Twigg 2015, 2018), and that individuals living with dementia may retain an acute sense of their appearance and place in their social world (Kontos 2004, 2005) hence highlighting the importance of paying attention to this aspect of a patient's care, rather than purely to basic medical and physical needs. Neglect of appearance may add to inadvertent dehumanisation and assumptions regarding capacity (Twigg and Buse 2013).

But people living with dementia on wards were found often to have personal grooming neglected, often with false teeth and glasses missing, with men unshaven, beards unkempt, and were less likely than other patients to have personal possessions on their bedside cabinets, adding to the unfamiliarity of the environment for a group less likely than other patients to be able to cope well in such a setting (Featherstone and Northcott 2021). Those living with dementia, and indeed, older patients in general, are less likely than other patients to be dressed in their own clothes, wearing instead ill-fitting hospital gowns which may fail to provide adequate coverage; loss or absence of familiar clothing on the ward sometimes produced considerable distress (Featherstone and Northcott 2021, pp. 50ff; Boddington et al. 2021). Featherstone and

Northcott describe the 'stripping practices' (Robb 1967) on admission to the ward for people living with dementia, compared to other patients, when personal possession are removed or hidden away: Roth and Eddy (1967: 69) wrote of 'the process of stripping the patient of moral and social identity'. The significance of this is underlined by observations which have shown significant improvements in behaviour following time taken to address such issues, such as improved communication and alertness (Boddington et al. 2021).

But for this to eventuate, the staff involved have to see any time devoted to the personal appearance of patients as well-spent, and they have to be free to choose to spend time in this way; such choice may be restricted by those higher in the hierarchy, by their own perceptions of what tasks are valuable within the setting, and by time pressures which persist despite – and in some cases because of – the introduction of technology. Featherstone and Northcott find the nurses subject to a fast-paced timetable of constant busyness, and that the hierarchical structures of the ward appear to prevent communication, reinforcing the invisibility of both the patients and the lower grade staff (2021, p. 105). Moreover, there is considerable evidence that nurses have preferences for task-based care over the psychosocial needs of patients (Kitson et al. 2014; Mieronkoski et al. 2017) but that the fragmentation of tasks may interfere with care provision (Feo and Kitson 2016).

Observations have shown that such barriers to freeing staff time persist within hospital wards, with pauses in work discouraged, continual self-surveillance as well as close monitoring of colleagues to enforce acceptable busyness (Featherstone and Northcott 2021, pp. 117, 144). In illustration, during periods of quiet on a ward, a healthcare assistant arranged for three men who were each living with dementia to have a 'race night' with a horse races on a games console, only to be reprimanded by senior nurses, following which a doctor arrived who publicly scolded the healthcare assistant for slowing his timetable and insisted patients be put back in bed (ibid.). Other examples could be given. Implicit attitudes towards more person-centred aspects of care can also be seen in how technology was used on the wards. Medical technology was in constant use, yet the wards frequently contained technology such as TV sets which were rarely if ever used (Featherstone and Northcott 2021, p. 24); attempts to use these could be foiled because nobody knew the password (Featherstone and Northcott 2021, p. 145).

11.6.2 Time and Communication: When Slow is Good

It is important to understand that the potential benefits of any saved time should also apply to tasks currently undertaken but under time pressures which hamper communication for those who have difficulties in comprehension or simply operate more slowly, a frequent issue on the wards. Let us examine one example, the medications round. The medications round is signalled as possessing a particular urgency, with nurses wearing 'do not disturb' tabards, and with the understandable requirement for careful logging and checking of the administration of medications. But people with dementia admitted to hospital are usually already on a regime of medication at home, which is often changed upon admission, hence often prompting queries or resistance, which staff may not have time to address or may explain simply as what the doctor ordered, and which resistance they may attempt to overcome (Featherstone and Northcott 2021). The person living with dementia thus also frequently becomes the 'non-adherent' patient in respect of medications. (The implications for the use of care robots for the administration of medications will be obvious and merits further consideration outside the scope of this paper.) The process of helping a patient with food is equally complex.

11.6.3 The Institutional Culture of Time, Task, and Efficiency

But for technology to be used in a way that frees up time for communication by the use of technology, the need for this must be recognised on the wards, including the validity of many often 'irrational' seeming forms of resistance and questioning, and including recognition of how tasks higher up the pecking order may be interfering in such a process. Spending time with patients in communication and personal care would need to be valued as one of the recognised 'tasks' of the hospital. But to do this requires certain views of the role of the hospital and the task of medicine, as well as certain views of the person. We need to see the whole human being in a humanistic way.

Providing food and medication to individuals is not simply getting fuel or drugs into a body, but involves interacting with a human being in a socially embedded way. The privations of the hospital ward may be harder to bear for some than for others, and again the group of people living with dementia – unfortunately for them – act as an indicator of neglect. It has been noted above the material familiarity of one's environment, such as clothing, can aid in the orientation and alertness of a person living with dementia, and likewise the social rituals of mealtimes may help a person maintain orientation to their place in a social world. Kontos (2004, 2005) has found that the rituals of dining and dress may be well understood even by those with profound cognitive difficulties. For some patients, this may be an added extra, a 'luxury'; for others, something more deeply necessary, especially as we remember the rapid decline and deconditioning that routinely happens to people living with dementia on hospital wards. Attention to such details is the warp and weft of a humanistic approach, and we must ensure that technology respects and enhances this, especially in the face of experience to date which shows how technology itself can become the focus of attention (Barnard 2002, p. 21). The introduction of technology itself needs to be cognizant of such issues, especially as the general institutional aim of efficiency which might spur its introduction assumes a task- and speed-oriented social world.

This means that we must simultaneously address the culture of the institutions including the local culture of wards onto which technology is introduced. Yet Featherstone and Northcott's findings showed the culture of the ward was profoundly shaped by its timetables and by the need for completing tasks efficiently, and concluded that roles which could not be quantified or reduced to data, such as talking to patients, were invisible (Featherstone and Northcott 2021, p. 86 ff). 'Value was placed on the prompt completion of a routine timetabled task, rather than the interactions with patients (or missed opportunities to do so) around them. Stopping to talk to a patient, to listen or to reassure them, despite its value for staff, patients, and the wider work of the shift … was typically overlooked and unrecognised. *These interactions could not be quantified or recorded with the available mechanisms, lacked organisational value, whereas the timing and completion of task-based care would be highly visible and documented.*' (p. 90, emphases added). We see then, the long arm of data and metrics.

11.6.4 Time and Timetables

Observations on the wards also reveal the need for flexibility in the timing of care. Here attention to the clashes or arrhythmias arising from the imposition of linear institutional rhythms upon the cyclical time of the body is useful, showing the necessity of understanding the full person living in their body within a social world including attention to local culture in integrating technology. Here the institutional context of the hospital is pertinent. Osborne, Lowe, and Meijering used rhythmanalysis to examine informal care practices for people living with dementia at home, finding that 'in dementia care, the body's circadian rhythms take precedence instead, broadly resisting dressage - with the only exception being for medical appointments' (2023, p. 5). In contrast, Northcott et al. (2025) found that the linear rhythms of the hospital ward frequently overrode the cyclical bodily rhythms of the person living with dementia. This had implications not simply for the provision of particular tasks, but for the dignity and social standing of the person.

Take for example, continence care such as the fitting of catheters and the changing of continence pads (which were often used even for continent patients 'just in case'). It was not simply that these means were used to help facilitate ward timekeeping; it was not simply that patients might be made to wait for pad changes or that they denied or discouraged from accessing the toilet; tasks which were seen to be 'medical' could interrupt other tasks, and tasks arising from hospital timetables, such as the provision of meals, were given priority over personal care tasks arising from the cyclical rhythms of the patient's body. Catheters caused discomfort and confusion and men living with dementia frequently removed them, meaning that they would then be refitted. The timing of this could be an issue. Catheters might be fitted, even though a patient had visitors or was in the middle of eating. Likewise, a patient in a soiled pad might be made to wait to have it changed, because lunch had arrived. The patient living with dementia suffers indignity with the socially inappropriate situation possibly adding to any confusion and disorientation. The ethnographer observing this is acutely aware of the social transgression and insult. It must be emphasised that these studies found no instance of abuse by staff but nonetheless, the routine nature of such events, otherwise acutely out of kilter with due respect for a person's social standing, renders them invisible to those swept up in the ever-present demands of busyness and the medical mandates of the hospital. Technology surely has the potential to help provide care that reflects the needs and rhythms of the individual person, but again, attention to such issues is vital for the adequate and humane implementation of technology.

11.6.5 Time, Technology, and the Construction of 'Disobedience'

Lastly, a few observations. We have noted the driver of efficiency both within the institution and implicit within many uses of AI and other technology. Observations on the hospital ward alert us to the fact that the notion of efficiency also helps to create the notion of the 'disobedient' patient, the one with the most trouble fitting into the timetabled efficiency of the ward, who requires too much explanation about why their tablets now look different, and so on, with the consequent hazard of a worsening of status and of behaviour via looping. People living with dementia have provided a useful test case to alert us to this possibility which surely lurks for many if not all of us as technology proliferates into the infrastructure all around us. We face a world where those most resistant to the use of particular applications of technology, or to the medical imperative, to passive data collection perhaps, are also, perhaps unknown to them, seen as disobedient or non-adherent, possibly then subject to further attempts at control. This possibility does not seem compatible with a humanistic approach to the adoption of AI and should be guarded against. It represents one of the many ways in which the use of AI may exert control in profound ways which arise from the socio-technical system into which it is embedded and hence, which might escape notice.

We have seen above that concern that patients living with dementia were 'wandering' and strategies to prevent this, arise at least in part because of the necessity of preventing falls, including the mandated recording and reporting of falls. Especially given the vast capacities of AI to capture and analyse data, this should alert us to the potential of recorded data to be used in ways that might assist patients but which might also be used to add to practices of discipline and control, especially if the recorded data feeds back into an institutional system of rigid hierarchically nested tasks, where attention is drawn to metrics and to technology at the expense of the person.

'Disobedience' is a strong term but can also be understood in terms of Lefebvre's notion of 'dressage', the ways in which linear rhythms are imposed via discipline upon the recalcitrant cyclical rhythms of the body, especially when arrhythmias occur. This was found to operate frequently for people living with dementia on the hospital ward in particular who had difficulty in otherwise 'obeying' the rules of the ward. 'Dressage is achieved in a number of ways: by the physical layout of the ward and its furniture; by the actions of staff such as repeatedly tucking patients into bed or raising the bedrail to prevent movement; by the use of objects and technologies, such as catheters and pads to discourage use of the toilets, and so on' (Northcott et al. 2022, 2025). Featherstone and Northcott (2021) found that on the wards, technology often had a dual use function to control the 'imperfect' patient. Any introduction of AI technologies into such a situation must be alert to such possibilities. To do so involves far more than simply abstract concern with 'autonomy' but will necessitate careful observation and critique. Even something so basic as the desire to use the toilet instead of a pad is worthy of attention and inclusion in any project to use AI in a way consistent with humanistic principles.

References

Alzheimer's Society (2016) Fix dementia care: hospitals. London: Alzheimer's Society, UK

Amini S, Zhang L, Hao B, Gupta A, Song M, Karjadi C, Paschalidis IC (2021) An artificial intelligence-assisted method for dementia detection using images from the clock drawing test. J Alzheimers Dis 83(2):581–589

Anscombe GEM (1957) Intention. Basil Blackwell, Oxford

Archibald MM, Barnard A (2018) Futurism in nursing: technology, robotics and the fundamentals of care. J Clin Nurs 27(11–12):2473–2480

Armstrong D, Byrne G (2011) Improving person-centred care in dementia. Nurs times 107:12–14

Astell AJ, Bouranis N, Hoey J, Lindauer A, Mihailidis A, Nugent C, Robillard JM (2019a) Technology and dementia: the future is now. Dement Geriatr Cogn Disord 47(3):131–139

Atkinson P, Housley W (2003) Interactionism. Sage

Barnard A (2002) Philosophy of technology and nursing. Nurs Philos 3(1):15–26

Barnard A, Sandelowski M (2001) Technology and humane nursing care: (ir) reconcilable or invented difference? J Adv Nurs 34(3):367–375

Bates J (2004) One day it could be you: wipe the term bed-blocker from your vocabulary. Nurs Stand 18(38):24–26

Berisha V, Krantsevich C, Hahn PR, Hahn S, Dasarathy G, Turaga P, Liss J (2021) Digital medicine and the curse of dimensionality. NPJ Dig Med 4(1):1–8, 153

Boddington P, Featherstone K, Northcott A (2021) Presentation of the clothed self on the hospital ward: an ethnographic account of perceptual attention and implications for the personhood of people living with dementia. Med Humanit 47(2):e3–e3

Buber M (1970) I and Thou. Simon and Schuste, New York

Buchanan C, Howitt ML, Wilson R, Booth RG, Risling T, Bamford M (2020) Predicted influences of artificial intelligence on the domains of nursing: scoping review. JMIR Nursing 3(1):e23939

Buchman D, Reiner PB (2009) Stigma and addiction: being and becoming. Am J Bioeth 9:18–19

Burton-Hill C (2016) The superhero of artificial intelligence: can this genius keep it in check? The Guardian, 16 Feb 2016. https://www.theguardian.com/technology/2016/feb/16/demis-hassabis-artificial-intelligence-deepmind-alphago#:~:text=Demis%20Hassabis%20has%20a,from%20him%2C%20not%20so%20much

Buse CE, Twigg J (2015) Clothing, embodied identity and dementia: maintaining the self through dress. Age Cult Hum (2)

Buse C, Twigg J (2018) Dressing disrupted: negotiating care through the materiality of dress in the context of dementia. Materialities of care: encountering health and illness through artefacts and architecture, pp 97–109

Caudill W (1958) The psychiatric hospital as a small society. Harvard University Press

Chen Y (2016) Practising rhythmanalysis: theories and methodologies. Rowman & Littlefield, Maryland
Chollet F (2019) On the measure of intelligence. arXiv preprint arXiv:1911.01547
Cope TE, Weil RS, Düzel E, Dickerson BC, Rowe JB (2021) Advances in neuroimaging to support translational medicine in dementia. J Neurol Neurosurg Psychiatry 92(3):263–270
Danso SO, Muniz-Terrera G, Luz S, Ritchie C (2019) Application of big data and artificial intelligence technologies to dementia prevention research: an opportunity for low-and-middle-income countries. J Glob Health 9(2)
Dashwood M, Churchhouse G, Young M, Kuruvilla T (2021) Artificial intelligence as an aid to diagnosing dementia: an overview. Prog Neurol Psychiatry 25(3):42–47
Davies T (2008) Humanism. Routledge
De Fauw J, Ledsam JR, Romera-Paredes B, Nikolov S, Tomasev N, Blackwell S, Askham H, Glorot X, O'Donoghue B, Visentin D, van den Driessche G (2018) Clinically applicable deep learning for diagnosis and referral in retinal disease. Nat Med 24(9):1342–1350
Dekkers W, Rikkert MO (2006) What is a genetic cause? The example of Alzheimer's disease. Med Health Care Philos 9(3):273–284.
de la Fuente Garcia S, Ritchie LS (2020) Artificial intelligence, speech, and language processing approaches to monitoring Alzheimer's disease: a systematic review. J Alzheimer's Dis 78:1547–1574
Dennett D (1988) Conditions of personhood. In What is a person? (pp. 145–167). Humana Press, Totowa and NJ
Department of Health and Social Care (DHSC) (2020) Genome UK: The future of healthcare. https://www.gov.uk/government/publications/genome-uk-the-future-of-healthcare
Featherstone K, Northcott A, Bridges J (2019) Routines of resistance: an ethnography of the care of people living with dementia in acute hospital wards and its consequences. Int J Nurs Stud 96:53–60
Featherstone K, Boddington P, Northcott A (2020) Using signs and symbols to label hospital patients with a dementia diagnosis: help or hindrance to care? Narrat Inq Bioeth 10(1):49–61
Featherstone K, Northcott A (2021) Wandering the wards: An ethnography of hospital care and its consequences for people living with dementia. Taylor & Francis, London and New York
Featherstone K, Northcott A, Boddington P, Edwards D, Vougioukalou S, Bale S, Harrison Dening K, Logan K, Tope R, Kelly D, Jones A (2022) Understanding approaches to continence care for people living with dementia in acute hospital settings: an ethnographic study. Health Soc Care Deliv Res 10
Feo R, Kitson A (2016) Promoting patient-centred fundamental care in acute healthcare systems. Int J Nurs Stud 57:1–11
Fioravante R, Vaccaro A (2025) Humanism, dehumanism, integral human development: an overview of boundaries and capabilities of human-centred artificial intelligence in business and organisations. In: Fioravante R, Vaccaro A (eds) Handbook on humanism and artificial intelligence. Springer
Frey AL, Karran M, Jimenez RC, Baxter J, Adeogun M, Bose N, ... Routledge C (2019) Harnessing the potential of digital technologies for the early detection of neurodegenerative diseases (EDoN)
Fuchs T (2018) The cyclical time of the body and its relation to linear time. J Conscious Stud 25(7–8):47–65
Fuchs T (2020) Embodiment and personal identity in dementia. Med Health Care Philos 23(4):665–676
Goffman E (1961/1991) Asylums: Essays on the social situation of mental patients and other inmates. Penguin Books, London
Hacking I (2007) Kinds of people: moving targets. In: Proceedings-British Academy, vol 151, p 285. Oxford University Press Inc
Higgs P, Gilleard C (2016) Interrogating personhood and dementia. Aging Ment Health 20(8):773–780

Insel TR (2017) Digital phenotyping: technology for a new science of behavior. JAMA 318(13):1215–1216

Jain SH, Powers BW, Hawkins JB, Brownstein JS (2015) The digital phenotype. Nat Biotechnol 33(5):462–463

Jiang H, Zhang Y, Zeng Z, Ji J, Wang Y, Chi Y, Miao C (2021, May) Mobile-based clock drawing test for detecting early signs of dementia. In: Proceedings of the AAAI conference on artificial intelligence, vol 35, No 18, pp 16048–16050

Kalafatis C, Modarres MH, Apostolou P, Marefat H, Khanbagi M, Karimi H, Khaligh-Razavi SM (2021) Validity and cultural generalisability of a 5-minute AI-based, computerised cognitive assessment in Mild Cognitive Impairment and Alzheimer's Dementia. Front Psych 12:1155

Khaligh-Razavi SM, Habibi S, Sadeghi M, Marefat H, Khanbagi M, Nabavi SM, Sadeghi E, Kalafatis C (2019) Integrated Cognitive assessment: speed and accuracy of visual processing as a reliable proxy to cognitive performance. Sci Rep 9(1):1–11

Kitson AL, Muntlin Athlin Å, Conroy T, International Learning Collaborative (2014) Anything but basic: nursing's challenge in meeting patients' fundamental care needs. J Nurs Sch 46(5):331–339

Kitwood T, Brooker D (2019) Dementia reconsidered revisited: the person still comes first. McGraw-Hill Education (UK)

Kitwood T (1997) Dementia reconsidered: the person comes first. Open University Press, Buckingham and Philadelphia

Kontos PC (2004) Ethnographic reflections on selfhood, embodiment and Alzheimer's disease. Ageing Soc 24(6):829–849

Kontos PC (2005) Embodied selfhood in Alzheimer's disease: rethinking person-centred care. Dementia 4(4):553–570

Kourtis LC, Regele OB, Wright JM, Jones GB (2019) Digital biomarkers for Alzheimer's disease: the mobile/wearable devices opportunity. NPJ Dig Medi 2(1):1–9

Larson E (2021) The myth of artificial intelligence: why computers can't think the way we do. Harvard University Press, Cambridge Mass

Leefmann J, Schaper M, Schicktanz S (2017) The concept of "genetic responsibility" and its meanings: a systematic review of qualitative medical sociology literature. Front Soc 18

Lefebvre H (2013) Rhythmanalysis: Space, time and everyday life. Bloomsbury Academic, London

Legg S, Hutter M (2007) A collection of definitions of intelligence. Front Artif Intell Appl 157:17

Leonardi F (2018) The definition of health: towards new perspectives. Int J Health Serv 48(4):735–748

Li R, Wang X, Lawler K, Garg S, Bai Q, Alty J (2021) Applications of Artificial Intelligence to aid detection of dementia: a narrative review on current capabilities and future directions. arXiv preprint arXiv:2104.14073

Liang CS, Li DJ, Yang FC, Tseng PT, Carvalho AF, Stubbs B, Thompson T, Mueller C, Shin JI, Radua J, Stewart R (2021) Mortality rates in Alzheimer's disease and non-Alzheimer's dementias: a systematic review and meta-analysis. Lancet Healthy Longev 2(8):e479–e488

Locsin RC (2005) Technological competency as caring in nursing: a model for practice. Sigma Theta Tau International, Indianapolis, IN

Lupton D (2016) The quantified self. John Wiley & Sons, Toronto

Lyon D (2020) Rhythmanalysis: Research Methods. Bloomsbury Academic

Menzies Lyth IEP (1960) A case-study in the functioning of social systems as a defence against anxiety: a report on a study of the nursing service of a general hospital. Hum Relat 13:95–121

Mieronkoski R, Azimi I, Rahmani AM, Aantaa R, Terävä V, Liljeberg P, Salanterä S (2017) The Internet of Things for basic nursing care—a scoping review. Int J Nurs Stud 69:78–90

Miled ZB, Haas K, Black CM, Khandker RK, Chandrasekaran V, Lipton R, Boustani MA (2020) Predicting dementia with routine care EMR data. Artif Intell Med 102:101771

Milne R, Costa A, Brenman N (2022) Digital phenotyping and the (data) shadow of Alzheimer's disease. Big Data Soc 9(1):20539517211070748

Mitchell G, Dupuis SL, Kontos P, Jonas-Simpson C, Gray J (2020) Disrupting dehumanising and intersecting patterns of modernity with a relational ethic of caring. Int Pract Dev J 10(1):1–15
Morozov E (2014) To save everything, click here: the folly of technological solutionism. J Inf Policy 4(2014):173–175
Mullard A (2021) Controversial Alzheimer's drug approval could affect other diseases. Nature 595(7866):162–163
Mwale S, Northcott A, Lambert I, Featherstone K (2024) 'Becoming restrained': Conceptualising restrictive practices in the care of people living with dementia in acute hospital settings. Sociol Health Illn 46(8):1730–1748.
Ng J, Kong H (2016, May) Not all who wander are lost: smart tracker for people with dementia. In: Proceedings of the 2016 CHI conference extended abstracts on human factors in computing systems (pp 2241–2248)
Northcott A, Boddington P, Featherstone K (2022) Pad cultures: an ethnography of continence care and its consequences for people living with dementia during a hospital admission. Dementia 21(7):2191–2209
Northcott A., Boddington P, Featherstone K (2025) The arrhythmia of bodily urgency: using Rhythmanalysis to understand the organisation of care people living with dementia experience within acute hospital wards. SSM-Qualitative Research in Health, 100535.
Osborne T, Lowe TA, Meijering L (2023) Care and rhythmanalysis: using metastability to understand the routines of dementia care. Soc Sci Med 331:116099
Park JH, Cho HE, Kim JH, Wall MM, Stern Y, Lim H, Cha J (2020) Machine learning prediction of incidence of Alzheimer's disease using large-scale administrative health data. NPJ Digit Med 3(1):1–7
Reith FH, Mormino EC, Zaharchuk G (2021) Predicting future amyloid biomarkers in dementia patients with machine learning to improve clinical trial patient selection. Alzheimer's Dementia Transl Res Clin Interv 7(1):e12212
Resnik D (2005) The patient's duty to adhere to prescribed treatment: an ethical analysis. J Med Philos 30:167–188
Robb B (1967) Sans Everything: a case to answer. Nelson, London
Roth J, Eddy EM (1967) Rehabilitation for the unwanted. Atherton Press, New York
Russell S (2019) Human compatible: AI and the problem of control. Allen Lane, UK
Schweda M, Jongsma K (2022) Death in advance? A critique of the "Zombification" of people with dementia. Hist Philos Life Sci 44(3):1–13
Shibata D, Ito K, Wakamiya S, Aramaki E (2019) Detecting early-stage dementia based on natural language processing. Trans Jpn Soc Artif Intell 34(4)
Shimoda A, Li Y, Hayashi H, Kondo N (2021) Dementia risks identified by vocal features via telephone conversations: a novel machine learning prediction model. PLoS ONE 16(7):e0253988
Spichak S (2021) UK rolls out new 5-minute Alzheimer's test, Being Patient, Oct 2021. https://www.beingpatient.com/ai-alzheimers-diagnosis-cognetivity/
Taylor C (1968) The explanation of behaviour
Twigg J, Buse CE (2013) Dress, dementia and the embodiment of identity. Dementia 12(3):326–336
Vahey DC, Aiken LH, Sloane DM, Clarke SP, Vargas D (2004) Nurse burnout and patient satisfaction. Med Care 42(2 Suppl):II57
Wasserman D, Asch A, Blustein J, Putnam D (2017) Cognitive disability and moral status. The Stanford Encyclopedia of Philosophy (Fall 2017 Edition), Zalta EN (ed). https://plato.stanford.edu/archives/fall2017/entries/cognitive-disability/
Weller J, Budson A (2018) Current understanding of Alzheimer's disease diagnosis and treatment. F1000Research 7
Weil S (2009) Waiting on god (Routledge Revivals). Routledge
Weinberg AM (1966) Can technology replace social engineering? Bull At Sci 22(10):4–8
Wise J (2022) Digital strategy promises more care at home to free up doctors' time

Chapter 12
Concluding Remarks

Fioravante Rosa and Vaccaro Antonino

The widening grey area between AI-driven ethical shortcomings and the lack of timely legislation calls for a careful assessment of its perils concerning its design and use. Such assessment involves dealing with a large number of ethical dilemmas: balancing potential harms and benefits yielded by AI for individuals, organizations, and institutions; identifying clear responsibilities for its design, its input–output managing, its process supervision; reshaping juridical norms regulating technology and its advances in organized social life, among others. Such questions, clearly having huge impacts on management, business opportunities, organizational reform, workforce reskilling, stakeholders' relationships, and others, are widely influenced by underpinning ethical stances to support ethical decision-making in solving continuously arising dilemmas.

Against a scenario of multiplication of ethical calls and guidelines for AI design and use, this book develops a unifying perspective that addresses different dimensions and sources of ethical AI risks and actual shortcomings through one moral anchor. The book aimed to answer questions such as: Which values and principles, aligned with the humanism tradition, can guide organizations in designing, implementing, and leveraging AI? What are the main ethical humanistic challenges that organizations relying on AI face? What ethical humanistic challenges do organizational stakeholders that depend on AI face? Which does humanism drive the critical recommendations on AI? How can AI-driven innovations positively or negatively affect human dignity? Human freedom? What dehumanization perils are tied to AI,

F. Rosa (✉)
Catolica Lisbon School of Business and Economics, Universidade Católica Portuguesa, Lisbon, Portugal
e-mail: rosa.fioravante@uniurb.it

V. Antonino
IESE Business School, Barcelona, Spain
e-mail: avaccaro@iese.edu

R. Fioravante and A. Vaccaro (eds.), *Humanism and Artificial Intelligence*, SpringerBriefs in Philosophy, https://doi.org/10.1007/978-3-031-85478-1_12

and how do we face them? This Chapter briefly presents the book's main takeaways to answer such questions and inform future research paths.

The book develops four central debates on AI and humanistic ethics: AI-related dehumanization of actual or potential risks, AI regulation between law-making and spirituality, AI as tied to human responsibility, and AI management between technical and value-laden governance.

The book's first part enhances our knowledge of the dynamics intertwining the mechanization of humans and the humanization of machines. From a humanistic ethics perspective, John Tasioulas develops a model based on three elements to assess human-AI relationships: plurality of values, focus on the procedures and centrality of individual and collective participation in determining scopes and wellbeing assessments. In this way, Tasioulas stresses how, within AI ethics, not all approaches are rooted in humanistic ethics, regardless of "human-centered AI" calls. At the same time, Simona Chiodo reflects on humans' quest to deploy AI to predict their future. Chiodo highlights the performativity of such pursuit, able to turn new technologies into a driver of human automation; through optimization processes, humans aim to machine performativity for themselves, while, through a quest for predicting the future, they develop prediction patterns that inform their existence, thus concurring in determining their future. The book's first part highlights how, from a humanistic perspective, the dynamics of human engineering while humanizing machines deploy an alienating use of technology, which aims to eliminate the burden of responsibility from the personal and collective sphere to machines. Against this scenario, humanistic ethics develops sensibilities, guidelines, and moral grounding for guidelines and codes of conduct, which aim, the other way around, to use automation for human purposes while focusing on its scopes and how innovation can serve human well-being in a more desirable society.

Regarding the latter, Fioravante and Vaccaro discuss dehumanization threats posed by AI deployment in working organizations: dehumanization happens in organizations daily, and AI deployment can either increase or decrease its presence. Fioravante and Vaccaro use humanistic ethics to focus on three dimensions, personal, organizational, and stakeholder relationships, to present practices and policies aimed at avoiding technological optimization to become the sole rationale of the organization while ensuring wellbeing and human integral development for internals and externals. Overall, the first part of the book contributes to the debate on augmentation/automation dynamics in AI design and use (Lindebaum et al. 2023; Raisch and Krakowski 2021): by applying humanistic ethics to business and organizational contexts, it presents a holistic perspective on how to tame dehumanization and build human-centered organizations (Pirson and Kimakowitz 2014; Sachs and Kujala 2022; Sandelands 2009).

The second part highlights the role of spirituality and virtue ethics in building a humanistic, enrooted approach to AI design and deployment. Mario Ferrante discusses how "algorithmics" can inform AI design and use by relying on moral universal guidance from Catholic social teaching and canonic rights as juridical streams enrooted in humanism. In this way, presenting "algorithmics" adds to widespread debates on regulating and guardrail AI to avoid common ethical shortcomings and its potentially harmful use. Martin Schlag presents the role of Christian spirituality and contemplation in assessing models of technological innovation that serve the human transcendental sphere, adding to a cornerstone tradition within business ethics of deploying Catholic Social Teaching and Christian ethics to socioeconomic, ethical dilemmas and informing human economy relationships. Ignacio Munoz Ferrero, Marta Rocchi, and Francesco Vincenzo Giarmoleo discuss the role of virtue ethics when deploying AI in the workplace, stressing the possibility of "virtuous AI," which enhances actions and moral behavior rather than undermining the role of virtues and virtuous characters in the workplace. Hence, the book adds to debates on the role of universal moral norms in informing AI regulation and policymaking (Attard-Frost et al. 2023; Melé 2021; Ryan and Stahl 2021). Furthermore, the volume contributes to debates on the ethics of AI by stressing the role of Catholic Social Teaching and spirituality-based approaches (Guillén et al. 2015) in informing humanistic management and human-centered organizations (Costa and Ramus 2012; Hooker and Kim 2022; Kim and Scheller-Wolf 2022; Melé 2015; Sandelands 2009; Zigarelli 1993).

The third part discusses how AI-related discourses are ethically informed and how their framing has performative effects on how AI is understood, regulated, and deployed in the private and public organized social spheres. João César das Neves underlines fundamental inconsistencies in how AI is characterized and debated in major developers and public documents, looking into threats of misconceiving AI projects as drivers of anti-humanism. By highlighting the moral borders of AI development, das Neves focuses on desirability of technological progress and its impact on human capabilities, as well as deceptive discourses on surpassing human boundaries to achieve God-like status. Alberto Romele discusses AI as a "floating signifier." He presents AI as a contradictory field where different definitions, meanings, and references are used in leading media outlets in major Western countries to circulate general discourses on AI ethics that do not bear concrete impacts on its understanding and ethical guardrail. David Gunkel presents current significant approaches to the distinction between "things" and "persons" to assess machines and AI's status, stressing the need to bestow moral considerations upon AI unfolding and rightly considering AI agency. Through such discussions, the third part of the book adds to debates on "Responsible AI" (Buhmann and Fieseler 2023) by enquiring into the moral agency and responsibility of those involved in AI public discourses, as well as in deceptive calls for ethical AI without significant humanistic ethics underpinning, policy informing and moral agency recognition (Sætra 2023; van Maanen 2022).

Furthermore, the book's fourth part discusses how to approach data management and human management within AI development by deploying a holistic humanistic perspective. Peggy Tsai presents a comprehensive model of ethical data governance, able to perform ethical guardrail of data management in all critical points of the AI pipeline. Thus contributing to mitigating ethical risks for the black box and insufficient transparency of AI tools and systems, arising bias and potential discriminatory and unwanted consequences of AI functioning. Paula Boddington presents a revelatory case study on AI deployed in the healthcare sector within facilities for dementia patients. By looking into one of the most fragile groups in society, Boddington presents a model to assess the impact of AI use on humanizing or dehumanizing fragile groups. This work elicits further debates on AI's impact in bettering or worsening personal wellbeing conditions and the relationship between the means and purposes of its use. Overall, the fourth part contributes to debates on AI responsible and sustainable governance by looking at all its pipelines and power structures (Crawford 2021; Widder and Whittaker nd). It proposes a humanistic-led perspective in data and human management by leveraging on human values to be safeguarded and human capabilities to be improved as the primary AI design and use goal while addressing AI efficiency and optimization as a means towards such greater good (Ammanath and Blackman 2021; Blackmann 2023; Kim et al. 2021a, b).

Overall, the book proposes the following contributions.

First, it bridges three bodies of literature: ethics of AI, humanistic ethics and organizational studies (de Colle et al. 2023; McAfee and Brynjolfsson 2017; Melé 2016; Floridi 1999; Vaccaro and Madsen 2009). In this way, it contributes to debates on debates refusing technological neutrality and enquiring into ethical streams suitable to be applied in everyday situations and contexts of ethical dilemmas and shortcomings arising from AI (Blackmann 2023; Floridi et al. 2018; Turilli et al. 2012). This contribution is crucial to inform future research paths, bridging philosophical foundations and normative approaches with empirical research (Rosenthal and Buchholz 2000), aiming to provide ethical guidance to practitioners and decision-makers in both public policy-making and within the private sector and hybrid organizations.

Second, the volume promotes a thorough discussion of what humanistic ethics is, how it is developed, and how it evolved in the light of AI's disruptive innovation. It highlights how the wide variety of ethical approaches used to underpin ethical guidelines, self-regulation, and current policymaking is seldom enrooted in humanistic ethics. AI design, in particular, is highly informed by other ethical approaches, such as utilitarian ethics; furthermore, projects like Artificial General Intelligence and Artificial Superintelligence are underpinned by ethical theories aiming to go beyond humanism. Against such a scenario, the book contributes to assessing dehumanization perils entailed by disregarding humanistic ethics, thus contributing to literature debating such dehumanization practices (Craze 2019; Fritts and Cabrera 2021; Väyrynen and Laari-Salmela 2018). More in-depth, the book highlights how organizations exploit AI-driven competitive advantage and opportunities for optimization while disregarding the safeguard of human wellbeing when affected by AI use. This can inform future research paths looking into AI-driven practices of dehumanization by enquiring into organizations' rationale and leading values as sources of potential ethical threats to dehumanized interpersonal relationships and organizational mission (Ammanath 2022)(Van Der Linden and Edward Freeman 2017). With this regard, the perspectives are focused on "AI not for bad" rather than "AI for good", thus aiming to tame undesirable consequences of its design and deployment. This volume offers a clear vision of desirable AI purposes and goals, enrooting them in human development and human capabilities approaches, informing desirable and fair societal and personal goals (Bietti 2021; Melé 2009, 2015).

Third, the volume contributes to assessing organizations' role in designing and using AI for humanistic or anti-humanistic purposes. Looking into the ethical shortcomings of current AI use clarifies the stakes of AI-driven exclusion rather than inclusion and the potential socially harmful impacts of unethical AI. It addresses AI in the workplace and its effect on workers' future and wellbeing (Brynjolfsson et al. nd; Melé 2021; Michaelson et al. 2014). In this way, the book contributes to enhancing the debate on work megatrend elicited by AI and assessing organizational responsibility towards its members (Brynjolfsson and McAfee 2014; D'Cruz et al. 2022; Reeves and Sinnicks 2023). Furthermore, it assesses AI's impact on fragile groups, thus contributing to literature highlighting how AI evaluation should be pursued through assessment of its consequences on human rights protection and human flourishing enabling, with a specific focus on weaker groups in society. The latter bear undesirable technological unfolding consequences in a disproportionate matter (Aguiñaga and Leal, nd; Crawford 2021), need to be included and have a say in the process of AI deployment (Buhmann and Fieseler 2023; Derry 2012). In this way, the book elicited bottom-up perspectives aimed at safeguarding humanizing stakeholders as ends in themselves rather than means to technological optimization. This perspective can inform future research on accountability of AI (Martin 2019; Novelli et al. 2023), transparency (das Neves and Vaccaro 2013; Shah et al. 2023) and suggest to practitioners novel forms of inclusion and trustworthy AI practices building (Ammanath 2022; Kim and Routledge 2022).

Fourth, the book provides a unique underpinning of the ethics of AI with moral norms derived from Catholic Social Teaching (Kim et al. 2021a, b; Melé 2021). Indeed, Catholic Social Teaching and Christian ethics appeal to secular and religious persons and organizations, thanks to their principles rooted in solidarity, subsidiarity, human dignity, and the Common Good. The latter have a universalistic reach and can elicit ethical dialogue and encounters between different confessions and confessional perspectives (Costa and Ramus 2012; Palacio et al. 2021; Schlag and Melé 2020). Given current loopholes in AI legislation and law enforcement, the book proposes a critical assessment of the role of Canonical law as a central juridical body explicitly enrooted in humanistic ethics (Melé and Cantón 2014; Zigarelli 1993). This contribution can inform future AI legislation by emphasizing the perks of enrooting lawmaking into universal moral norms. Furthermore, it can promote future research on the role of spirituality in the business decision-making process in light of AI automation and values alignment issues (Gabriel 2020; Kim et al. 2021a, b) (Spirituality and Business in the Anthropocene Era nd).

The book presents a unique, multidisciplinary approach to ethical risks and personal, organizational, and societal impacts of current tendencies of humanizing machines and automating humans. This holds vast consequences regarding business ethics approaches, balancing economic, social, and environmental sustainability and bearing specific moral responsibility for AI developers and users. Humanistic ethics can inform all relevant debates in the field by being applied, in each inherent context and level, as a morally informed ethical stance aiming at integral development and shared prosperity for each person and all communities.

References

Aguiñaga E, Leal AR (nd) Supply chain management. Humanistic management and circular economy: fostering industry innovation and decent work through responsible consumption and production through partnership. https://doi.org/10.4324/9780429351117

Ammanath B (2022) Trustworthy AI: a business guide for navigating trust and ethics in AI. John Wiley & Sons

Ammanath B, Blackman R (2021, July) Everyone in your organization needs to understand AI ethics. Harvard Business Review. https://hbr.org/2021/07/everyone-in-your-organization-needs-to-understand-ai-ethics

Attard-Frost B, De los Ríos A, Walters DR (2023) The ethics of AI business practices: a review of 47 AI ethics guidelines. AI Ethics 3(2):389–406. https://doi.org/10.1007/s43681-022-00156-6

Bietti E (2021) From ethics washing to ethics bashing: a moral philosophy view on tech ethics. J Soc Comput 2(3):266–283. https://doi.org/10.23919/JSC.2021.0031

Blackman R, Niño C (2023) How to avoid the ethical nightmares of emerging technology.

Blackmann R (2023) Ethical machines: your concise guide to totally unbiased, transparent, and respectful AI. Harvard Business Review Press.

Brynjolfsson E, Li D, Raymond LR (nd) Generative AI at work

Brynjolfsson E, McAfee A (2014) The second Machine Age: work, progress, and prosperity in a time of brilliant technologies. WW Norton & Company

Buhmann A, Fieseler C (2023) Deep learning meets deep democracy: deliberative governance and responsible innovation in artificial intelligence. Bus Ethics Q 33(1):146–179. https://doi.org/10.1017/beq.2021.42

Costa E, Ramus T (2012) The Italian Economia Aziendale and catholic social teaching: how to apply the common good principle at the managerial level. J Bus Ethics 106(1):103–116. https://doi.org/10.1007/s10551-011-1056-x

Crawford K (2021) Atlas of AI. Power, politics, and the planetary costs of artificial intelligence. Yale University Press

Craze G (2019) Corporate social responsibility and dehumanization. Philos Manag 18(1):43–53. https://doi.org/10.1007/s40926-018-0085-2

das Neves JC, Vaccaro A (2013) Corporate transparency: a perspective from Thomas Aquinas' Summa Theologiae. J Bus Ethics 113(4):639–648. https://doi.org/10.1007/S10551-013-1682-6/METRICS

D'Cruz P, Du S, Noronha E, Parboteeah KP, Trittin-Ulbrich H, Whelan G (2022) Technology, megatrends and work: thoughts on the future of business ethics. J Bus Ethics 180(3):879–902. https://doi.org/10.1007/S10551-022-05240-9/FIGURES/1

de Colle S, Freeman RE, Wicks AC (2023) Toward humanistic business ethics. Bus Soc. https://doi.org/10.1177/00076503231183681/ASSET/IMAGES/LARGE/10.1177_00076503231183681-FIG2.JPEG

Derry R (2012) Reclaiming marginalized stakeholders. J Bus Ethics 111(2):253–264. https://doi.org/10.1007/S10551-012-1205-X/METRICS

Floridi L (1999) Information ethics: on the philosophical foundations of computer ethics. Ethics Inf Technol 1(1):37–56. https://doi.org/10.1023/a:1010018611096

Floridi L, Cowls J, Beltrametti M, Chatila R, Chazerand P, Dignum V, Luetge C, Madelin R, Pagallo U, Rossi F, Schafer B, Valcke P, Vayena E (2018) AI4People—an ethical framework for a good AI society: opportunities, risks, principles, and recommendations. Mind Mach 28(4):689–707. https://doi.org/10.1007/s11023-018-9482-5

Fritts M, Cabrera F (2021) AI recruitment algorithms and the dehumanization problem, vol 23, pp 791–801. https://doi.org/10.1007/s10676-021-09615-w

Gabriel I (2020) Artificial intelligence, values, and alignment. Mind Mach 30(3):411–437. https://doi.org/10.1007/s11023-020-09539-2

Guillén M, Ferrero I, Hoffman WM (2015) The neglected ethical and spiritual motivations in the workplace. J Bus Ethics 128(4):803–816. https://doi.org/10.1007/s10551-013-1985-7

Hooker J, Kim TW (2022) Humanizing business in the age of artificial intelligence. In: Dion M, Freeman RE, Dmytriyev SD (eds) Humanizing business. issues in business ethics, vol 53. Springer, Cham (pp 601–613). https://doi.org/10.1007/978-3-030-72204-3_40

Kim TW, Hooker J, Donaldson T (2021) Taking principles seriously: a hybrid approach to value alignment in artificial intelligence. J Artif Intell Res:70, 871–890. https://doi.org/10.1613/JAIR.1.12481

Kim TW, Maimone F, Pattit K, Sison AJ, Teehankee B (2021b) Master and slave: the dialectic of human-artificial intelligence engagement. Hum Manag J 6(3):355–371. https://doi.org/10.1007/s41463-021-00118-w

Kim TW, Routledge BR (2022) Why a right to an explanation of algorithmic decision-making should exist: a trust-based approach. Bus Ethics Q 32(1):75–102. https://doi.org/10.1017/beq.2021.3

Kim TW, Scheller-Wolf A (2022) Technological unemployment, meaning in life, purpose of business, and the future of stakeholders. In: Business and the ethical implications of technology. Springer Nature Switzerland (pp 13–31). https://doi.org/10.1007/978-3-031-18794-0_2

Lindebaum D, Moser C, Ashraf M, Glaser VL (2023) Reading the technological society to understand the mechanization of values and its ontological consequences. In: Academy of management review (vol 48, Issue 3, pp 575–592). Academy of Management. https://doi.org/10.5465/amr.2021.0159

Martin K (2019) Ethical implications and accountability of algorithms. J Bus Ethics 160(4):835–850. https://doi.org/10.1007/S10551-018-3921-3

Mazzi F, Floridi L (nd) Philosophical studies series the ethics of artificial intelligence for the sustainable development goals

McAfee A, Brynjolfsson E (2017) Machine, platform, crowd: Harnessing our digital future. WW Norton & Company

Melé D (2009) Integrating personalism into virtue-based business ethics: the personalist and the common good principles. J Bus Ethics 88(1):227–244. https://doi.org/10.1007/s10551-009-0108-y

Melé D (2015) Three keys concepts of catholic humanism for economic activity: human dignity, human rights and integral human development. Issues Bus Ethics, 43, 113–136. https://doi.org/10.1007/978-94-017-9704-7_7/COVER

Melé D (2016) Understanding humanistic management. Hum Manag J 1(1):33–55. https://doi.org/10.1007/S41463-016-0011-5/METRICS

Melé D (2021) Ethics at the workplace in the fourth industrial revolution: a Catholic social teaching perspective. Bus Ethics Environ Responsib 30(4):772–783. https://doi.org/10.1111/BEER.12368

Melé D, Cantón CG (2014) The homo economicus model. In: Human foundations of management. Palgrave Macmillan UK (pp 9–29). https://doi.org/10.1057/9781137462619_2

Michaelson C, Pratt MG, Grant AM, Dunn CP (2014) Meaningful work: connecting business ethics and organization studies. J Bus Ethics 121(1):77–90. https://doi.org/10.1007/S10551-013-1675-5

Novelli C, Taddeo M, Floridi L (2023) Accountability in artificial intelligence: what it is and how it works. AI Soc. https://doi.org/10.1007/s00146-023-01635-y

Palacio JRS, Climent VC, Catalá AE (2021) The organizational model of the economy for the common good and its comparison with other approaches to Sustainability. CIRIEC-Espana Revista De Economia Publica, Social y Cooperativa 101:143–163. https://doi.org/10.7203/CIRIEC-E.101.16399

Pirson M, Kimakowitz E Von (2014) Towards a human-centered theory and practice of the firm. Presenting the humanistic paradigm of business and management. J Manag Glob Sustain 2(1):17–48. https://doi.org/10.13185/jm2014.02102

Raisch S, Krakowski S (2021) Artificial intelligence and management: the automation–augmentation paradox. Acad Manag Rev 46(1):192–210. https://doi.org/10.5465/AMR.2018.0072

Reeves C, Sinnicks M (2023) Totally administered heteronomy: adorno on work, leisure, and politics in the age of digital capitalism. J Bus Ethics. https://doi.org/10.1007/S10551-023-05570-2
Rosenthal SB, Buchholz RA (2000) The empirical-normative split in business ethics. Bus Ethics Q 10(2):399–408. https://doi.org/10.2307/3857883
Ryan M, Stahl BC (2021) Artificial intelligence ethics guidelines for developers and users: clarifying their content and normative implications. J Inf Commun Ethics Soc 19(1):1477–1996. https://doi.org/10.1108/JICES-12-2019-0138
Sachs S, Kujala J (2022) Stakeholder engagement in humanizing business. In: Issues in business ethics (vol 53). Springer Science and Business Media B.V. (pp 559–572). https://doi.org/10.1007/978-3-030-72204-3_37
Sætra HS (2023) Against the conflation of corporate strategy, ethics, and the politics of AI. Digit Soc 2(1). https://doi.org/10.1007/s44206-023-00035-5
Sandelands L (2009) The business of business is the human person: lessons from the catholic social tradition. J Bus Ethics 85(1):93–101. https://doi.org/10.1007/s10551-008-9751-y
Schlag M, Melé D (2020) Building institutions for the common good. The practice and purpose of business in an inclusive economy. Hum Manag J 5(1):1–6. https://doi.org/10.1007/s41463-020-00092-9
Shah MU, Rehman U, Parmar B, Ismail I (2023) Effects of moral violation on algorithmic transparency: an empirical investigation. J Bus Ethics. https://doi.org/10.1007/S10551-023-05472-3
Spirituality & Business in the Anthropocene Era (nd). https://www.businessethicscenter.com/
Turilli M, Vaccaro A, Taddeo M (2012) Internet neutrality: ethical issues in the internet environment. Philos Technol 25(2):133–151. https://doi.org/10.1007/S13347-011-0039-2/TABLES/1
Vaccaro A, Madsen P (2009) Corporate dynamic transparency: the new ICT-driven ethics? Ethics Inf Technol 11(2):113–122. https://doi.org/10.1007/s10676-009-9190-1
Van Der Linden B, Edward Freeman R (2017) Profit and other values: thick evaluation in decision making. Bus Ethics Q 27(3):353–379. https://doi.org/10.1017/beq.2017.1
van Maanen G (2022) AI ethics, ethics washing, and the need to politicize data ethics. Dig Soc 1(2). https://doi.org/10.1007/s44206-022-00013-3
Väyrynen T, Laari-Salmela S (2018) Men, mammals, or machines? Dehumanization embedded in organizational practices. J Bus Ethics 147(1):95–113. https://doi.org/10.1007/s10551-015-2947-z
Widder DG, Whittaker M (nd) Open (for business): big tech, concentrated power, and the political economy of open AI. https://ssrn.com/abstract=4543807
Zigarelli MA (1993) Catholic social teaching and the employment relationship: a model for managing human resources in accordance with Vatican Doctrine. J Bus Ethics 12(1):75–82. https://doi.org/10.1007/bf01845789

Author Index

R. Fioravante and A. Vaccaro (eds.), *Humanism and Artificial Intelligence*, SpringerBriefs in Philosophy, https://doi.org/10.1007/978-3-031-85478-1

Made in the USA
Monee, IL
14 September 2026

62974051R00136